D0983244

THE CLASH

Tempo
Series Editor: Scott Calhoun

Tempo offers titles that explore rock and popular music through the lens of social and cultural history, revealing the dynamic relationship between musicians, music, and their milieu. Like other major art forms, rock and pop music comment on their cultural, political, and even economic situation, reflecting the technological advances, psychological concerns, religious feelings, and artistic trends of their times. Contributions to the **Tempo** series are the ideal introduction to major pop and rock artists and genres.

Bob Dylan: American Troubadour, by Donald Brown
Bon Jovi: America's Ultimate Band, by Margaret Olson
British Invasion: The Crosscurrents of Musical Influence, by Simon Philo
Bruce Springsteen: American Poet and Prophet, by Donald L. Deardorff II
The Clash: The Only Band That Mattered, by Sean Egan
Patti Smith: America's Punk Rock Rhapsodist, by Eric Wendell
Paul Simon: An American Tune, by Cornel Bonca
Ska: The Rhythm of Liberation, by Heather Augustyn

THE CLASH

The Only Band That Mattered

Sean Egan

ROWMAN & LITTLEFIELD
Lanham • Boulder • New York • London

Published by Rowman & Littlefield
A wholly owned subsidary of The Rowman & Littlefield Publishing Group, Inc.
4501 Forbes Boulevard, Suite 200, Lanham, Maryland 20706
www.rowman.com

16 Carlisle Street, London W1D 3BT, United Kingdom

British Library Cataloguing in Publication Information Available

Library of Congress Cataloging-in-Publication Data

Egan, Sean, author.
The Clash : the only band that mattered / Sean Egan.
pages cm – (Tempo : a Rowman & Littlefield music series on rock, pop, and culture)
Includes bibliographical references, discography, and index.
Summary: "In The Clash: The Only Band That Mattered, respected music critic Sean Egan examines The Clash's career and art through the prism of the uniquely interesting and fractious UK politics of the Seventies and Eighties, without which they simply would not have existed. Tackling subjects such as The Clash's self-conscious tussles with their record label, the accusations of sell-out that dogged their footsteps, their rivalry with the similarly leaning but less purist Jam, the paradoxical quality of their achieving multi-platinum success and even whether their denunciations of Thatcherism were proven wrong, Egan has come up with new insights into a much discussed group"—Provided by publisher.
ISBN 978-0-8108-8875-3 (cloth : alk. paper) – ISBN 978-0-8108-8876-0 (ebook)
1. Clash (Musical group) 2. Punk rock musicians–England–Biography. I. Title.
ML421.C57E43 2015
782.42166092'2–dc23
2014024677

Printed in the United States of America

CONTENTS

INTRODUCTION

The Clash are a truly ideal subject for Tempo, a series that aims to set the legacy of recording artists in a wider sociological context.

Today, The Clash are universally recognized as one of the greatest, most exhilarating bands ever to either make use of recording tape or step on a stage. Their works regularly appear in high positions in critics' polls to find the greatest albums in history. However, they were more than just a great rock band. The Clash were convinced that they could change the world with their art, and their art itself sprang from the uniquely interesting and fractious social conditions and politics of Britain in the Seventies and Eighties.

The fond regard in which they are held, therefore, is not merely the normal gratitude felt by those for whom artists have provided aural pleasure. They were a group whose music was, and is, special to their audience because that music insisted on addressing the conditions of poverty, petty injustice, and mundane life experienced by the people who bought their records. Moreover, although their rebel stances were often no more than posturing, from The Clash's stubborn principles came a fundamental change in the perception of what is possible in the music industry, from subject matter to authenticity to quality control to price ceilings.

Yet The Clash's high standing was not ever thus. The slogan "The Only Band That Matters" was devised by The Clash's American record label Epic. The Clash began to resent it, but it was deemed accurate (and snappy) by enough people to be quickly and widely taken up. It was a slogan that summed them up, not just in terms of the social relevance of their songs but their penchant for self-mythologizing. Initially, critics and fans accepted, even loved, their endless self-aggrandizement. However, their multiple vainglorious anthems about themselves began to grate when The Clash started to be perceived as losing relevance and even selling out. From day one, The Clash had made proclamations to the music press about their integrity—which encompassed promises to spread around any wealth they made, to keep their ticket and record prices below certain levels, to spurn crass commercialism, and to remain in touch with their fans. Unfortunately, a function of the global success engendered by their excellent music meant the betrayal of some of those promises, with an inevitable backlash. The increasing frequency of substandard product didn't help either.

Having clawed back some respectability with their best-selling 1982 *Combat Rock* album, band dissension and egotistical behavior unseemly for people with collectivist ideals produced a rupture in their ranks. A new version of The Clash released in 1985 *Cut the Crap*, an album whose self-parody made it a sad finale.

After the dust had settled and the purist punk credo receded into history, The Clash's catalog could be assessed in more objective terms. The consensus is that it is mostly superb.

This book seeks to explore both why The Clash's music was so powerful and to give an idea of why The Clash aroused passions, pro and anti, for reasons that often had nothing directly to do with their music.

I

GARAGELAND—MORE OR LESS

Twin forces of decline—the economic decay of Britain and the waning powers of the rock aristocracy—created the musical movement that was punk.

It's difficult to convey to those who didn't experience it the perennial sense of crisis in Great Britain in the Seventies. Not long after the turn of the decade, it already felt like an age since the nation had been able to fool itself into believing that, in a post-Empire era, it retained an importance by dint of the world turning its eyes toward its pop culture. *Time* magazine may have conferred the adjective "swinging" on London in April 1966, but the UK's contemporaneous currency and labor crises were already working to undermine even the small amount of national pride that engendered.

From 1966 to 1974, the position of prime minister in Britain was the exclusive preserve of two men: Harold Wilson of the center-left Labour Party and Edward Heath of the center-right Conservative Party. (The "Mr. Wilson" and "Mr. Heath" whose names are cooed by The Beatles in "Taxman.") In that time, Wilson's party won three general elections to Heath's one, although the clear-cut dominance that implies is an illusion created by the vagaries of Britain's electoral system. Not that it mattered much: at the time there was little to choose between the two parties as a result of the long-standing "Post-War Consensus." During the Second World War, the rich sheltered from German bombs cheek-by-jowl with the poor in London's Underground stations, with the consequence that the ruling classes properly understood poverty for the first time. Accordingly, in the first post-war general election in July 1945, both of Britain's major parties offered a platform designed to appeal to the newly altruistic sentiment in the air: the creation of an all-encompassing welfare state.

Labour won that election by a landslide, and by the time they left office in 1951, many millions of Britons knew—courtesy of National Assistance—the once-unimaginable relief of not having the worry of joblessness-induced penury. Old age, meanwhile, was stripped of its association with terrible suffering or humiliating dependence on younger relatives by virtue of a pension system. Courtesy of the National Health Service—predicated on medical care free at the point of use—the sick no longer literally died for inability to pay doctor bills. Once created, the welfare state could never be abolished by any political party that continued to be in the business of re-election. The new order thus engendered was newly susceptible to Keynesian economics, which dictated that the answer to economic problems was for government to spend its way out of them. Government had plenty of money to spend, courtesy of a unanimous belief in progressive taxation levels.

There were eventually other improvements in the quality of post-war life separate from the installation of a welfare safety net. The loosening of Hire Purchase agreement terms—essentially the precursor to the credit card—saw the proletariat begin to fills its homes with consumer goods beyond the dreams of its parents. This gave many of the low-waged a stake in society, a sense that the system was not necessarily there to oppress them and could reward them for effort. Yet while this may have diluted the allure of full-blown collectivism, let alone revolutionary ideology, it did not make Britain a land of tranquillity. As the decades wore on, the sound track to British life was increasingly bellicose pay demands.

Britain has always been seen as a country riven by class division. Over the course of the twentieth century and beyond, the class system became progressively less pronounced (and in the Sixties being proletarian was actually a virtue). However, although caste divisions are nothing like as pitiless today, visitors to the UK continue to proclaim themselves shocked at the fact of how laughable it remains that white-collar and blue-collar workers might move in the same social circles.

Seventies Britain was still a place where people were judged by their accent or their education. To many (not by any means all middle- or upper-class) the idea of someone with a cockney or scouse or Glaswegian accent working as a lawyer, banker, or television presenter was absurd. Barriers to advancement were not even always informal: up until 1986, it was nearly impossible to gain a job as a stockbroker unless you had attended a public school (British parlance for a private school wreathed in history and tradition).

So ingrained were notions of class and privilege that some members of the Establishment clearly felt that democracy itself could be an affront to what they considered the natural order. It was later claimed by MI5 officer Peter Wright that in the Seventies the British secret services manipulated the financial markets to cause a run on the pound in an attempt to discredit the Wilson government and cause the electorate to remove it from power.

While the militancy of the trade unions might have been counterproductive, for many on the left it was the inevitable consequence of maltreatment in the workplace. Britain's workplaces were at least leaving behind the rigid attitudes that still prevailed in the Sixties and which were summed up by Ian MacDonald in his book *Revolution in the Head*: ". . . all males below one's own level being addressed by their surnames as if the whole country was in the army." However, in the Seventies, there existed a more-than-insignificant residue of that authoritarianism: workers were treated like cogs in a machine, and little value was attached by their overlords to their opinions or rights. The division between the workers and management created a confrontational ambience. Extreme practices that in other counties might have been the stuff of parody were, in the UK, day-to-day reality: any employer who allowed the slightest blurring of demarcation of trades—such as a plumber picking up an electrician's cable—or failed to agree to negotiated manning levels—such as two employees lifting a piece of equipment that could easily be handled by one—could, and often did, find themselves the victim of a mass walkout. Few in Britain, left or right, disputed that there was a "them and us" situation on factory and office floors. Related to this, was a chronic overmanning in British industry.

That division of class was reflected throughout society. Up until 1985, the BBC, which broadcast two of the nation's three television channels and had a monopoly on national radio, employed someone to secretly vet employees for left-wing sympathies. Newspapers frequently carried stories of how some bewigged, elderly member of the judiciary had expressed bewilderment at a common phrase or social trend, or had even incarcerated someone in the courtroom for saying the wrong thing or smiling at an inappropriate moment. Such arbitrary exercise of power was subject to no comeback: nobody had the power to fire a judge. If corruption wasn't a problem among the judiciary—they generally earned far too much to bother—the same could not be said for the police, especially London's Metropolitan Police. Allegations of frame-ups at the time were many, and in the following decades—when many convicted on terrorism and murder charges had their life terms quashed by the appeal courts—were proven to be more than the conspiracy theories and mischief-making alleged at the time (including by some members of Parliament).

Whatever stake the never-had-it-so-good working class might feel they had in society was, therefore, purely a financial one. For many of them, it remained difficult not to perceive figures of authority—which description encompassed bosses, employers, judges, politicians, broadcasters, and others—as "posh," a byword for people with such different life experience and values as to have no idea about, and no interest in, them, their beliefs, and their lives. Going on strike, therefore, seemed not just the logical thing to do when the working man and woman had a grievance about their treatment in their place of work, but the only course of action that would be taken seriously.

Thrown into this mix was an unusual link between labor and the executive: because the trade unions funded the Labour Party, they had a massive influence on party policy both in and out of government. It was difficult for Labour governments to resist union suggestions about labor legislation or pay and conditions in nationalized (and even private) industry. When they did, and unions called strikes, many of them (if not quite as many as popular memory suggests) were non-balloted—"wildcat"—strikes. Moreover, a strike could easily bring the country to a standstill. Rail, coal mining, steel, electricity, gas, post, and the telephonic system were all nationalized (or, to use the term more common in America, "socialized"). Moreover, cross-industry "sympathy" strikes were perfectly legal. Not only did legislation make it nearly impossible to dismiss difficult workers, but breaking strikes was also rare because of a sense of solidarity among workers, as well as the persuasive powers/intimidation (delete according to opinion) of "flying pickets" (mobile pickets who could literally number in the thousands).

Accordingly, confrontation between organized labor and both employers and government defined British life in the Seventies. That decade was pocked by news footage of picket lines, power blackouts, and spiraling inflation, which averaged 13 percent per year and in 1975 reached a peak of 25 percent. Unemployment rose inexorably. Pay rises of 20 and even 30 percent achieved by unions inevitably resulted in industry passing on its increased costs to the consumer, with those mushrooming retail prices then prompting a fresh pay demand. The 1973 oil crisis only made the situation worse. With the miners currently striking in protest at public-sector pay caps and with imported coal too expensive to make up the shortfall their industrial action was causing, the nation was reduced in 1974 to a state-mandated three-day working week in order to conserve electricity.

Nationalization caused other problems. Anyone wanting a telephone installed had to wait several months before the General Post Office would oblige, such was the inertia induced by state monopoly. If the gas board or electricity board was coming round to read the meter, people had to take the day off work to let them in upon pain of disconnection. If that was due to inferior technology for reading meters, it may be the case that the lack of impetus for improving that technology came from a lack of competition which made companies unresponsive to consumers. Moreover, energy prices were often raised not because of necessity but because it was a handy means of indirect taxation for the Exchequer.

The British have always been admired for being able to laugh at their own country, but in the Seventies the nation's self-deprecation took on a quality of self-loathing. A popular motif of UK stand-up comedians of the era was that the sign "Made in Britain" on any consumer good was shorthand for substandard. That British workmanship was a laughing stock was another manifestation of both centralization and union power. When the muscle of unions meant that workers could win almost any dispute with management, there was little incentive for conscientiousness. This worked on a macro level, too: nationalized industries always had the comfort blanket of a government bailout. Moreover, even much private enterprise was deemed too big to fail: when car manufacturer British Leyland entered bankruptcy in 1975, the government—desperate not to add more numbers to the unemployment rolls—took it into state hands. The latter company was another boon to comics, a byword for bad practice and low productivity, while Derek

Robinson—Communist union convener of the company's Longbridge plant in Birmingham—was made a tabloid pantomime villain ("Red Robbo") by virtue of his apparent determination to bring his members out on strike at the drop of a hat.

This all created another vicious circle: the worsening balance of trade created by the resulting preference for cheaper and more reliable foreign goods only further jeopardized Britons' jobs and standards of living.

It is no exaggeration to say that unions could bring down a government. In the wake of the miners' opportunistic strike for a 13 percent pay rise during the oil crisis, Edward Heath called an election specifically on the issue of whether it was the unions or the democratically elected government who ran the country. Although it could be argued that it was less labor muscle that saw the Tories consigned to opposition in 1974 than the vagaries of the country's first-past-the-post electoral system (the Conservatives won more votes than Labour but lost the election because they secured fewer seats in the House of Commons), the election would never have been called had not Heath been frustrated in his attempts to maintain a pay restraint policy. Naturally, the incoming minority Labour government adopted a craven attitude toward unions—or even more craven than usual—to avoid the same fate. Little wonder that, in January 1977, 53 percent of respondents to an opinion poll stated that a trade union leader (Jack Jones, general secretary of the Transport and General Workers' Union) was the most powerful man in the country. (Prime Minister James Callaghan was nominated by 25 percent.)

Britain's continental neighbors during this period looked askance across the English Channel at what they called the "Sick Man of Europe."

In 1979, another government was brought down by the unions, but not in the way one might expect. The victory secured by the Conservatives over Labour that year was down to the chaotic conditions created by the wave of public sector strikes in 1978/79, popularly dubbed the Winter of Discontent and characterized by rubbish being uncollected and the dead being unburied. That 1979 victory by the Conservatives epitomized the strange brew of the nation's problems and the prevailing crisis of confidence on the left. The Tories picked up votes from areas they never previously had because for many millions of working-class people who might ordinarily be sympathetic to collectivist ideology, unions were responsible for the crises afflicting their country. Conservative leader Margaret Thatcher was a figure with ideas for clamping down on wage demands and the right to strike that might be termed hard-right, but a measure of the complicated times is the fact that British novelist Graham Greene—notably left-wing his entire life—said that, had he lived in his home country at the time of the 1979 general election, he would have voted Conservative. Little could better summarize the way that the problems of the Seventies left many Britons' assumptions and belief systems shaken to the core.

Roughly in the middle of that tumultuous decade came punk rock.

Punk musicians were disenchanted not just by their gray, broken society but also by a similarly dysfunctional rock scene. Rock, a form of popular music that had always been associated with rejecting convention, had become moribund, its aging idols evidently no longer keen to excel artistically while at the same time being plainly as keen as ever to succeed financially. The Sex Pistols played their first gig in November 1975. They were a new breed. They extended the traditional irreverence of rock 'n' roll to previously hallowed totems, dismissing The Rolling Stones—for more than a decade the epitome of the rebel—as Establishment and spurning the long hair which for the same amount of time had been a yardstick for the rejection of conventionality. They accordingly captured the imagination of a certain subset of society. Their disgust with virtuoso self-indulgence in rock and advocacy of a back-to-basics musical credo inspired both a following and a wave of bands who emulated their attitude. Of course, part of this was false: whatever their recent failings, the back catalogs of the Stones, Bob Dylan, The Who, The Kinks, et al., were precious to them. However, destroying those whom one really loves is in the best Oedipal tradition.

Rhythm guitarist and vocalist Joe Strummer (born John Mellor in Ankara, Turkey, in August 1952; raised in Warlingham, in the county of Surrey just outside London, when not at boarding school) saw the Sex Pistols firsthand on April 3, 1976, when his R&B revivalist group, the 101'ers, found them to be their support at a gig at London venue the Nashville. He was exhilarated by their rejection of the cheesy show-business approaches by which rock had become infected. He told *Record Collector* in August 2000, "I saw the future—with a snotty handkerchief—right in front of me. . . . Their attitude was, 'Here's our tunes, and we couldn't give a flying fuck whether you like them or not. In fact, we're gonna play them even if you fucking hate them.' . . . Punk hit London and suddenly, which side of the line were you on?"

The 101'ers's fate was sealed when Strummer was approached by Bernard Rhodes, who wanted to set up a band like the one managed by his friend, Sex Pistols Svengali Malcolm McLaren. That Rhodes band became The Clash. Although Rhodes's penchant for self-mythologizing, spurious left-wing ideology and even comical speech impediment seems to have made some reluctant to acknowledge his contributions to The Clash, there seems little dispute that he was key in assembling their personnel, devising their image, and nudging them toward political subject matter. On the latter, Strummer told Gavin Martin of *Uncut* in September 1999, "He would listen to rehearsals and the famous quote he came out with was, 'Write about what you know.' Which was just as well, because we couldn't have written about Mick's girlfriends forever."

The Mick referred to in that quote is Mick Jones, born in Clapham, southwest London, in June 1955 and raised in various areas of southwest London. While Strummer might have been The Clash's voice through his trio of roles as stage front man, main lyricist, and main press spokesman, Jones being a man with an effortless knack for melody and arrangement made him as important, even if his lyrics never matched the best of Strummer's street-poet songwords. The two formed the songwriting axis of the group.

Paul Simonon (born in Croydon, then just outside London, in December 1955; raised in Brixton, south London) was picked for the band primarily because of his heartthrob looks rather than musical ability. At first his basslines were written by Jones, and taught him by rote. Keith Levene was third guitarist for a brief period, and although he was technically more proficient than any of his colleagues, the consensus was that his departure from the ranks in September 1976 after five gigs had the effect of streamlining the group to its optimum configuration. The band was completed by drummer Terry Chimes, a diffident man who always had the air of a semi-detached member simply because he had no interest in the band's political bent or self-aggrandizing ways.

The Clash's entrée appeared on March 18, 1977: the single "White Riot" backed with "1977." (All dates herein are for UK releases unless otherwise stated.) Joe Strummer was motivated to write the A-side's lyric out of fury that his race weren't prepared to mount violent demonstrations against social injustice in the way that black youths had in the riot that attended the 1976 Notting Hill carnival.

Afro-Caribbean immigration to Britain began in earnest in 1948 with the Windrush Generation, so called because of the title of the ship that brought the first lot of Jamaican immigrants to the country following the signing into law of the 1948 British Nationality Act, which gave a commitment to allow any resident of the Commonwealth (essentially what used to be the British Empire before the process of the granting of independence started) the right to settle in the United Kingdom. A clash of cultures soon followed. Crime committed by blacks was massively disproportionate to their numbers: by 2009, the Home Office revealed that they accounted for well over 60 percent of street robberies in London despite only representing about 15 percent of the capital's population. The consequent targeting of black male youth by police officers—now commonly referred to as "racial profiling"—inspired deep resentment at its discriminatory and even abusive application.

The Notting Hill carnival is an annual event in west London and is largely Afro-Caribbean themed and organized. The high attendance levels necessitate a large police presence. As such, it created a ready-made flashpoint where black grievance against heavy-handed police tactics might erupt into violence. Such transpired to be the case on August 30, 1976. Joe Strummer and Paul Simonon were caught in the middle of the conflagration, with some reports even having one or both of them as participants in terms of throwing stones at police and trying to set alight a police vehicle. The experience got Strummer's creative juices flowing. In "White Riot" he bellows that he wants "a riot of my own" as he lambasts himself and his fellow Caucasians for being chicken, spurning civil disobedience in favor of education.

It was sometimes said that The Clash's recordings of "White Riot" were performed at half the speed the song was always played live. That applies especially to this version, which is a different take to that which would appear on the band's eponymous debut album. Although the single has a certain power—and sounded unspeakably raw in the MOR wasteland that was the mid-Seventies—it sounds absolutely tame in comparison to the variant on *The Clash*. Strummer's rage isn't done justice by the relatively measured accompaniment and bobbing beat,

even if the sound effects that don't feature on the album version—
police sirens, smashing glass, alarm bells—add a certain gritty frisson.

Despite its flaws, "White Riot" is the equivalent of The Who's "I
Can't Explain": an introduction that became a signature song. It also
punched way above its weight in the sense of achieving a chart position—no. 38—incongruous for the scant radio play its confrontational,
uncommercial bent engendered.

Like almost all self-generated Clash tracks up until the *Sandinista!*
album, "White Riot" was credited to Strummer/Jones, a publishing attribution that made perfect sense to rock consumers used to seeing
joint credits like "Lennon/McCartney" and "Jagger/Richards" in the pa-
rentheses beneath song titles on record labels. Although Strummer and
Jones were undeniably the compositional axis of The Clash, the mechanics behind the public façade of collaboration were—as with the
aforementioned Beatles and Rolling Stones songwriting teams—complicated. Sometimes they wrote alone; more often together. Although it
was never the case that either restricted himself to one role, it would be
fair to say that Strummer specialized in one department, Jones another.
As Strummer, slightly tactlessly, summarized to Gavin Martin of *Uncut*
in September 1999, "It was obvious from the start that Jonesy was great
at melody and totally useless on lyrics. So it dovetailed into me—not so
bad on the lyrics, not so great on the melody."

Up until 1976, dismissal of established rock icons had been almost
sacrilegious except in terms of the commonly aired grievance "Not as
good as they used to be," a phrase which itself implied acknowledgment
of respect for past artistic achievement. As mentioned, The Sex Pistols
broke that mold of veneration with interview comments in which they
sweepingly dismissed the artists without whom they would never have
been inspired to venture into music-making, and, if some of their rhetoric was willfully provocative, that itself was in the celebrated rock tradition of rebelliousness and callowness. It should be recognized, though,
just how genuinely cheated many people had come to feel in the last
few years each time they purchased a new album by the Stones, an ex-
Beatle, Bob Dylan, or Eric Clapton and found it was either mediocre,
somnambulant, or both. The key line—and effectively chorus—of
"1977" is "No Elvis, Beatles or the Rolling Stones in 1977," an articula-
tion of punk's Year Zero credo: that the rock idols who had made their
name in the Sixties had outlived their usefulness as either interesting

artists or totems of social progression. Or in more colloquial terms, they were a bunch of old farts who didn't understand the kids anymore.

If "1977" is a shot across the bows of the rock aristocracy, that's not all it is. Its lyric also targets a group who, like the rock aristocracy, could only view an increasingly gray and strife-torn Britain from veritable ivory towers: the ruling class. The lyric bristles with talk of sten guns and knives being flourished in upmarket areas of London like Knightsbridge. It is asserted that in the remainder of the titular calendar year, being rich will not necessarily any longer be an advantage.

It would become a motif in Clash interviews that the band's lyrics had been misunderstood, the most common example of which gripe being, "I'm So Bored with the U.S.A." "1977" provides the earliest example of this phenomenon. Strummer told Allan Jones in *Melody Maker* on November 25, 1978, "We have been misunderstood . . . I imagined sten guns in Knightsbridge pointed at me. But people took it to mean that *we* had them and we were pointing them at other people." Similarly, Mick Jones told Alexis Petridis of *The Guardian* on November 3 , 2006, "The 'Sten guns in Knightsbridge' thing wasn't like we had Sten guns in Knightsbridge, it was like, we're concerned about that kind of thing, it was around the time of the Spaghetti House siege." The trouble is that it's not necessarily possible to take such denials at face value: The Clash's interviews are littered with lies, half-truths, and rationalizations, partly the result of their early absolutism in lyrics and myth-making when holding court to journalists, partly the consequence of their subsequent squirming attempts to explain away their previous posturing dishonesty and studied belligerence, with the added complication that in some cases, as in the origin of "I'm So Bored with the U.S.A.," they seem to have made a transition into believing their own falsehoods.

Suffice it to say that the lyric's statement that in 1977 it ain't so lucky to be rich that provides a rhyme for Knightsbridge seems pretty unambiguous. The ambience, meanwhile, is deliberately—and impressively—menacing, although for neither the first nor last time one wishes Strummer had sung his lyric better. The accompaniment is a mid-tempo affair propelled by buzz-saw guitar with a drama-heightening respite and a climax that sees Strummer enumerating the years that will follow 1977. His final resounding "Nineteen eighty-*four!*" coincides with the music stopping dead, a portentousness more easily understood at the time due to the fact that it was a year which—because still in the future—retained the dread of dystopia injected in it by George Orwell.

Although now considered an impressive opening shot from a group destined for legendary status, it should be noted that several critics found The Clash's debut record laughable. In the wake of the taboo-busting of The Sex Pistols's public pronouncements, the band were felt to have a point about the diminishing allure of aging rock icons. (That argument would come to be considered lost in the following decades as the concept of "heritage" acts took hold.) However, it wasn't only the old guard who found preposterous the implication that these young upstarts whose musical skills were demonstrably rudimentary and whose singer's syntax was almost comically mangled were the ones to take over the established acts' mantle. Moreover, that none of the apoc-alyptical predictions of the lyric of the B-side would ever come true was patently obvious and urban guerrilla posturing as risible as the record's sleeve, which depicted the band standing in frisk position against a wall so as to better display the political slogans daubed on their clothes. The back cover was more agitprop: inner-city imagery of tower blocks and police officers with quotes about youth culture riots and class warfare pulled from *The Floodgates of Anarchy* and *Generation X*, tomes which presumably resided on Rhodes's bookshelf but which were destined never to be tackled by The Clash's fanbase.

Despite it being acknowledged that The Sex Pistols were both the origi-nators of punk and its most important artists, it is also widely accepted that the movement/genre's major artistic statement is The Clash's epon-ymous debut long player, released on April 8, 1977.

The LP was recorded in three four-day sessions in February 1977 at CBS Studio 3, London. Although Terry Chimes played drums on the record, he was doing so as a favor, having already left the group at the end of 1976. Various reasons were given down the years for his spurn-ing the wealth and success then staring The Clash in the face, but when he gave his side of the story in his 2013 autobiography *Dr. Terry and Mr. Chimes* he explained that it was because, as a product of a happy home, he found it difficult being around bandmates whose worldviews and demeanors seemed to be dictated by their unhappy domestic hin-terlands. His reward for rendering this favor was to be credited on the sleeve as "Tory Crimes." This play on words—"Tory" being another name for an adherent of the British Conservative Party—is one of the only party-political statements The Clash ever made. (That the surname of Keith Levene—credited for his contribution to "What's My Name"—is misspelled "Levine" is probably accidental.)

Ironically, Chimes is second only to Jones in being the album's most consistent performer, his imaginative patterns always defying the songs' minimalist structures. Jones's professionalism on his instrument is a marked contrast to Simonon's lip-bitten rendering of the Jones-dictated basslines and Strummer's mostly nondescript guitar and mediocre, often awful, singing. This hardly suggests a good-to-bad ratio liable to produce art much above average, but *The Clash* is one of the greatest albums ever recorded, its technical deficiencies overcome by the quality of the arrangements, riffs, melodies, and lyrics and by its overall passion, power, and sheer vitality.

In one respect, a technical deficiency even became a virtue. The album's producer credit is given to the band's live soundman Mickey Foote, but in reality, CBS staff engineer Simon Humphrey merits that designation. Foote was from all accounts merely a presence who would occasionally throw in ideas. Not that many studio hands would want to lay claim to the producer's role for this work. The murky mix is undeniably incompetent. However, in one of the miracles of serendipity surprisingly common in art, the maladroit mix improves the record, giving its seething songs an apposite nocturne, menacing atmosphere. It's difficult to imagine the album sounding quite as good had it possessed more conventional, clean-limbed sonics.

Although lauded all over the world, *The Clash* had a particular resonance in the UK. This was a British rock album through and through in a day and age when there was—the odd Kinks LP aside—no such thing. It was also that (then) rare beast: a socially relevant album. For many thousands of young people this album described their lifestyle and their mind-set: anthems articulating disaffection with dreary everyday life, low wages, grim employment prospects, power-drunk authority figures and pusillanimous, blustering politicians. Yet the album is somehow exhilarating rather than depressing. This is mostly due to its breakneck pace. Except for "Police & Thieves," everything here is fast. Short, too. Most of the fourteen tracks are under three minutes. Five are under two minutes. In a counterblast to the rock aristocracy's preening virtu-

osity, the band are almost fanatical—sometimes to the point of parody—in their determination to make their point and depart the stage.

Opener "Janie Jones" sets the tone for *The Clash*. There are better
songs on the record —the underrated "Cheat," for example—but "Janie
Jones" is part of an iconic quartet that also includes "White Riot," "Police & Thieves," and "Garageland" that sums up the spirit of the album
and the times, and that was played in concert by the band throughout
their career.

Chimes' opening minimalist tattoo serves as a businesslike album
fanfare. The cut's galvanizing blurred, continuous lead guitar illustrates
the influence of American proto-punks The Ramones. The lyric is a
twist on what would be a familiar Clash theme: the aching need to
escape the tedium of conventional life. Strummer sings in the third
person of an office worker who takes refuge from the gray routine of
the shift rota and the photocopy room by rock 'n' roll, Janie Jones, and
getting stoned, in that order.

In 1973, Janie Jones—a former minor pop star—briefly became a
household name in Britain when she was put on trial for blackmail,
attempting to pervert the course of justice, and controlling prostitutes.
She was found not guilty on the blackmail charges but guilty on the
others. Many found disproportionate her seven-year prison sentence,
large fine, and order to pay costs, and highlighted the way that famous
celebrities who were her clients and alleged blackmail victims were
ordered not to be named. It was a point of view summed up in a 1982
single titled "House of the Ju-Ju Queen" featuring Janie Jones on vocals
and members of The Clash backing her under the pseudonym The
Lash. The lyric of this latter record summarized an allegedly two-faced
attitude of the Establishment to her notorious sex parties via a line of
dialogue from a chief of police: "Later I'll raid, but first make me behave." The same juxtaposition was also implicit in "Janie Jones."

It's a juxtaposition that has attracted little discussion—or chal-
lenge—down the years. Yet its acceptance as a valid broadside against
the hypocrisies of the ruling class seems open to question. The facts—
long in the public domain by the time "Janie Jones" was written—as
well as the guilty verdicts, support the contention made by several at
the time of her trial that Jones lured young women into prostitution on
the pretext of securing them stardom if they slept with high-placed
media figures and that she then threatened them with exposure when

they attempted to break free from her professional circle. The Clash may have had grounds for a generalized point about upper-class double standards regarding morality and punishment, but Jones was not—contrary to what might be inferred by their tributes, which also included smilingly posing for photographs with her—some kind of delightful figure of rebellion tweaking the nose of the Establishment.

"Remote Control" is a track The Clash have effectively disowned. For instance, it was the only song from their debut album not to be included in some form on the 1991 *Clash on Broadway* box set. This is nominally because it was without their consent released by CBS as the follow-up to the "White Riot" single, but one suspects that the main reason for its low visibility is that they find it rather embarrassing.

Although ignorant youthful aggression is the album's touchstone, Mick Jones's lyric is so simplistic as to be toe-curling. In the vocal lines that he alternates with Strummer's, he wails about those who would seek to control the song's listeners and keep them down, yet these people are referred to only in generic terms such as the civic hall, big business, Parliament, the House of Lords, denizens of upmarket London area Mayfair, and the fat and old. The song is partly the result of The Sex Pistols's recent Anarchy Tour—on which The Clash were a support act—having been decimated by local councilors following a profane Pistols television appearance: twenty-two of the planned twenty-nine shows were cancelled due to official objection. This penchant for low-level officialdom to arbitrarily flex its petty powers is a valid subject that is not done justice by the song's lyric. Meanwhile, officialdom's methods of remote control are no better defined than "Ree-preessh-uun!," which forms one of the more cringe-making vocal refrains in popular music history. This inchoate assertion of subjugation and litany of banality is compounded by a staccato guitar riff that is merely a transposed hand-clap rhythm well known from the nation's soccer stadiums.

Yet the track is not entirely without merit. Jones's inventive guitar solo sees him showing supple-wristed virtuosity despite the era's prevailing ethos obliging him to make it a model of brevity. More importantly, the combination of his mordant melody and the better parts of his bleak songwords summarize with surprising acuity a particular quality of Seventies London life for those without money. Set aside for the moment Britain's Sick-Man-of-Europe status. Even without that state of affairs, Mick Jones's sung lament "Iiiit's so gray in Lahndan Tahn!" would still have had a resonance, and to some extent still does.

The British are, if not a glum race, then not exactly the life and soul of the party. One can cite several possible reasons for this, not least a median average standard of living well below those of comparable industrialized countries. However, another key reason is the weather. The phrase Seasonal Affective Disorder was not in common currency in the Seventies, but had it been, its use would have instantly caused many British heads to nod in understanding. Britain is indeed gray. The sun doesn't shine much. It rains a lot, moreover rains in a depressingly feeble, somehow non-elemental way: the famous English drizzle. Even when it's not raining, the weather can be miserable. Sometimes walking along a quiet street in the capital on an overcast afternoon, one is put in mind by the indiscernible atmosphere almost of the lunar surface.

All of that is implicit in "Remote Control." Explicit is the aching misery of feeling one is on the bottom of society's ladder with no easily accessible way to do anything about it and the fact that this is compounded by the paucity of ways to alleviate the misery arising therefrom: in 1977, continental sidewalk culture was out of the question in a land where pubs and venues serving alcohol closed promptly at eleven p.m. The combination of all those things gave rise to the sense of sheer dreariness in England's capital that, for all its profound faults, "Remote Control" adroitly describes.

In the Seventies, British culture was absolutely drenched in Americana. British weekly "comics" printed primarily in black-and-white on pulp paper had to compete at the newsagents with Marvel and DC "comic books" which, although only monthly, boasted glossy covers and color interiors. So low-key and parochial were British movies compared to American productions with big budgets and glamorous locales that nobody in their right mind going to "the pictures" would prefer to see a British film. The national humiliation attached to this, however, was made easier to stomach by the pleasure the humiliated nation obtained from the superior craftsmanship proffered them by their transatlantic cousins.

Some things, however, irritated Britons about Americans. For instance, American sports were all clearly British sports, only—as in the way of America—blown up to cartoon level. Baseball was just rounders.

Basketball was just netball. American football was just rugby, only its players dressed up in helmets and huge shoulder pads like they were going to fight a war. Said players always seemed to be crouched down and enunciating things like "Hup 25! Hup 61!" What they hell did that mean? And why did they call it football when they used their hands?

Why were the bonnets of their cars so bloody big? Come to that, why were they called "hoods"? And why did they say "mom" instead of "mum"? Or call trousers "pants"? Or petrol "gas"? They spelled colour "color," as well. *Stupid.*

Some things went beyond irritation and induced contempt. American foreign interventions like Vietnam conveyed the impression of a nation that thought it owned the planet. That the extraordinary wealth and economic muscle of the country prompted the discomforting underlying thought that said assumption might well be justified only made things worse. Media reports of U.S. politicians or public figures being gunned down—unthinkable in Britain where handguns were banned—were startling enough, but the impressionistic notion of American cops, provided by both TV drama and documentary reportage, was of gum-chewing, self-dramatizing brutes barely morally distinguishable from those they apprehended. Also astounding was the apparent proliferation of serial killers in America. Equally astounding in its own way were reports of American judges quipping such things as "That's all, folks!" as they pounded their gavels to conclude a case. Even British judges—whom nobody could fire—would never behave with such crassness.

"Faakin' 'ell—what a bloody country!" and "God—only in America!" were the sorts of phrases that often filled British living rooms at the sight of these people who looked and sounded so much like Britons but whose national character and, particularly, flaws seemed to mark them out as extraterrestrials from the planet Moron.

Then there was television, the most pervasive American import. It may be easy to forget the fact in a day and age of *Six Feet Under,* *Frasier, Mad Men,* and other peerless American small-screen productions, but American TV in the Seventies was atrocious. Even high production values and a backdrop that was glamorous to Britons by default couldn't compensate for techniques so hackneyed as to be tut-inducing. Where Britain had gritty, naturalistic cop shows like *Special Branch* and *The Sweeney,* America had the bland, formulaic likes of *Kojak* and

Starsky and Hutch. Even UK law enforcement shows which gravitated toward the fantasy end of the spectrum had a twinkle-eyed approach (*The New Avengers*) or a muscularity (*The Professionals*) that offset cartoonish qualities. Moreover, *all* British shows somehow sidestepped the fault that afflicted American product of being laid out, storywise, like a grid. The dazzling beauty of its lead actresses couldn't disguise *Charlie's Angels*'s emptiness. In *The Incredible Hulk*, the creature always threw antagonists harmlessly onto cardboard boxes and rubbish bins—sorry, trash cans—and his tormented human alter ego ended each and every episode walking into the distance to a piano theme that would be sad had not endless repetition drained it of its original pathos. All American television courtroom scenes seemed to inexorably make their way to the groan-making heated exchange of "Objection, Your Honor!"/"Objection overruled!," just as every episode of *The Six Million Dollar Man* seemed to wind up with Steve Austin squinting soberly at a scientist-type as he enunciated the deathless line, "Can we reverse the praw-cess?" Even a supposedly cutting-edge and daring show like *Hill Street Blues* (or, from a different genre, *Soap*) was still laughably prescriptive compared to UK television. This creakingly rigid American approach was epitomized, of course, by the episode endings of *Hawaii Five-O*: it was surreally pathetic how unvarying was its climactic formula of Detective Steve McGarrett instructing his colleague, "Book him Danno—murder one." Were they taking the piss?

American TV comedy, meanwhile, was just unspeakable. Fifties nostalgia show *Happy Days* had a wit and warmth to it in the beginning, but it shockingly quickly became so desperate as to bequeath the term "jumping the shark." Everything else comedy-oriented coming out of the States was guilty of a mirthlessness that was only compounded by infuriatingly presumptuous fake laughter tracks. The best American TV could do comedywise was *M*A*S*H*, which was enjoyable in its merry gentleness but hardly full of belly laughs. It was inconceivable that "Yanks" could produce anything as hilarious as *Monty Python's Flying Circus*, *Fawlty Towers*, *Some Mothers Do 'ave 'em*, or *Rising Damp*, let alone that they could have the discipline UK writers displayed: British programs didn't know the concept of jumping the shark because their creators declined to flog them to death and instead made sure they were cancelled at their apex after two or three seasons. The legendary reputation of *Fawlty Towers* is predicated on just twelve episodes.

Yet, Britons had little choice but to watch American TV shows. The combination of low-ish disposable income, a total of three national channels, and the low market penetration of VCRs all meant that television had a captive market. As buying American imports was cheaper for British broadcasters than original programming, U.S. programs flooded the "telly."

All of this fed into The Clash's "I'm So Bored with the U.S.A." Strummer snarls and spits his contempt for the culture whose status as originator of his beloved rock 'n' roll is not quite recompense for the fact that "Yankee detectives are always on the TV." The backing to this venom is alternately punchy and soaring, and begins with an ear-splitting, acetylene-torch sound that is one of the most intense guitar riffs of all time.

Despite its high quality, this song epitomizes The Clash's penchant for dishonesty and myth-making in interview. Strummer told this author in 2002 that the composition was a fairly uncomplicated put-down of a lover which assumed a political dimension only through a misunderstanding: "[Jones] said, 'Here's one of mine—it's called "I'm So Bored With The U.S.A."' And I said, Great title! So I wrote it on a bit of paper to make a note of it. He went, 'No, no—"I'm So Bored With You."' I went, 'No, this is better.' He went, 'No, no—it's about my girlfriend.' I went, 'Not anymore!'" This variant of a story Strummer had told several times before cannot possibly be true: "I'm So Bored with You" was in The Clash's early set, played on more than one occasion with its original, non-political lyric intact. Yet Strummer didn't sound like he knew he was lying. It would seem that he had got so used to telling this story that he had ended up thinking it was the truth.

While myth-making has always been part and parcel of the rock tradition that The Clash loved—from name changes to invented romantic backstories—it sat oddly with The Clash, who, like so many punk acts, insisted they were inordinately genuine. This tension between seeking to tell it like it is in their songs and their determination in interviews to give their biographies and activities a mythos would frequently and increasingly leave them open to ridicule and hostility.

Although the band's dissatisfaction with the tameness of the single version may have been a factor in their decision to include a different recording of "White Riot" on *The Clash*, fears of accusations of "selling out" almost certainly contributed to it.

When in 1971 The Rolling Stones released in Britain the single "Brown Sugar," it marked a watershed. Not one of the Stones's previous fifteen UK singles had appeared on album. They were works of art and commercial entities in and of themselves. While their first 45 rpm release of the Seventies was indubitably a work of art—to many Stones fans, their greatest ever—it was a commercial entity on a new level. "Brown Sugar" was put out primarily to promote its parent album, *Sticky Fingers*. There would never again be a "stand-alone" Rolling Stones single in their home country.

Although it had long been the practice in America to both include singles on albums and to release singles from albums, such policy simply seemed crass to natives of the UK. This may have had something to do with the country's class consciousness engendering a more sensitive antennae when it came to suspicions of being taken for a ride. Either way, British record companies were nervous of harming an album's potential sales by generating bad will via the act of including tracks available elsewhere.

Come the Seventies, though, times had changed. Rock music was perceived as big business with a future, not a mere flash in the pan to be exploited before the next craze hit. As a consequence of this, musicians began to finally get the riches they had long deserved but which in many cases had been denied them by philistine and rapacious record company executives. However, it can't be denied that this new mentality also introduced a dismaying corporatism into an art form that had always been implicitly anti-corporate.

Another issue that rang the changes was the fact of the longevity of the idols of the Sixties. Acts like the Stones had now been around so long that the consumers of their product were less likely to be kids spending their pocket money than grown adults parting with some of their wage packet.

For all those reasons, the notion of "ripping off the kids"—taking advantage of those with little money or ability to make sensible decisions—became increasingly less relevant over the course of the Seventies.

Yet these assumptions by the breed that was beginning to be referred to as the rock aristocracy were, as far as British punks were concerned, precisely the point. Bands who no longer felt obliged to issue tri-monthly manifestos on single but instead annual albums simply didn't feel part of a fan's life. Consequently, low productivity became as much a bone of contention for punks with regard to their former idols as substandard product and drug-addled hauteur. As such, many former fans of The Sex Pistols reacted with dismay when they learned that their debut album *Never Mind The Bollocks, Here's The Sex Pistols* (October 1977) was to feature all four of their previously released singles. It reeked of the mercenaryism of the hated likes of Queen, who famously had no compunction about many of their fans paying twice for the same songs. This may have been less to do with band greed than the determination of the Pistols's new record company, Virgin, to financially cover themselves as they picked up the contract of the most notorious band in the world. However, it was still shocking that the standard bearers for what seemed a new age of integrity should have so quickly appeared to betray their principles.

The Clash would have been acutely conscious of these sorts of sentiments when they set about compiling their first album. Although the fact of its title gave "1977" a limited shelf life, its very topicality had made it one of their signature songs. Yet it did not appear on *The Clash*. "White Riot" did, but the band elected to fend off criticism for its inclusion as much as they could. The album version of "White Riot" is the only track on the record not to originate from the album's sessions. It is instead a remix of a recording which precedes their recording contract with CBS, one of the rough demos the band recorded at the National Film and Television School in Beaconsfield in January 1977 through the aegis of their student friend Julien Temple (later to become a famous film director).

In an example of just how blessed this album seems to have been, it was a decision that was as unexpectedly beneficial as the LP's inept mix. The album version of "White Riot" is not only profoundly different to the single version but one of the most exciting rock recordings of all time. Sandwiched between Mick Jones's just-audible "One-two-free-four!" count-in and the track's brutally curtailed ending is one minute and fifty-six seconds of rage translated into tuned sound. A relentless double-time tempo, flaming guitar lines, and a vocal performance from Strummer that sees the microphone drenched in spittle all contribute to a concoction that is heart-stopping. Sometimes Strummer is so angry that he can't even form words properly: in verse three, he departs from demanding to know whether the listeners prefer taking over or taking orders (as enunciated clearly in the single version) to growl and howl something agonized and indecipherable.

There was actually another studio version of "White Riot" in circulation from 1998 when, through some vagary of international copyright law, Italian record company Stampa Alternativa managed to get the right to make available the entire demo tape The Clash recorded through the aegis of Polydor before signing with CBS. It appeared on a CD bundled with a CD-sized book entitled *The Clash Story* (although the product had an ASIN—found on CDs—rather than an International Standard Book Number). Two of these tracks—"Janie Jones" and "Career Opportunities"—had already appeared on the *Clash on Broadway* box set, but "White Riot," "London's Burning," and "1977" were exclusive.

The Polydor tracks were recorded in November 1976 in Polydor Studios in Stratford Place, Central London. They had been commissioned as a demo tape by the label's Chris Parry who was trying to impress his so-far uninterested superiors of the group's viability. The performances feature a Strummer struggling to make his diction clear at the request of Polydor staff engineer Vic Smith. This creates an almost comical incongruity on "White Riot," which serves to make clear that Strummer's descent into manic spluttering on the album version is actually the preferable approach.

In "Hate & War," the contrast between the fluidity of Jones's lead guitar and the unimaginative stabbing on rhythm guitar by Strummer is at its most risible. Simonon's stodgy basslines are given unmerited prominence. Despite this, the music—a loping rhythm with several stop-starts—is decent.

Strummer wrote the lyric but, perhaps subconsciously aware of its shortcomings, gave it to Jones to sing. The songwords embarrassingly confuse radical fervor with macho bravado in their declaration, "If I get aggression, I'll give it two time back." Jones compounds this shortcoming with a singing style that still gauchely carries traces of the American accent that all of The Clash's peers had until recently used in their vocals until they suddenly decided to be bored with the U.S.A. There is also a bizarre coda spat by Strummer in which he declares loathing for Englishmen, "wops," politeness, the police, and "kebab Greeks." Although any suggestion of racism can be refuted by the sheer all-encompassing nature of his resentments, such scattershot anomie hardly suggests the moral superiority and philosophical certainties on which both this album's songs and The Clash's media image were predicated.

The song's central conceit, however, is valid and interesting. Its title, of course, is an inversion of "Love and Peace" and an extension of the loathing professed by UK punks for the hippies for whom that phrase was famously a mantra. "Never Trust a Hippie" became, courtesy of The Sex Pistols, another punk slogan and was itself a play on the hippie catchphrase "Never Trust Anybody over Thirty." As with most punk stances, a touch of gleeful affectation was involved in the attitude articulated in "Hate & War," but, also as with most punk stances, a certain truth lay behind it.

Only ten years previously, the hippies, radicals, and freaks—collectively the "counterculture"—had been the beautiful young people who it was assumed simply by dint of the passage of time would take their values into the centers of power in society. Rather excitingly for the young (and alternative of outlook of any age), this meant that, in a future no further distant than the retirement of the youngest of the "old farts" currently in office, the world would be run by people who were less obsessed with authority than liberty, tradition than new frontiers, formal laws than natural justice, career ladders than personal fulfillment, war than peace. . . . A decade on, however, the world seemed on the surface not to be advancing toward that chilled-out utopia at all, but rather to be either no better than it had been before, or even regressing. In 1977, those in power—seemingly qualitatively unchanged by an influx of younger blood—were committing all the same "crimes" as before: making war, passing censorious laws, demanding conformist lives, and generally failing to evince an outlook that suggested repudiation of old values. The kaleidoscopic tinge of the psychedelic age had drained away and revealed a gray place indeed. The merciless march of time had transformed hippies (shockingly quickly when one thinks about it) from vital, thrusting crusaders for a new world order into irrelevant old farts who represented a failed revolution. Although punks had not reached puberty let alone been politically conscious when the hippies were at their most prominent, they shared this sense of failure. As Strummer said to Caroline Coon of *Melody Maker* on November 13, 1976, "The hippy movement was a failure. All hippies around now just represent complete apathy." This was really an illusion and a symptom of both the young's impatience and their naïveté about how achievable is rapid social change. By just about any measure, life had changed considerably in Western democracies since the heyday of "flower power" and, according to the values of the liberal-left, for the better. Incomes had risen, workplace rights had improved, freedom of expression in the media had been expanded, and liberal reforms had been enacted in the areas of abortion, homosexuality, divorce, racial discrimination, women's rights, the penal system, and several other areas only recently considered rife with grievous injustice. However, this vast progress was disguised for anyone viewing life from the perspective of the left by the perplexing fact that Western societies remained essentially capitalistic: it would be another two decades before the belief in collectivism and the conviction of the unequivocal evil of the free market began to be restricted to a hard core on the far left. The issue was further clouded by inflation, oil shortages, and industrial unrest. The reasons for these problems were varied and not all attributable to old-fartdom, but they created an overarching impression of stagnation or decay that it was difficult for some not to assume to be a symptom of the persistence of the Old Ways.

"Hate & War" goes some way toward encapsulating that combination of disappointment and contempt that punks felt over the fact that the beautiful people hadn't bequeathed them the promised social bounty. Like a disproportionate number of young people, punks desired something in which to believe. With Love and Peace having failed as a cause, that only seemed to leave the opposite/photo negative—an example of the way that the punk credo so often ended up being the antithesis of previous youth and rock culture values.

Purposefully or not, "Hate & War" also demonstrates that, in some ways, the punks' jeering contempt for their predecessors in youth culture is reminiscent of the disdain felt by rebellious teenagers—of any generation—for the supposedly outdated approaches of their parents.

Primitive though the production is on *The Clash*, that it is also not without keen intelligence is illustrated by the consecutive tracks "What's My Name" and "Deny." Both cuts demonstrate apprehension of the need for sonic variety so as to stave off feelings of one-dimensionality, and are accordingly skillfully tweaked to bring about marginal but definite differentiation from the surrounding material.

In the case of "What's My Name," this takes the form of guitars treated to echo spookily and backing choruses doctored to confer a surreal tone. This is apposite for a song intended to convey—even more than the hardly cheerful remainder of the songs—dread. Strummer spits out a lyric depicting the adventures of a young urban malcontent: rowing with his dad, appearing in court on disorder offenses, and effecting entry to strangers' houses with the aid of a "celloid strip." Jones, meanwhile, displays his arrangement skills with tension-building wailing harmonies. The multiple chanting of the title phrase that constitutes the chorus only adds to the song's deliciously disquieting feel. Credited to "Strummer/Jones/Levene," this sole compositional remnant of the Keith Levene lineup of the band is of sufficiently high quality to make one think that a Clash album featuring and co-written by Levene would have been intriguing.

However, this praise comes with a profound caveat. Pretty much everything on *The Clash* is a hostage to fortune, rife with posturing and a snapshot of the immature mentality of uneducated twentysomethings. Yet in its glamorization—even endorsement—of crime against the person (as opposed to the crime against property recommended by "White Riot"), "What's My Name" goes beyond that level of acceptable juvenile folly.

To some extent, the lyric is a symptom of how a class-conscious society, particularly at a time of economic difficulty, engenders an almost Robin Hood perspective on crime. As long as the victim is well-off, such a perspective dictates, there can be considered to be a justification for robbing, or even committing violence against, him. Even the act of fighting in the road for which the narrator gets "nicked" assumes the status of a gesture of rebellion when it transpires that the judge who sentences him doesn't know his identity: it would have been already assumed by the listener that the judge hails from a rarefied public school background because almost all of the British judiciary did in those days; the lack of knowledge of the defendant's name would have chimed with the conviction felt by many that, to such upper-class figures of authority, working-class people were "just a number." (This notwithstanding the fact that the judge's ignorance is a contrived way to lead back into the title vocal refrain.)

Yet the song also dismayingly demonstrates something altogether different to the altruism practiced by a certain Merry Band of Men: the fact that theft and violence can possess a patina of glamour to those too young to fully grasp their effect on individual lives, and too physically sturdy and too materially poor to properly understand that they could one day be the helpless victims of such ordeals. However aesthetically enjoyable is "What's My Name," it is, at heart, morally indefensible.

"Deny" is granted differentiation via a fade-in, plus more eerie production treatment of guitar lines and harmony singing. (It also has one of only three fade-outs on the album, the others being those of "Cheat" and "Police & Thieves.")

Although it is a success on that level, it's unfortunately on this track that the shortcomings of the album's rough-hewn production are most apparent. Repeated listens and hard concentration reveal the verses and coda to be remarkably intricate, but the full effect of the nocturnal tapestry created by the interplay of Strummer's vocals, Jones's guitar, and the otherworldly backing vocals is somewhat obscured, the sonic murk for once detracting from, rather than enhancing, the power of the music.

In terms of its lyric, "Deny" is the closest thing to a song about a sexual relationship that The Clash dared put on the album, and even then, the climate of the times dictated it be far from a love song. It wouldn't be true to say that there was no such thing as a punk love song. The Damned's "New Rose" (October 1976), cited by many as the first-ever punk record, unquestionably fits that description. However, creations of that ilk were thin on the ground. To many punks, love songs somehow seemed a mark of philosophical softness, their composition a deliberate refusal to address the burning issues of a country in crisis. Add to that a pinch of leather-jacketed hard-man posturing—seeming to not need to depend on other people's affections or approval often inspires awe in the young—and it all led to an attitude to romance best summarized by a quote from Mark Perry, editor of punk fanzine/bible *Sniffin' Glue*, who told Val Hennessy in *In The Gutter*, "What is it when you work it out, a mucky dribble, spunk running down some bird's leg, just lust." As such, although it is the only track on this record on which the traditional rock term of romantic affectation "baby" is to be heard, "Deny" is actually anti-romance.

Written in the second person, it constitutes a litany of grievances on the part of a man about a woman (implicitly his lover) who is both a congenital liar (hence the title) and a drug user. Perhaps to provide another buffer against the accusation of soppy love song, the lyric sets the dysfunctional relationship against the backdrop of the punk scene, with one of the narrator's complaints being that the woman lied to him about attending the 100 Club, the London venue that for a period was one of the few places prepared to host punk acts.

Even despite the sonic murk, the track's end is sublime: Jones's hypnotic repetition of the phrase "Whadda liar!" is counterpointed by an extraordinarily sustained spoken-word rant from Strummer that is so varied and lengthy that it sounds like it was scripted but which was, by all accounts, testament to his remarkable powers of stream-of-consciousness spontaneity.

The capital is not literally aflame in "London's Burning." Instead, The Clash co-opt the title of the English nursery rhyme to posit their city as one being consumed by boredom.

To get a caveat out of the way first, Strummer weakens "London's Burning" by the way he renders the line he usually sang live as "Dial 999!" (the UK equivalent of 911). Roaring instead, as he does, "Dial nine, nine, nine, nine, nine!" destroys a good couplet (not least because he sounds like he's enunciating what would be an excruciating rhyme: "To-night-night-night-night-night!"). This is a small misgiving, though, about another powerful blast of invective against sepia-toned inner-city life married to a fine, strident riff and more massed, defiant chorus chanting. For the first time, there is more than one good guitar part: chopped rhythm perfectly complements snarling lead. The track brought side one of the original vinyl *The Clash* album to a dramatic conclusion with a brief but deafening blast of feedback.

The song began life on a balcony of Wilmcote House, part of the Warwick Estate, Notting Hill, where Jones's grandmother—who had raised the guitarist after he was abandoned successively by his parents—lived in a flat on the 18th floor. Strummer told this author in 2002, "We'd go and hang out up there, just lean on the rail and look down across where Westway crosses over Royal Oak. We'd spend night after night up there and one night I went home to [my] squat on Orsett Terrace and just sat down and wrote it, whispering because my girlfriend was asleep." The first two verses of the song are devoted to the Westway. The noisy, soulless flyover that takes motor vehicles west out of London would become a fixture in Clash mythology, a totem of their inner-city origins and concerns. So too would Wilmcote House and

buildings like it, to which verse three is addressed, for they represented
the way that the powers-that-be had somehow contrived to degrade the
lives of the British proletariat even in an era of rising living standards.
Significantly, Clash acolyte Tony Parsons of the *NME* termed their
music "Towerblock Rock."

Tower blocks, also referred to as high-rises, were created with the
best of intentions. In the Sixties, British society was obsessed with slum
clearances, a process whereby the inner-city poor were moved out of
terraces no longer deemed suitable for a decent society by dint of their
dilapidation and outdated facilities. Said slums were demolished and
replaced by buildings that were not only modern but tall, a handy solution to a housing shortage caused by German bombing in World War II
and the rapidly rising population brought about by what Britons then
still referred to as the Baby Bulge, the precipitous post-war birthrate
rise known to Americans as the Baby Boom. At first, the displaced were
grateful: indoor lavatories, central heating, and a general feeling of being a privileged part of a streamlined future created a honeymoon period. Very quickly, however, the drawbacks of tower blocks became apparent. They were soulless, creating little opportunity for neighborly
interaction and hence the sense of community that the slums, for all
their faults, possessed in abundance. They were also ugly. The sense of
their design being futuristic was soon replaced by a consensus that their
architecture was grim. The term "New Brutalism"—later shortened to
merely "Brutalism"—was coined to describe tower blocks. As a consequence of all this, they instilled little sense of proprietorial pride. This
was manifested in vandalism. This problem was squared by the fact that
local councils began using the blocks as dumping grounds for anti-social
tenants in lieu of a queue of "respectable" families willing to be housed
in them.

It even transpired that the logistics regarding building toward the
sky were flawed: planning regulations requiring specific distances between blocks meant that it would have been possible to accommodate
the same number of people in conventional houses. Disasters like Ro-
nan Point—the partial collapse of an East London high-rise in 1968
following a gas explosion—only added to the impression of one of the
biggest catastrophes in the history of social planning.

It was an issue to which The Clash would return, although never as
successfully as in "London's Burning."

Side two of the album's original vinyl configuration opened with "Career Opportunities," yet another display of the band's apparently effortless ability to compose anthems that instantly rang true for their disaffected constituency. A theme of anti-work defiance—Strummer affirms he ain't gonna be a shop assistant, civil servant, bus driver, ambulance man, or any other kind of menial worker—is complemented perfectly by an exhilarating militaristic tempo; a clipped, stop-start chorus; and a breathless, drumstick-flailing finale. The cumulative effect is that the listener wants to punch his fist in the air in solidarity.

The title phrase was one familiar from the Situations Vacant sections of newspapers. By snarling in response to it, "The ones that never knock," Strummer is sardonically playing on the phrase "opportunity knocks," which itself was famous to most Britons as the title of a contemporaneous cheesy (if very popular) TV talent show.

Rock 'n' roll stardom had traditionally been viewed by musicians as their potential salvation from a humdrum existence oriented around jobs in which they were not particularity interested and for which the remuneration was not particularly high. Both Strummer and Jones had had some experience of conventional working life—Strummer had been a gravedigger, Jones a clerical worker at a Social Security (the current name for National Assistance) office. They had stomached just enough of that life to confirm their assumptions of it being soul-destroying. Both had opted for the alternative life then open to them through Britain's generous welfare system: it was very easy to remain "on the dole" for long stretches: no more was demanded of them in exchange for their fortnightly Giro check than that they turn up to "sign on" every fortnight and that they give the impression of actively seeking employment by occasionally visiting a Job Centre.

It was an era where there was little moral compunction about such behavior. Had they contemplated the fact of them effectively stealing from the taxes paid by the very lower-waged whose plight their songs sought to highlight, the Clash members would have quickly squared it with their consciences on the grounds that they didn't want to be part of the rat race and didn't care if they were taking from people who had made that contemptible choice. There may even have been a feeling that, when they became rock stars, they would be paying back in taxes and philanthropy anything they'd taken, although that would have been complicated by The Clash's avowed determination not to follow the conventional path to riches.

Nonetheless, it was an entire mind-set that would have aroused nothing but disgust from the working class of the era of Robert Tressell's *The Ragged-Trousered Philanthropists*, the famous novel that depicted proletarian life in Britain at the turn of the twentieth century. The workers therein had to work long, grinding hours simply to acquire the basics in a life that had little real meaning and, when work was not available, literally starved because of the lack of any welfare provision. Any such workers who had survived into The Clash's era would surely have insisted that youth of The Clash's generation "didn't know they were born"—that they should be grateful for a lifestyle and opportunities that had been beyond the wildest dreams of the working class in their day, including a mere forty-hour week, as well as a totally free education system that theoretically enabled anyone with the desire to do so to actually redefine their class. The notion of demanding from jobs such things as "fulfillment" would have caused bitter amusement to such old-timers.

It raises the interesting point that the welfare state, contrary to the assumptions of its founders, cannot ever bring about a situation where all the problems of society—particularly the grievances of those on the bottom of its hierarchal pyramid—are definitively considered solved. Even in a world without want, there will always be people unhappy with their lot.

"Career Opportunities" gave way to "Cheat" via a between-track gap unusually short for the vinyl era. This meant nothing in the CD age, let alone the era of the download/individual track purchase, but the impression created by the near-segue–one classic snapping at the heels of another–brought home what a veritable embarrassment of riches was *The Clash*. "Cheat" is breathless, snarling, and galvanizing. Its quality is further underlined by the fact that, as though realizing that even another brilliant anthem for the dispossessed would be too similar, the band once more vary the sonic tone, this time with some impressive special effects and an intricate arrangement.

Strummer's lyric sums up a frustration felt from time to time by all who consider themselves on the side of enlightenment in the battle against injustice: the conviction that rules which serve to prevent injustice being corrected should be flouted. "If you play the game, you get nothing out of it," he avers. As discussed in the section on "Career Opportunities," this is a suggestion that is immensely arguable: people of older vintage would be inclined to suggest that Britain in the late Seventies demonstrably rewarded endeavor and the adherence to society's parameters in a way it never had before. This, though, doesn't make the sentiment completely invalid. Many of the unskilled genuinely feel that avenues to betterment are not open to them, and if their viewpoint is dictated by their lack of formal qualifications and resistance to obeying orders from people of spurious authority, that in itself is often a legacy of a needlessly authoritarian education system which seems to them another way of enabling their oppression. In the UK, schoolchildren are far more likely to see teachers as jailers than benefactors by dint of the existence of school uniforms and the dictatorial atmosphere it produces: endless conflict is created by teachers upholding petty rules that have nothing to do with education, with the result that kids from working-class homes where there is no tradition of, or interest in, educational attainment leave school at the earliest opportunity.

It has to be admitted that all of this po-faced analysis of the validity of the song's argument seems slightly preposterous in the context of its sonic impact. You would have to be the most horrendous old fart not to be swept up in the exquisite aural assault Jones constructs around the songwords. The arrangement is incredibly complex: starting with an exciting opening salvo from Chimes, through the staccato guitar underpinning Strummer's barked lyric, through a short instrumental break that soars sky high thanks to it being treated with phasing. Said larger-than-life whooshing gives way to some earthy guitar strumming—creating a sublime contrast —before we're back to more Strummer condemnations of "goody-goodies," followed by a respite from which a marching Chimes brings the band forward. This is followed by a fine, taut guitar solo and the emergence once more of phasing to take the song to a celestial fade. The cumulative effect is awe-inspiring: it seems amazing that all this is crammed into just over two minutes.

"Protex Blue"—on which Jones takes the lead vocal—is named after a make of condom (or "rubber Johnny," hence the closing cry of "Johnny! Johnny!"). Although marred by some unattractive scrabbly guitar, it's a sprightly depiction of young male lust. The narrator fends off a homosexual importuning him in a public lavatory to purchase the archetypal "packet of three" from a vending machine and is then disappointed when he opens it to find it does not contain the brand he desired: he is worried that they won't fit him as he ruminates on the lady whose company he had planned to enjoy. The rather glib and staccato nature of the lyric makes the last verse a little confusing. That the narrator is traveling on London's Underground service —sitting in a tube carriage on the Bakerloo line, then studying the advertisements along the escalator stairs leading up from the platforms—is clear enough, but the songwords throw in a slightly perplexing twist in which, apparently apropos of nothing, he spurns "skin flicks" (porn movies) and insists he wants to be alone.

That "Protex Blue" is one of the few tracks on *The Clash* that doesn't bear much sociological analysis is probably down to the fact that it predates Joe Strummer's influence on Mick Jones's songwriting. Tony James, Jones's ex-colleague in the band London SS, has even stated that it was the first-ever Mick Jones original. If true, that would make the track particularly impressive, not just because of its precociously able construction and witty, self-deprecating tone, but because of its punk prescience. Songs depicting the mundane mechanics of preparing for sex phrased in an English working-class vernacular speckled with contemporary references (Jones calls his penis his "P. D. drill," a type of power tool) were simply not being written in the mid-Seventies. As such, a song whose vintage might have been assumed to render it out of place actually fitted in perfectly on an album—and with a musical movement—that both spurned conventional subjects (especially chocolate-box romance imagery) and delighted in breaching taboos.

Unlike most acts in rock history who are ultimately recognized as great artists, The Clash were disdained by many critics before they had product in the stores. The same, of course, applies to The Sex Pistols: during a changing of the guard, the old order is usually not receptive to the idea of the necessity for its replacement (or, in this case, the replacement of its musical and philosophical values). The derision directed at The Clash, though, was on a deeper level: unlike The Sex Pistols, they couldn't claim the cachet of being the first example of their type, nor the mantle of Outsider that the Pistols acquired as soon as they started playing live, let alone the glamorous status of social outlaw forced on the Pistols when they became nationally famous after their controversial December 1976 television appearance. Moreover, their rudimentary skills and unconventional approach made The Clash very much an acquired taste in their early days. A confrontational stage manner and grim subject matter—vaguely disturbing to graduates of the Summer of Love—only increased a repugnance factor that even applied with those who had been partial to the bad-boy mien of The Rolling Stones.

Although not too many could sustain that contempt for The Clash once their manifestly high-quality first album was available, it's also doubtful that quite so many detractors would have been converted without the presence on the first Clash album of two particular tracks: "Police & Thieves" and "Garageland." Without that brace, the record would have evinced a paucity of three things considered essential to a halfway competent and worthwhile rock release: complexity of instrumentation, emotional warmth, and variety of timbre. Instead it would have been—as well as a rather short album—a collection of tracks limited by their broadly uniform brevity, primitivism, and attitudinal bent. In short, "Police & Thieves" and "Garageland" conferred on the album the breadth necessary to take it from the realms of minor to major work.

Interestingly—almost frighteningly—neither "Police & Thieves" nor (at least up until a month before the release of *The Clash*) "Garageland" were part of The Clash's live set before the release of their first album, giving rise to the discomforting suspicion that those who dismissed the band as insignificant at that point in time were expressing a justifiable position based on the evidence presented to them.

"Police and Thieves" was a 1976 reggae single by Junior Murvin, written by him and his producer Lee "Scratch" Perry. Although it hadn't been a UK hit (that would come in 1980, when it made no. 23), reggae was not in Britain the underground music it was in the United States, but rather a de facto mainstream sound.

The first reason for this was the fact that UK pop chart positions were not in any way dependent on airplay. It was purely sales that determined what appeared in the nation's charts. If this still left musicians at the mercy of radio programmers, it should be noted that the latter had a less conservative attitude than their U.S. counterparts partly because of the exposure to more alternative sorts of music engendered by that sales-oriented process. The will of the people, not the whims or prejudices of "straights," dictated the UK charts.

In a country with only three television stations and one national radio channel, and in which commercial local radio had only begun in 1973, the media was compact (and, it must be said, limited) in a way beyond comprehension to the average American. Whereas in America in order to enter the charts a record would have to weave its way into the affections of DJs or programmers in multiples of states of a vast country, in the UK it would simply have to prompt enough people to go out and purchase it after they'd heard it on, say, John Peel's Radio One program. Either that, or seen it reviewed in one of the music papers, whose proliferation (four) and regularity (weekly) enabled a speedy throughput of promotion and availability information. Once a record had surmounted the hurdle of being deemed broadcast-worthy by a sufficient number of programmers or DJs—both because it had already appeared in the charts and there was no easy way to claim it unacceptable for a family audience—becoming a hit was a relatively easy matter.

An appearance on BBC TV chart program *Top of the Pops* cemented that hit status. It also underlined the impossibility of consigning reggae, punk, or any other genre to the underground status no doubt desired for it by many in the country's establishment. The BBC show did nothing more than represent what was currently selling well and was therefore obliged to offer a slot to anybody who qualified.

As far back as the late Sixties, reggae began achieving footholds in the UK chart when skinheads—perhaps a little self-consciously—decided to adopt it as their preferred music. Its slow, lilting, repetitive structures sounded strange—even at first absurd—to the pop consumer's ear, and many parents of the era were apt to express disapproval of their children listening to "darkie music." However, the likes of Desmond Dekker's "Israelites" and "It Mek," The Upsetters's "Return of Django," Dave and Ansel Collins's "Monkey Spanner," Bob and Marcia's "Young, Gifted and Black," and Nicky Thomas's "Love of the Common People" achieved a popularity in Britain that served to make reggae simply another branch of the tree of popular music. By the time of the point in 1971 when the pastiche record "Johnny Reggae" made a UK no. 3, reggae's sense of danger and exotica had dissipated.

A similar thing happened with punk. Although a genre that was the epitome of underground in the States, the mass of the British public were exposed to just about all of the major punk acts and records. The Sex Pistols's first two singles, "Anarchy in the UK" and "God Save The

Queen," were banned from playlists for very particular reasons (the first because of a firestorm of bad publicity after their aforementioned pro-fane TV appearance, the second due to the taboo of republicanism in a Royal Jubilee year), but the same fate did not afflict the Pistols's subse-quent records, nor product by Sham 69, The Adverts, X-Ray Spex, Buzzcocks, The Stranglers, The Boomtown Rats, and sundry other acts who were palpably New Wave.

Those acts had little difficulty securing hits despite the supposed anti-commerciality of the harsh and self-aggrandizing punk sound be-cause, New Wave or no, their records were often catchy, as well as intriguing almost by default. *Top of the Pops* helped because, as the only regular music show on the box, it was the nation's meeting place for pop and a family viewing staple. Its fifteen million viewers meant that a quarter of the country was regularly tuning in. As such, house-wives, businessmen, and babes in arms—as well as those more directly interested—were in the late Seventies treated to the regular sight of spiky-haired malcontents bellowing their grievances into microphones against the show's usual garish light entertainment-oriented backdrops. (That wasn't too great a culture shock for Britons, however. Parents had long become used to being reduced to spluttering rage by the sights on *Top of the Pops*: only a few years before punk had come the mildly grotesque, pouting quasi-transvestitism of Sweet's Steve Priest and the gilded orangutan image of Wizzard's Roy Wood.)

The spiritual link between British punk and reggae may have been overplayed by music historians. The punk bands certainly had Rastafar-ian mates like Lee Perry, Don Letts, and Bob Marley, and incorporated reggae covers and originals into their repertoires partly as a gesture toward a fellow form of outsider/rebel music. However, the speedy tempos and belligerent attitudes by which punk audiences were en-thralled was a world removed from the general musical tranquility of "riddim." While it's true that reggae shared punk's lyrical penchant for social protest, the average inner-city youth in Britain did not really feel much kinship with—or, whisper it lightly, sympathy for—the downtrod-den black Jamaican.

Nonetheless, reggae was sometimes a big influence on British punk bands either by osmosis (Johnny Rotten of The Sex Pistols had a long-standing love of the genre) or imitation (The Clash and Stiff Little Fingers were among punk bands who always tried to include at least one reggae number on their albums). "Police & Thieves" (as they rendered the title) was The Clash's first foray into the medium, and an unexpected triumph. Originally a band warm-up song, it was included on *The Clash* to bulk it up to a standard playing length without having to resort to lesser originals.

Part of its success is the consequence of it being far more than a cover of the Murvin record. By lengthening and adding intensity to Murvin's fine but rather soft-focus original, it improves it. Jones's arrangement—guitars hit on both the off-beat and the on-beat—is sublime, but Terry Chimes's drumming plays just as large a part in the track's brilliance. His piston-regular pattern nails itself into the listener's brain, ultimately inducing a state approaching a trance. Even Simonon puts in a bravura performance with his mesmerizing lugubrious bass throb. Although, at six minutes, it is three times as long as most of the album's tracks, "Police & Thieves" doesn't feel bloated in comparison. Instead, its leisurely atmosphericness allows it to make its point in its own time.

The lyric about the misery engendered by criminals and the methods used by the authorities to combat them had, of course, a resonance in life-is-cheap Jamaica that it never could in what Mick Jagger described in "Street Fighting Man" as "sleepy London town." However, while the words might be a mere cops 'n' robbers nursery rhyme in the mouth of a child of a temperate welfare state like Strummer, the conviction of his delivery ensures that at no point does he come over as laughable or presumptuous. In fact, the track feels no less valid than material surrounding it informed by direct knowledge.

Toward the end of the track, Strummer is ranting in another of his climactic ad-libs while the instrumentation behind him quietly builds to a towering height. Just as a musical crescendo is expected, his franticly scrubbed guitar abruptly falls away to leave just the spare sound of Jones's stabbed guitar, Simonon's calm bassline and Chimes's piston-regular drumming. It's a stunning moment. A clear nod to reggae's "drop out" tradition, it's as inspired and hypnotic as anything from the average progressive rock virtuoso, but possessed of far more grit.

"48 Hours" tackles the same subject matter as "Janie Jones" and "Career Opportunities" but embraces just about all the musical clichés and ham-fisted means of expression that those songs managed to deftly sidestep.

Its line "Monday is coming like a jail on wheels" is a worthy successor to that melancholy desperation once articulated by The Easybeats as "Monday I've got Friday on my mind" (and in less succinctly quotable terms by Fats Domino in "Blue Monday"). That, though, is about the extent of the track's cleverness. The lyric is lazy, in particular a third, final verse wherein the narrator switches from a straightforward, if hardly poetic, litany of grievances about his unfulfilling, unskilled life to a claim that he can't make his way around because his legs are broken. Just a little more exercise of the gray matter would have seen Strummer/Jones make the small jump to realizing that they really meant the narrator's spirit was broken and thus turn a risible line into something with a poignancy the subject deserved.

"48 Hours" is uninspired musically, as well. Not disgraceful as such, but in its marching featurelessness and failed anthemic chorus it's the only thing on the LP with nothing sonically to write home about. As though realizing it amounts to nothing more than a nondescript bridge between two profoundly superior tracks, The Clash make it, at 1:36, the shortest song on the record.

Charles Shaar Murray has been an intelligent commentator on rock since the late Sixties. He, however, was one of those observers who failed to see the potential of The Clash. The Clash's first-ever gig was a support slot to The Sex Pistols at the Black Swan, Sheffield, on July 4, 1976. Their second was an invitation-only performance for booking agents and music journalists at their rehearsal space (the tautologously named Rehearsals Rehearsals) in Camden, north London, on August 13. Their third was another Pistols support slot, this one at The Screen on the Green, Islington, London, on August 29. Reviewing the latter event for *New Musical Express* (known to one and all as "the *NME*"), Murray said, "The Clash are the kind of garage band who should be speedily returned to the garage, preferably with the motor still running, which would undoubtedly be more of a loss to their friends and families than to rock and roll." Such a reception to their proper London entrée hardly seems the sort of thing to induce anything other than despair in The Clash. Strummer, though, seemed to be as much honored as angry. "Joe was really excited about this idea of a garage band," Terry Chimes said in Chris Salewicz's 2006 Strummer biography *Redemption Song*. "That led to the song 'Garageland'."

Garage rock was a phenomenon that began in America in the wake of the "British Invasion." Following The Beatles's storming of the U.S.A. in 1964 and the subsequent cultural takeover by their compatriots, teens up and down America were inspired to pick up guitars and take up drums. Their rehearsal space was usually somewhere conveniently local and free of charge: the family garage. The proliferation of small local labels in the States ensured that it wasn't too difficult for garage bands with a modicum of talent to make a record. The music heard on such singles was often primitive but also sometimes brilliant, the combination of lack of finesse and presence of naïve enthusiasm making for the likes of primal classics such as "Laugh, Laugh" by The Beau Brummels, "Dirty Water" by The Standells, and "96 Tears" by ? & the Mysterians.

Although groups like Paul Revere and the Raiders and Tommy James and the Shondells both translated their arguable garage band roots into mainstream careers, most purveyors of such records were one-hit wonders. Several of them, however, were in 1972 unexpectedly granted immortality when Elektra Records compiled the double-LP *Nuggets*, which collected notable examples of the genre. Subtitled *Original Artyfacts from the First Psychedelic Era, 1965–1968*, it was one of the first industry releases to evince a genuinely archival approach to rock music. It became one of the half-dozen biggest influences on the UK punk scene, along with the eponymous debut albums of The New York Dolls (1973) and The Ramones (1976), *Back in the U.S.A.* by MC5 (1970), *Raw Power* by the Stooges (1973), and *The Velvet Underground and Nico* (1967).

In his liner notes, *Nuggets* compiler Lenny Kaye did not use "garage rock" to describe the LP's tracks. Instead, he said, "The name that has been unofficially coined for them—'punk-rock'—seems particularly fitting in this case, for if nothing else they exemplified the berserk pleasure that comes with being on-stage outrageous, the relentless middle-finger drive and determination offered only by rock and roll at its finest." Although the quote indicates that he was not making a claim for devising the term "punk rock," *Nuggets* was unquestionably the first place many encountered it, particularly in Britain, where "punk" had not hitherto been part of the lexicon, musical or general.

In 1976, a pair of British music journalists decided to give a new musical movement in their country a convenient handle. Sex Pistols bassist Glen Matlock told this author in 1999, "Caroline Coon and Jonh [sic] Ingham came up with it 'cos they had to call it something. I think one week there was all of a sudden two major articles. Caroline [of *Melody Maker*] knew Jonh Ingham of *Sounds* and they kind of colluded and both decided to call it 'punk rock' for want of something else. I didn't like being called punk rock—neither did John [Johnny Rotten]— 'cos we thought it was a loser kind of term and it reminded us of all that Sixties *Nuggets* kind of thing."

Joe Strummer clearly decided he liked being called a garage rocker. Perhaps it was because of the intoxicatingly snotty quality of the music to which Kaye referred or its purity of intent, the kind of which can only come from people too young to have known disillusion. Strummer may even have had a notion that the ad hoc amateurism of the garage rock scene was something in keeping with the poverty-dwelling punk spirit, although that would have been misguided: unlike American homes in the Sixties, British households—many of whom still didn't have access to indoor toilets—could usually only dream of having their own garages. In any event, Strummer defiantly appropriated the garage band title for a powerful new song about the punk movement, thus unknowingly completing some sort of terminology circle.

"Garageland" sees Strummer lament the commercialization of the punk scene and the attendant corruption of its ethos of No Compromise. The Clash, of course, were perceived to not be without sin in that department, what with their receipt of a check for £100,000 as an advance against royalties when they signed to CBS Records in January 1977. As such, it is possibly a certain sense of guilt that motivated the song as much as idealism.

"Garageland" is a farewell to punk and a scene that—reliant as it was on an outsider status that ceased to exist when the punk acts were welcomed in by the music establishment—was dying even as he wrote the lyric. This is shot through with the knowledge of a dichotomy: success involved making money, which would inevitably cause agonizing because, while they hated the imagined values of the wealthy, the band had never been fans of poverty. Strummer's impassioned declaration that he will not give in to record company executives who want the group to wear suits and that he will have no truck with the rich and their priorities ("The truth is only known by guttersnipes") is undercut by the overall melancholy, one that is heartrending. Jones's wonderful melody once again has the attributes of an anthem, but this time it's the anthem of a defeated, retreating army, an impression underlined by his keening guitar and blasts of mournful mouth harp. It all makes for an unexpectedly thoughtful and poignant closer to the record.

Charles Shaar Murray, incidentally, recanted and became a champion of The Clash.

The Clash came housed in a cover featuring a photograph of Strummer, Jones, and Simonon in a legs-planted pose whose drama was cranked up by it being rendered in negative-effect. The back cover featured a similarly bleached-out photo of a police charge, with the track listing spelled out in scruffy faux-typewriter lettering.

The high UK chart position achieved by the record—no. 12; astounding for a product with little mainstream media coverage—was one of the things which made some conclude that The Clash were now the most important punk act. They had started out as quite open disciples of The Sex Pistols, but the Pistols had fallen behind in the race because they were unable to issue product as they lurched from record company to record company. While their being kicked off EMI and A&M in quick succession naturally enhanced the Pistols's outlaw credentials, it meant that, in an era where fans and critics were permanently hungry for product, they hadn't even released their second single by the time The Clash issued their debut album.

When The Sex Pistols's album entrée did appear six months after The Clash's debut, it was something of a disappointment. Few doubted the awesome and revolutionary quality of the string of singles that had preceded *Never Mind The Bollocks, Here's The Sex Pistols*—"Anarchy in the UK," "God Save The Queen," "Pretty Vacant," and "Holidays in the Sun"—but, as previously mentioned, their very presence on the album was ideologically offensive. Moreover, although several of the previously unheard tracks were of very high quality, the album was cumulatively exhausting in its endless stream of invective and relentless wall of guitar sludge. That emotional and musical monotone was exactly what The Clash had managed to sidestep with their own LP, and The Clash's rough-hewn humanity was in many ways more appealing than the Pistols's more abstract nihilism.

The Clash became the darling of the younger music critics, particularly those on the left-leaning *NME* and alternative-minded *Sounds*, even if that relationship very quickly developed into one in which the music papers adopted the pious role of Jiminy Cricket to The Clash's supposedly wayward Pinocchio.

By January 1978, the debate about who were the punk figureheads was over: Johnny Rotten's departure from their ranks meant that the Pistols were history in all but name. The Pistols staggering on without him only added to the sense of their having been usurped by the pretenders to the crown: Sid Vicious, guitarist Steve Jones, or even drummer Paul Cook took lead vocals on record releases (which continued for a further eighteen months) that traded on The Sex Pistols's notoriety to increasingly cartoonish effect.

Although *The Clash* put its creators in the vanguard of the New Wave, and although it remains a brilliant snapshot of a particular age and state of mind, a quarter of a century after its release logic dictates that it cannot have the same resonance. With endless strikes and hyperinflation no longer part of the UK landscape, it has been a long time since a generation was born into such difficult times that it felt self-abnegation to be its appropriate means of expression. Punks who once averred there was "No Future" now have bald spots in place of spikes and mortgages to offset their enthusiasm for white riots. Meanwhile, while social authoritarianism and financial poverty still exist, the endless incremental Western process of reform has ensured they are less pronounced than ever before.

Yet different though contemporary circumstances are, the album doesn't feel profoundly dated. The reason for this is that The Clash—as they would throughout their career—wisely disdained specific references in their songs to current-day events. Contrast this to the approach of The Tom Robinson Band, a hard-rock act inspired by The Clash who would achieve prominence in 1978. While the very topicality of TRB's songs temporarily gave them a greater power than The Clash's works— a "relevance," to use a common superlative of the day—it also quickly dated them and thereby drained them of resonance. Nowadays, not even its musical excellence can save TRB's work from largely being interesting in only an abstract sense. It is so peppered with references to half-forgotten public figures, barely remembered proposed government legislation, and now-moot talking points that it sometimes seems as stale and unworthy of attention as an old newspaper. *The Clash* has avoided acquiring a patina of age because its contents stick to generalities. Essentially, it lists grievances that will always be concerns for the questioning young of any era.

The Clash is now widely revered, regularly featuring in critics' polls to determine the greatest albums in popular music history. Although this exalted status is justified, it has to be conceded that, in a sense, *The Clash* always seems the odd-man-out in such tables. Compared to other fixtures of such polls such as The Beatles's *Sgt. Pepper's Lonely Hearts Club Band*, The Rolling Stones's *Exile on Main St.*, Bob Dylan's *Highway 61 Revisited*, The Jimi Hendrix Experience's *Are You Experienced*, The Who's *Who's Next*, Love's *Forever Changes*—or, indeed, The Clash's own later work *London Calling*—*The Clash* looks like a presumptuous interloper. How can such a badly produced, rudimentarily played, and often spiritually mean-spirited work be considered fit to stand beside such examples of fine craftsmanship, high production values, and touching compassion? It's also more of a mood album than most other acknowledged classics, and becomes more so the older one gets. Its moral absolutism and spiritual aggression are the stuff to strike a chord with those who are unfulfilled, property-less, and loveless. Greater nuance of thought comes into play the more emotional validation and material comforts an individual acquires, while less venom seems appropriate the more one's private life confers peace of mind. This fact was perfectly summarized by American rock critic Robert Christgau in his book *Albums of the '90s* when, noting that his two favorite rock albums were the debuts of The New York Dolls and The Clash, he admitted that he didn't play either of them often because they are "loud and harsh, and don't fit very neatly into my middle-aged, nuke-fam leisure schedule."

Perhaps in the end, though, this odd-man-out status is a superlative—just another way of saying that *The Clash* is a unique album.

2

SELLOUT ALERT

After having worked with interim members following Chimes's departure, in April 1977 The Clash recruited Nick Headon—born in Kent in March 1955, raised in coastal Dover—as their new drummer. It's a measure of how long ago this now is that, for a while, there was a certain air of mystery about what he looked like: it wasn't until Lester Bangs's famous three-part *NME* Clash feature in December that year that a photograph of Headon appeared publicly.

Some long-term Clash camp followers always had their doubts about Headon, who seemed to them disturbingly insecure and erratic. For them, such misgivings about him would ultimately be seen to be justified. However, the existing members of the band took him to their hearts, not least because of his excellent drumming skills and unusual multi-instrumentalist abilities. Despite his not being a founding member, Headon came to be considered by both his new colleagues and the public as part of The Clash's definitive lineup.

In the month of the release of their first album, The Clash entered into a mutually beneficial agreement with the *NME* over an Extended Play release called *Capital Radio*. This three-track, 7-inch disc was given away free to those readers who sent in a sticker supplied with the first 10,000 copies of *The Clash* attached to a coupon that had been printed in the music weekly.

Although it might be churlish to quibble about the substantiality of an item that was gratis, the offer immediately seemed less impressive when it was realized that one of the tracks, "Interview with The Clash on the Circle Line," consisted of twelve minutes (spread across two parts) of The Clash responding to questions. These days, the interview has some historical value, particularly the band's tough-guy posturing and ostentatiously dropped *h*'s. It's a snapshot of a time when working-class vernacular was a much rarer presence in "straight" media than it is today, leading to a conviction that emphasis of accent was a rebellious act in and of itself. Additionally, at the time musical artists were not as all-pervasive in the culture as they would later be made by home video/ DVD, multiple-channel television, and the Internet, so there was still a certain frisson that came with the relative unfamiliarity of hearing their speaking voices. However, it would probably be fair to say that, even then, most fans would have preferred another new Clash song. Tony Parsons's fawning questions and the band's self-conscious answers are intellectually barren.

One of the EP's two musical tracks didn't even quite merit the description "song," "Listen" being an instrumental. It also barely merited the description "new." Although a pleasing enough piece of music with a stiletto-sharp riff, it's not exactly dissimilar to "London's Burning." Moreover, it is a mere 27 seconds in length. The band could have opted to include the full-length (2:44) version heard playing beneath the Parsons interview, but made the world wait until 1994, when it was placed on the rarities album *Super Black Market Clash*. Said version reduced the impression of a "London's Burning" clone but without creating the feeling of a substantial piece of music in the tradition of acclaimed instrumentals like "Green Onions" by Booker T and the MGs and "Grow Your Own" by The Small Faces.

The one cut on the record that could be said to be substantial is the title track. "Capital Radio"—the first Clash recording to feature the drumming of Headon—resulted from Strummer's mixture of emotions at the appearance of The Clash's first release. Although he could be said to be different to his colleagues in having prior experience of being a recording artist, it could also be appended: "only just." The first and last single by the 101'ers—"Keys to Your Heart"—appeared on Chiswick in July 1976, the very month after he had abandoned the 101'ers to join the band that would become The Clash. When "White Riot" rolled off the production lines, therefore, his thrill would have been little different to that of Jones and Simonon at the fact of his voice and instrumentation emanating from a piece of round black plastic just like all the ones bearing the strains of his heroes that had spun on his turntable since youth.

Strummer sat expectantly down at the radio, waiting for "White Riot" to be played over the airwaves. When it became apparent that his masterpiece was going to be ignored by "suits" more interested in pumping out banal love songs than compositions that spoke to the concerns of his countrymen, he and Jones wrote "Capital Radio" in fury, turning the titular London radio station's lilting slogan "In tune with London, yeah, yeah, yeah" into the put-down "In tune with nothing" and effectively likening their head of music Aidan Day to Josef Goebbels. By the point of the closing notes of "Capital Radio," Strummer is at the state of apoplectic speechlessness into which he had descended in the final verse of the album version of "White Riot." In this case, this is not impressive: his fury feels completely out of proportion to its subject and seems to somewhat miss the point.

The arrival of Capital Radio on the airwaves in October 1973 had been quite an exciting event. It was the first time the British government had permitted anybody but the BBC to broadcast music. Other local independent stations were subsequently brought into existence up and down the country by the same 1972 Sound Broadcasting Act that bequeathed Capital, but the London contract was obviously the most important in terms of exposure and prestige.

Foreign music industry figures were often bewildered by the fact that a record would flop in the UK if it failed to make the Radio One playlists or secure an appearance on *Top of the Pops*. Although at the time of Strummer's composition Capital remained the sole commercial pop radio station in Britain's hub city, its arrival theoretically meant that the BBC stranglehold on the British media was over. To some extent the monopoly-smashing theory was true. However, that did not mean that a record like "White Riot" would receive much attention from disc jockeys. The average housewife or window cleaner turning on their radio to help their day go quicker did not want the harsh sounds of punk assaulting their eardrums. As such, it was unreasonable to expect stations like Capital to risk alienating their audience. Punks could not have it both ways by setting their face against mellow musical strains and shallow sentiment and still expect to have access to the audience that favored such undemanding stylings. This particularly applied to "White Riot." Even the average working-class Labour voter did not want a riot of their own and would have been disgusted by agitprop which reduced such a disturbing phenomenon as civil disorder to facile sloganeering.

In any event, Strummer's claim of a marathon listening session in which he waited in vain for a broadcast of his record should be treated with caution. Self-mythologizing and martyrdom were by now becoming second nature to The Clash. Although airplay during the daytime was out of the question, the record received exposure on Radio One, the country's only national station, albeit probably restricted to the late-night show of John Peel, an old hippie who had made a Damascene conversion to punk. While it may not have got airplay on Capital, said station's Nicky Horne–fronted nightly show *Your Mother Wouldn't Like It* (later *The Rock Show*) would prove very amenable to New Wave. Moreover, the Clash camp were probably predisposed to hate Capital Radio. In 1974, Bernard Rhodes had been involved in designing a T-shirt to be sold in Malcom and Vivienne McLaren's shop Sex, the now-famous (and valuable) "You're gonna wake up one morning and KNOW what side of the bed you've been lying on." It was essentially an "In" and "Out" listing. "Loves" were on the right. Among the uncool stuff ("Hates") on the left was "Capital Radio."

The music of "Capital Radio" is as unimpressive as the lyric. While the riff is in the staccato vein of the likes of The Who's "I Can't Explain" and The Kinks's "You Really Got Me," it doesn't galvanize sufficiently to feel part of a noble tradition. The melody is competent but undermined by the circularity, banality, and quasi-dishonesty of the argument borne on it.

Whatever the cheap jibes one could make about the *Capital Radio* EP not representing value for money even though it was free, those who did obtain it were ultimately rewarded: the fact that there were only a limited number pressed led to an inevitable rarity status and mushrooming of worth.

The Clash were one of the last great singles bands. That phrase has since been devalued by it being applied to acts who release endless singles as a way to advertise an album, attached to multiple, otherwise unavailable B-sides to encourage purchase by fans who already have the album. The proper meaning of the phrase—artists who view singles as stand-alone entities—may not have quite described The Clash, who by the time of their second album had bowed to the exigencies of being signed to a major label and abandoned their preferred policy of never releasing LP tracks as 45 rpm records. However, they continued to value the single form as something other than a promotional tool, releasing non-album 45s and, especially, B-sides for almost the whole of the rest of their career.

A measure of how pure a singles band were The Clash in the early days is provided by the fact that when on May 13, 1977, CBS released "Remote Control" as the band's second 45 without the group's consent, not only did they refuse to promote it, but they proceeded to write a song about their anger over the issue. Although it featured the enticement of an otherwise unavailable live version of "London's Burning" on its flip side, "Remote Control" failed to chart. The live "London's Burning" has effectively been as much disowned by The Clash as the A-side, turning up very infrequently on Clash product since.

The legendary figure of the record company ogre was by this juncture in history becoming a thing of the past. Over the course of the Seventies, the young men and women entering the music business were increasingly people who had been weaned on popular music. Within a decade, those at the other end of the age scale whom they were replacing—people who were really devotees of classical music, easy listening, or pre-rock pop, and who had no more passion for what they were marketing than for shoes or pork chops—would be on the way to the same fate as the dinosaurs they were already dismissed as by their would-be successors. However, CBS had managed to live up to the outmoded ogre cliché to perfection.

By a supreme irony, the unauthorized release with which CBS attempted to bolster The Clash's commercial fortunes only did so via a circuitous manner in the sense of inspiring a song that became a minor hit. "Complete Control," the single that The Clash wrote partly about the "Remote Control" issue, climbed to no. 28 upon its September 23, 1977, release. Not only was it a commercial success, "Complete Control" is one of The Clash's most celebrated recordings. The record has also become part of that confrontation- and rebellion-oriented myth so assiduously cultivated by the band, a veritable yardstick of their integrity.

Although its title seems designed to be a bookend to that of the previous single in its usage of the word "control" and a preceding adjective, it was actually bequeathed by a comment from Bernard Rhodes,

who, in a typically outlandish public bar rant, demanded "complete
control" over his charges. Although Strummer sings, the lyric is entirely
the work of Mick Jones, who, furious at what he felt to be the meaning-
lessness of CBS promises of artistic control that the "Remote Control"
affair exposed, dashed out a catalog of this and other band grievances,
ranging from "Remote Control" ("We didn't want it on the label!" barks
line two) to the band not being able to get their mates into their gigs to
the group being harassed by the media and the police at a time when
punks were considered enemies of society.

There is a tinge of childish whine created by the fact that many of
the lines start with *"They* said . . ." The overall fury is once again
disproportionate to the injustice. The mix is slightly muddy (reggae man
Lee Perry produced both A- and B-sides, although Jones remixed his
work). However, all this is largely offset by the flaming quality of the
music. The record begins with a hefty riff counterpointed by a pulsing
drumbeat and proceeds with dramatic tom-tom rolls and vocal yodels.
It climaxes with a section where an echoed Strummer rants freeform
against a backdrop of Jones both peeling off guitar runs and wailing the
second word of the title.

It's interesting how quickly The Clash abandoned the minimalist
policy of the previous year, captured for posterity on their debut album:
from here on, their song length would be conventional ("Complete
Control" is 3¼ minutes) and their instrumentation markedly less primitive ("Complete Control" has more than one virtuoso guitar solo).

If the guitar virtuosity of "Complete Control" confirmed that the
studied minimalism of punk had been destined to last no longer than
the advent of the increased proficiency inevitably brought about by
regular live work, its B-side suggested that The Clash were going a
taboo-breaking step further in being actively interested in adopting musical trappings against which punk had been assumed to have set its
face.

Lyrically, "City of the Dead" is very much a punk song. It speaks
once again of a dreariness to London life, one that this time the protagonist and his lover vainly try to escape via the momentary pleasures of
sex, a dreariness so acute that the narrator finds himself even envying
the fate of a drowned friend. In later verses, the narrator alternately
laments and exults in the danger of walking the streets in punk clothing.
The bridge sees him recalling that a New York acquaintance had ridi-

culed him for not knowing where to score drugs in his own city. (This apparently was Johnny Thunders, formerly of The New York Dolls and recently a support act to The Clash as frontman of The Heartbreakers.)

All of this would be considered by the average punk musician or fan to be suitable only for a three-chord thrash setting. The Clash, however, opt for an arrangement at the center of which is saxophone. John Earle—the first auxiliary musician employed on a Clash recording—blows a mournful riff that gels surprisingly well with the traditional guitar-oriented Clash approach. He then duets with his overdubbed self to bring the song to a close. Despite the quality of the track, such was the purist credo of the time that it would have caused alarm bells to ring with some, manifested in reactions ranging from a snorting amusement that the Clash were "poncing about" to feelings that it was a sign of a sellout.

The Clash had spent large chunks of 1976 lapping up the almost parodic minimalism of the first Ramones LP. (They sometimes played The Ramones's signature song "Blitzkrieg Bop" in concert, and a live version of it—actually an exclusive medley of that and "Police & Thieves"—appeared as a hidden track on a 1999 promo CD titled *Rockers Galore* manufactured to publicize their live album, *From Here to Eternity*.) However, whereas The Ramones effectively spent their two-decade, fourteen-album career re-creating their entrée, both "Complete Control" and "City of the Dead" demonstrated that The Clash were too talented and imaginative to be content to plow the same limited furrow forever. Having made their point about the rock aristocracy's "wanky" tendencies, they were now already moving on to forms of music that would retain punk's urgency and political commitment but which would enable them to give full vent to their ever-deepening musical sophistication. Many of the UK class of '76/'77 failed to make this transition and were one-album wonders whose fate was one of reduced circumstances, either in or out of the music business.

The Clash's first record of 1978 was the single "Clash City Rockers," released on February 17, which achieved a UK chart peak of 35.

The song started life as a reference to the powerhouse Jamaican Reggae Rockers style, but ended up being interpreted as a description of the group's fans, something assisted by the photographs of Clash gig attendees that graced the picture sleeve. The recording certainly bore no resemblance to reggae, being instead riff-driven, mid-tempo, blasting rock.

"Clash City Rockers" marked a further incremental enriching of the band's sound: piano (played by Steve Nieve of Elvis Costello's Attractions) can be discerned on the rhythm track. Despite this, and the fact that Jones's guitar sound is his most intoxicatingly abrasive yet, the entire record has the feel of a piece of hackwork. Partly this is because of the clear debt owed to the riff of The Who's "I Can't Explain," an example of plagiarism with a double-kick: joining in the condemnatory chorus of the old farts who had betrayed the kids was always going to come back to bite the band on the backside when they inevitably began betraying the influence those old farts had had on their music. There is also a verse with, if not the tune, then the meter and rhythm of the nursery rhyme "Oranges and Lemons," an effete act which itself contains more hostages to fortune in gratuitous pops at established musicians, including "old" David Bowie. "Clash City Rockers" mostly fails, though because of how ill-thought-out and objectionable is what passes for its message.

Lyrically, this is another of the self-referential-cum-self-mythologizing songs that already dotted The Clash's catalog, and would continue to do so. Mick Jones had once been a camp follower of early-Seventies rockers Mott The Hoople, who had a similar penchant for dissection of their own career in song, as well as a corresponding knack for an anthem. It's difficult not to come to the conclusion that his grounding in this area was the reason The Clash trod the same path, even if a rocker and romantic like Strummer hardly needed any encouragement when it came to defiance-inflected, solidarity-inspiring theme songs. Sometimes, such numbers were effective. "Garageland" and "Complete Control" had already succeeded gloriously; in the future "Cheapskates," "Four Horsemen," and "Radio Clash" would also work to a greater or lesser degree. All of those songs, however, conveyed a message above and beyond the sort of self-aggrandizement so reflexive to working-class men in their twenties, especially ones who happen to have a receptive audience for the sort of strutting, studied arrogance that can double as a sociopolitical statement of self-determination. "Clash City Rockers," though, does not use self-assertion to make a melancholy point about the dying of an ideal like "Garageland" or to issue a defiant statement about personal integrity like "Complete Control." Instead, it is deployed to tell its audience that they are worthless.

In the lyric, Strummer states that that he wants to rock the town and get his message across, and that anybody who wants to knock the group or hinder them in this objective should leave the vicinity. This is bog-standard rock 'n' roll, chest-beating and harmless as such, even if there is some more "White Riot"/"What's My Name"–style toying with violence in its stated desire to burn down the suburbs.

However, the bridge is an example of a surprisingly nasty strain to early Clash philosophy. Strummer hectors his followers to "Shut your mouth about your useless employment," telling them to either quit their jobs or take comfort in their financial remuneration.

The Clash were not stupid. They understood full well that the alternative to unskilled labor for such people was penury: not many had the opportunities open to men of The Clash's talent. Yet such glib contempt for those who complained of being stranded in unfulfilling lives was not uncommon in their lyrics of this period. In "All the Young Punks" on *Give 'em Enough Rope*, The Clash were to be found adopting a stance about those consigned to factory floors which though it conveyed empathy, hardly amounted to sympathy. In "Bankrobber" (1980), the narrator scornfully dismisses the resignation of those who think they are condemned to poverty by birth and says he doesn't believe in lying back and saying how bad is one's luck.

Paradoxically, this could easily be posited as Thatcherite. The then-leader of the Conservative opposition in Parliament, who would become prime minister in May 1979, famously had no patience with people who complained about their lot in life and insisted that Britain was a country where opportunity for self-advancement was open to any with the right attitude. Yet whereas the average left-leaning rock writer disdained this attitude as one based on a false assumption of everyone starting out with the same advantages, The Clash received no censure from them for sentiments that seemed to buy into Thatcherite tenets. This is particularly puzzling considering that when similar sentiments were articulated—in actually less obnoxious terms—in Mick Jagger's 1987 solo single "Let's Work," they were condemned by the same sort of journalists as a betrayal of The Rolling Stones's alternative values.

Nor were The Clash's lyrics a stranger to a more generalized contempt for those supposedly on the same side of the spiritual fence as them: just think of the declaration to punks in "Remote Control" that the people who thought punks were useless were right, or the claim in "Complete Control" that punks were controlled by the price of the first drugs they could find. Even if we are to accept that in each case the band had a valid point on some level, it's one that hardly seems logical within songs that otherwise express camaraderie with the objects of their contempt.

The hectoring within "Clash City Rockers" would be offensive in itself, but being served up in the bridge ratchets up the effect. Because a bridge marks a shift in key, it has the result of drawing the listener's attention, akin to a dramatic flourish to frame a declaration. In short, The Clash couldn't have been more offensive had they tried.

The original vinyl version of "Clash City Rockers" was vari-speeded by Clash live sound man Mickey Foote to make the song faster. He was sacked from production work for his pains. Subsequent releases have seen the intended slower rendition reinstated.

On the flip side of "Clash City Rockers," Jones cannibalized "Lonely Mother's Son," a Strummer composition from the days of the 101'ers. Jones (who sings) wrote new verses to create a theme of guitar slingers as martyrs. Verse one is dedicated to Wayne Kramer of MC5, a band who could be posited as the American Sixties equivalent of The Clash. Kramer was currently doing time for selling drugs. That the people to whom he had tried to offload cocaine turned out to be undercover federal agents enabled Jones to portray him as the victim of injustice. The second verse concerns Peter Green, the ex–Fleetwood Mac frontman who had been committed to psychiatric care the previous year after threatening an accountant with a gun. The fact of the circumstances being disputed and Green's rumored disdain for money (some reports have him telling his accountant in profane language not to send any more royalty checks upon pain of physical harm) also justified, in Jones's mind, a martyr's tag.

He was on more difficult ground with Keith Richards, subject of the final verse. The Rolling Stones guitarist—whose distinctive shoulder-length mane of tangled black hair was adopted by Jones this year, making him look eerily like a younger brother of "Keef"—was currently on bail after transporting industrial levels of heroin into Canada. Richards had been charged with intent to traffic, which carried a maximum sentence of life imprisonment. However, instead of focusing on that overkill by the authorities, Jones complains that if Richards should be incarcerated, his guess was that the Stones would callously continue their career ("But his friends carry on anyway"). Even at a time when the problems caused the Stones by Richards's heroin addiction and neverending brushes with the law were not so well known, it was patently obvious that Richards's irresponsibility had jeopardized the band's future. Jones clearly gravitated to the opinion of many music fans that Jagger had sold out the Stones's anti-establishment credentials with his recent social climbing while Richards had clung to a semblance of rock 'n' roll integrity. That this integrity seems to have been a matter of Richards's inhabitation of a demi-monde in which smack was central betrays an inverted logic whereby self-destruction acquires a validity by virtue of it marking a refusal to lead a life hemmed in by conventionality.

This confused and dubious litany is set to an average melody made disjointed by its insistence on onomatopoeic reference to the clanging made by jail doors when they close. Those things, nondescript instrumentation, and Jones's mediocre singing make for probably the worst track released by the band up to that point. However, in 2007, "Jail Guitar Doors" was adopted for the title of a program started by UK musician Billy Bragg which attempts to help rehabilitate prison inmates by providing them instruments.

Although The Clash's song lengths had latterly been creeping upward, in running to four minutes, "(White Man) in Hammersmith Palais"—released as a single on June 16, 1978—was a veritable marathon. But, then, Strummer had something to get off his chest.

The title refers to a fracas that occurred when Strummer visited the titular London music venue on a reggae all-nighter. As well as inauthentic music, he was left disappointed by a menacing atmosphere: he became a target for violence when he tried to stop some black youths snatching handbags.

The fracas is really only alluded to, not explained or explored—such was the symbiotic relationship the group had with parts of the music press, and such was the frequency of the British papers, that there was sometimes more clarification to be had about their songs in print than on their records. Rather, it serves as a peculiar framing device for a rumination on the state of punk whose pessimism was typical of The Clash. Not until "Dirty Punk" in 1985 would the band posit the movement (in song at least) as anything other than one possessed of dubious motive, philosophical inconsistency, and an uncertain future.

Strummer—whose voice is treated with echo appropriate to an address to disciples—states that violence is not the answer for either white or black disenfranchised youth because they do not have the means to take on the forces at the command of the powers-that-be. Fair enough, but his sarcastic solution—that they should phone up Robin Hood and ask him for some wealth distribution—is another of the glib, mean-spirited, and unhelpful pieces of advice he and his colleagues were often to be heard dispensing to punks in song.

In the remainder of the increasingly mournful track, Strummer notes that punk musicians are too busy fighting for a good place under the lighting to be concerned about self-improvement, reserving particular contempt for a group who wear Burton suits. This is clearly a reference to The Jam, who incongruously played punk in collar-and-tie, although the fact that Strummer's problem with them was their recent revelation that they would probably be voting Conservative at the next general election is suggested by a verse in which he talks of people changing their voting preferences as thoughtlessly as they do their overcoats—a point that might or might not have some validity but which is somewhat destroyed by being followed by a suggestion that The Jam can be bracketed with Nazis.

Strummer's accusation that The Jam were "Turning rebellion into money" was a powerful line and much quoted. It was, however, an allegation that would come back to haunt him in more ways than one. The first was that The Jam would—inconceivable at the time—eventually acquire so much street-cred as to effectively snatch the crown as leaders of the New Wave—at least in Britain—that The Clash had so recently obtained from The Sex Pistols. The second reason would start to bite toward the end of The Clash's recording career and persist thereafter as they increasingly began to exhibit corporate and even mercenary marketing methods unthinkable to them when they recorded this track.

The music on which Strummer's confused but heartfelt rhetoric rides is what makes the record. "(White Man) in Hammersmith Palais" sees the band return to the blend they pioneered on "Police & Thieves," marrying reggae's stabbed guitar style to punk's (or, probably more accurately in this case, rock's) muscularity. Although it doesn't possess the hypnotic quality of that track from *The Clash*, it does have both a pulsing, busy bassline and an arrangement which alternately swells, subsides, and roars, punctuated by some of Jones's most keening playing. Subtle piano and mouth harp decorate the proceedings. Cooing Jones harmony adds color to Strummer's vocals.

For once, you can decipher Strummer's every word, helped by a clean and clear mix unusual for a Clash single. Strummer puts in a bravura vocal performance, rolling his *r*'s adroitly. There is a magical moment when he finishes enunciating the line about The Jam's suits, just before his claim that they think their behavior funny. He stumbles, reduced—appropriately—to laughter. It's clearly contrived but sounds anything but, and leaves the listener smiling.

Although it could only manage a peak chart position of 32, "(White Man) in Hammersmith Palais" was widely admired at the time, viewed like "Complete Control" as a barometer of the group's punk conscience. It remains a favorite of many longtime Clash fans.

Hammersmith Palais, incidentally, closed its doors for the final time in 2007 after eighty-eight years as an entertainment venue. The land on which the demolished building stood is now host to a students hall of residence.

A version of "(White Man) . . ." appeared on the January 1980 multi-artist collection *Rock Against Racism Greatest Hits* (Virgin RAR.1), whose aim was to raise money for the titular pressure group. This book won't go into the bewildering and not particularly enlightening byways of alternate and live versions (nor, generally, guest appearances on other artists' product), but this merits mention simply because, although listed as a live performance, it is reputed to actually be a studio outtake. It has a slightly different lyric (a reference to dollars in the U.S.A. instead of Burton suits) and a less punchy Strummer vocal.

Had the group not been intent on delivering a state-of-the-nation address with "(White Man) in Hammersmith Palais," it's difficult not to assume that its flip would have been a Clash A-side. A taut, fast-paced, and anthemic number with a defiant tone and a galvanizing heavy metal–style blam-blam! guitar trick in the chorus, "The Prisoner" is quintessential Clash.

The definitive article in a title that could just as effectively have employed the word "a" is a, perhaps not even fully conscious, nod to a television series from the Clash members' boyhoods in which Patrick

McGoohan played a secret agent confined to a weird, manipulative resort when his superiors refused to accept his resignation. McGoohan's protestation, and series motif, "I am not a number! I am a free man!," was right up punk's ideological street.

Although Jones belts it out with impressive authority—his best vocal yet—the lyric came from the pen of Strummer, who employs the term "The Prisoner" to mean somebody stuck in a life so dreary that it never gets much better than the daily routine of washing up, gardening, saving discount coupons, and hanging out washing—and for whom disillusion all too easily leads to seeking oblivion in the likes of heroin. "You're only free to dodge the cops and bunk the train to stardom," the song declares. Although the track has a melancholy tinge, "The Prisoner" doesn't feel confined in the way that its subjects' lives are. The recounting of various incidents across named London locales gives it a vitality and sweep. There is a degree of contempt for the pliant little nobodies depicted, but there is also some compassion. Additionally, there is a noticeable lack of posturing: The Clash are beginning to realize the value of observation rather than sloganeering. "The Prisoner" is one of the most overlooked songs in The Clash's oeuvre.

Although their high posthumous status—and often laudatory reviews of the time—might suggest they were perennially popular in their lifetime, accusations of sellout and decline began to dog The Clash as soon as they signed a record deal. The accusations gathered in pace and volume from November 10, 1978, when *Give 'em Enough Rope* hit the shelves.

Once removed, the outrage which greeted the news that The Clash's second album was to be produced by Sandy Pearlman, a man best known for his work for American mainstream rock act Blue Oyster Cult, seems a little arcane. Although he was also renowned for bringing a sheen to the work of proto-punk act The Dictators without sacrificing their sonic oomph, to the New Wave he reeked of the smugness, blandness, and artificiality of the rock aristocracy, the music business, and the aspects of America of which "I'm So Bored with the U.S.A." was a condemnation.

It was long assumed that his retention was a gutless acquiescence by The Clash to an insistence by Epic, their record company in the United States. Epic (who were doubtlessly referring to The Clash's second album as their sophomore effort) had thus far declined to release the debut Clash album on the grounds that it sounded too raw. However, Strummer later asserted that Rhodes selected Pearlman off a list of potential producers presented to him (and furthermore presented by CBS, not Epic). Pearlman himself told Pat Gilbert of *Mojo* in March 2003, "It wasn't CBS that hired me, it was The Clash." Pearlman added, "It wasn't to create an American sound, it was to create an *extreme* sound. And I did. I resent the idea that I lamed them out."

The ten tracks on *Rope* were hardly exemplars of bloated progressive rock, but the fact that they were of conventional rock album track length, rather than brief and snappy like on the debut, also got sellout-attuned nostrils sniffing suspiciously. (That the band's recent singles had been fairly long was not so obvious a fact by dint of them not being on album.) Although there seems no suggestion of The Clash not recording more or less what they wanted, the more standard playing times, streamlined tunes, and glittering guitar solos couldn't help resemble a way of making punk palatable to the "plebs," i.e., a mainstream audience. Any suggestion that it was nothing of the sort but simply the result of increasing sophistication of technique only made things worse. Everyone knew that absolutely nothing could prevent a musician's skill improving with practice, and not even the most hardcore punks would expect The Clash or any of their peers to play to a lower quality than they were able, but this record uncomfortably reminded those who had reveled in punk's back-to-basics, anti-virtuoso philosophy that it had always been a transient thing. *Give 'em Enough Rope* brought home the fact that punk had unavoidably started dying the second that its practitioners began learning more chords. Then there was the fact that the album spun off not one but two singles, just as with a conventional rock band flogging an album to death.

For all those reasons, the record was a crossing of a Rubicon in the almost hysterically purist climate engendered by punk. The scrutiny of the band would become increasingly uncharitable from here on, with the quality of their music, for many, almost a side issue to an ongoing debate about whether or not they were measuring up to ideals which even the rebels of the previous generation, The Rolling Stones, had never needed to worry about conveying. The British music papers were desperate that rock not lose its relevance again like it had in the first half of the Seventies. *Melody Maker* was more old-guard oriented than the *NME* and *Sounds*, and *Record Mirror* more well disposed toward pop than all of the others, but they too had punk-inclined writers with Jiminy Cricket tendencies. Four music weeklies created a sense of No Hiding Place. Many erstwhile band champions would over the years turn against them. The first major ones were Julie Burchill and Tony Parsons. Their 1978 "obituary of rock and roll," *The Boy Looked at Johnny*, even before the release of *Give 'em Enough Rope*, effectively recanted all their previous praise to portray the group as a joke hauling an already tired repertoire around the country and showing no signs of developing.

That the UK music press would always find The Clash wanting after a certain point was both inevitable and the band's own fault. The bravado of young men meant that The Clash were always pledging in print what they would never do, no way, no how. At various stages, members of the group explicitly promised that they would set up a club or live venue for the kids and a radio station for people who liked less-mainstream sounds, that there would never be a Clash album costing £6 or more, that they would never agree to perform on *Top of the Pops*, that they would not allow exorbitantly priced tickets, and that they would not play seated venues. Implicitly, their image and music also promised that they would always put art before commerce and that they would never compromise their vision and ideals for the sake of career advancement. In the inaugural piece of Clash press in *Melody Maker* on November 13, 1976, Strummer had said he wanted "to do something useful" with any money he made; Simonon had said, "We can put money back into the situation we were in before and get something going for the kids our own age." By the time Strummer told Tony Parsons in the *NME* on April 2, 1977, "I ain't gonna fuck myself up like I seen all those other guys fuck themselves up. Keeping all their money for themselves and getting into their head and thinking they're the greatest," the myth The Clash were cultivating was already holed below the water line.

Many felt that they sold out upon signing a £100,000 contract with CBS, not least *Sniffin' Glue*'s founder Mark Perry, who famously stated that the punk movement died that day. The exigencies of life meant it got worse from there. In the early days, The Clash allowed fans to sleep on the floor in their hotel rooms rather than face a long trek home after concerts. This policy inevitably had to be abandoned as impractical, but as soon as it was, another plank of the band's men-of-the-people image was lost. Insisting on stand-alone singles and their live soundman acting as their producer inevitably went up in smoke because CBS needed to recoup their £100,000 investment; employing professional producers and promoting albums with singles containing songs on those albums was the safest way of doing so. Meanwhile, all the grandiose plans The Clash had about creating an alternative platform such as a simpatico radio station and live venue never came to pass chiefly because their finances were undermined by their insistence on low ticket and album prices. Strummer told Vic Garbarini of *Musician* magazine in June 1981, "The thing I like about making a stand on prices is that it's *here and now*, and not just a promise. It's dealing with reality: how many bucks you're going to have to part with at the counter to get it. It's one of the few opportunities we have to manifest our ideals, to make them exist in a real plane." Another phrase for "here and now" is instant gratification: The Clash's inability to defer victory for their fans meant the abandonment of greater glories.

Even on the occasions when The Clash's behavior showed impeccable integrity, there was one piece of critical ammunition they could never nullify: Joe Strummer's bourgeois background. The facts of him having gone to private boarding school and being the son of a man in the Foreign Office who had been made a Member of the British Empire (at seventeen, he attended the investiture at Buckingham Palace) marked Strummer as privileged and therefore somehow lesser. For some, it meant his poverty tableaux lyrics were slumming at best, fraud at worst. That he had had a fairly wretched childhood involving minimum contact with his parents and the suicide of his brother in the same year as his father's acceptance of his MBE, and that he had oodles more compassion for the underprivileged than did many of the underprivileged themselves, cut no ice with some punks, music journalists, and leftists. Even one of The Clash's greatest, most unequivocal moments of triumphant rebellion—securing the UK release of "Bankrobber" after a standoff with their reluctant record company—was somewhat spoiled by people taking issue with the lyric's statement that the narrator's daddy robbed banks: "Actually, John Mellor's daddy was a Second Secretary of Information at the Foreign Office," sneered *Sounds*, as though that proved the singer had no right to inhabit a different character for the duration of a song. (Perhaps because of witnessing this sort of treatment, Headon kept his mouth shut about his not much less middle-class hinterland.)

The nadir of the intense scrutiny The Clash were under came in late 1977 when the homeless Strummer moved into a house occupied by Sebastian Conran, now a successful designer but at the time just starting out in his career and working for The Clash. The accommodation he offered Strummer was by all accounts a Spartan servant's room at the top of the house, but the fact that Conran was the son of Terence Conran—a famous and rich designer and author—and that the house was located in plush Regent's Park was all the music press's sellout-o-meter needed to start spinning. The ridicule and accusations of hypocrisy ensured Strummer felt compelled to vacate and move into a squat.

Recording on the second Clash album started in Utopia Studio, London, in spring 1978, relocating after the fallout from some rock star excess to Basing Street Studios, also in the capital. Whereas *The Clash* had been completed in the space of three weekends, the first three days of the recording of the follow-up were spent simply getting the drum sound right. Despite such care, Epic rejected the band's first master, and extensive re-recording was done by Strummer and Jones in America before a satisfactory acetate was finally achieved in September of that year, a period that had seen the band decamp to both the Automatt in San Francisco and the Record Plant in New York City.

The album's cover artwork co-opted *End of the Trail*, a famous postcard image of a cowboy being picked at by vultures, to make a point a couple of steps beyond "I'm So Bored with the U.S.A.": sitting on horseback over the corpse is an invading Chinese soldier, with, on the back cover, a column of his comrades disappearing into the distance. The Clash's name is spelled out in an oriental font to hammer home the point. The first pressings of the album were intended to include a free double-sided poster which further insisted that the most powerful country in the world was careening toward self-lynching. The "Clash Atlas," which occupied one side of the poster, posited a serial killer as representative of the States. Although the poster was mentioned in reviews, it wasn't distributed beyond the media because of a printing error. The other side of the poster, incidentally, showed The Clash as they now looked: all peaked caps, biker jackets, leather trousers, studded wristbands, and sunglasses.

The Clash were an incredibly visual group right from the get-go. Their early image saw their clothes stenciled with slogans and splattered—Jackson Pollack–style—with arbitrary paint patterns. From March 1977, band friend Alex Michon briefly gave them a unique look: trousers and jackets (often military in appearance) festooned with zips in weird places.

That middle period exemplified by the *Give 'em Enough Rope* poster also took in rebel gear like Doc Marten boots, brothel creepers, waistcoats, and bootlace ties. The Clash image became rather a mess in the period around *Sandinista!*: there exist from this juncture painful pictures of the group groaning under the weight of big hats and cartridge belts. In the *Combat Rock* period, the group simplified things to a sort of designer military look, perhaps to chime with that album's title, if not their pacifist beliefs. Strummer's post-Jones Clash similarly dressed like they were about to go on urban guerrilla maneuvers.

Hand in hand with attention to their threads was The Clash's stagecraft. In the beginning they had an almost disturbingly hyperactive live act which saw the perennially intense Strummer bookended by the figures of Jones and Simonon furiously swinging their instruments. This performance style continued into their middle phase, when it was abandoned, possibly for reasons of sheer exhaustion. They remained a riveting collective stage presence even despite Jones taking to staring fixedly before him. Strummer was talkative and witty and gave 110 percent to every vocal. Paul Simonon, meanwhile, became unrecognizable from the skinny, spike-headed waif of the early years, building up his muscles and adopting a quiff to create a Charles-Atlas-meets-James-Dean image that was classic rock 'n' roll iconography. In 1982, it prompted the readers of *Playgirl* magazine to vote him one of the ten sexiest men in the world.

Despite Pearlman and the U.S. sessions, *Give 'em Enough Rope* is really no less English than its predecessor. Although its lyrics sometimes address the world outside the one depicted on the debut, and its music sometimes comes close to conventional rock roar, no American act could ever have made a record like this. It is suffused with the concerns of British culture—particularly then-modern British youth culture. Meanwhile, the allegation that Pearlman swamped the record with cacophonous overkill was misplaced: The Clash were themselves responsible for the occasional sameness due to them mystifyingly holding over the acoustic "Groovy Times" and the playful "Gates of the West" for the *Cost of Living* EP well into the following year. The inclusion of those tracks would have nicely leavened *Rope*'s thunder. Moreover, although there is no denying that this record is more rock than punk, it is also indisputable that it would have been impossible without punk, whose values and attitudes inform its every note.

The album reached no. 2 in the UK and number 128 in the United States. Although nowhere near as good as the first album, the follow-up to *The Clash* is a very good work forever destined to be under-appreciated due to the uniquely unyielding flavor of the era of its release.

That the *NME* granted *Rope* a full-page review was a recognition that, at least as far as its demographic was concerned, The Clash were the most important band in the world. The paper's verdict on the LP was mixed, but Nick Kent did go so far as to say that the opening track knocked everything else the band had thus far recorded into a cocked hat. The critical consensus over the years has been that "Safe European Home" is, indeed, a powerful number. It's a puzzling conclusion.

"Safe European Home" resulted from a visit by Strummer and Jones to Kingston, Jamaica, with the purpose of writing material for that all-important second album, a sort of streetwise variant of the tactic of "getting it together in the country" favored in the late Sixties/early Seventies by rock acts in need of new songs to meet a recording schedule. Here the pair encountered the sobering reality behind writing "White Riot," covering reggae tunes and other ostentatious displays of solidarity with Caribbean black culture. The pair turned up in their multi-zipped Alex Michon clothes. What looked confrontational and mildly disturbing on London streets cut little ice in a country where a lack of the kind of welfare state and relatively egalitarian spirit to which The Clash and their countrymen were used had engendered a coarseness of attitude and atmosphere of danger beyond Strummer and Jones's experience. Even if their Western clothes hadn't betrayed them as interlopers, for the nation's black populace their white skin marked them out as an example of an oppressive presence in their lives. Confronted with abuse and hostility, the pair realized they could actually be in danger.

"I went to the place where every white face is an invitation to robbery," runs one of the lines in the song that came out of their disconcerting experience. The track expresses thankfulness for being back in comparatively tranquil Blighty and a simultaneous self-disgust at that relief. This acknowledgement of the relative luxury enjoyed even by guttersnipes in the First World is certainly an inversion of the philosophical certitude and breast-beating insistence on underprivilege central to punk and, on that level, commands admiration. However, that doesn't qualify "Safe European Home" for entry into the pantheon of Clash classics.

Musically, it's mediocre. Although it starts with a bang and occasionally its guitar assault suggests the ferocity and sweep of a hurricane—proof that the group could evince even more blazing power when their sound was marshaled by sophisticated recording techniques—it's mostly rather uninspired riffarama, which is itself compounded by the fact that the riff is the same as the song's melody line. The sense of repetition brought about by the latter is added to by a chanting Jones monotonously asking where Strummer, the narrator, has been at the end of each and every verse line. An interlude sees a guitar repeatedly hitting a chord in a ham-fisted approximation of reggae rhythm, the only aural overture to Jamaica apart from Jones's spoken-word patois.

Moreover, although the songwriters had stumbled upon the myth-deflating truth that, at the end of the day, they and their compatriots didn't really didn't have much about which to complain, it was no epiphany. Instead, it was a moment of self-knowledge soon washed over by the exigencies of career, peer pressure, and psychological comfort. The rest of the album—and, with the exception of "Death or Glory," the rest of their existence as a group—saw a return to un-nuanced Clash grousing about the iniquitous lot of the Western working class.

The 1978 10cc single "Dreadlock Holiday" uncannily paralleled "Safe European Home" in describing distressing experiences (in this case being mugged) while visiting the West Indies. Its superbly authentic, percussion-heavy reggae groove and infectious vocal hook "I don't like reggae—I love it!" deservedly took it to the top of the UK charts. (It made no. 44 Stateside.) However, where "Safe European Home" was hailed as enlightened, 10cc's creation was condemned as racist. The fact that it was partly based on true-life incidents cut no more ice with critics than the fact that "Safe European Home" had, like it, deployed patois. The reality is that "Dreadlock Holiday" knocks "Safe European Home" into a cocked hat.

During the Seventies, particularly toward the decade's end, there was much talk of civil war in Britain. Every Western democracy of the period had its problems as the combination of the rising oil prices of an increasingly assertive Middle East and the ballooning costs of the welfare state began to bite. The difficulties of the UK, however, were on another level altogether. With unions acknowledged as being as powerful as government, there was a sense of two big guns staring at each other that was very different to the overlord-underdog relationship between the state and labor in other industrialized democracies, with the inevitable negative consequences for the perception of how meaningful was casting a vote at the ballot box. Confrontations on picket lines and fracas at demonstrations—as well as violence outside the political sphere like street muggings and soccer hooliganism—all meant that physical unrest was a common fixture on television news broadcasts in a way it hadn't been only a decade before. It therefore seemed a component of life that needed a solution. That solution seemed obvious to some: if soldiers could be called in—as they were in the winter of 1978/1979—to clear from the streets rubbish that striking trade union members refused to touch in the latest of an apparently never-ending series of disputes with their employers, then it was just a small step to deploying the army to preserve the rule of law, possibly freedom itself. Mixed into all this was the Soviet threat. While few expected Russian tanks to roll down their high street any time soon, there was a real, ever-present dread about Soviet expansionism that provided an additional dimension of anxiety to every conflagration. Moreover, the Soviet threat didn't always seem distant or abstract. Few today remember that the late former Labour minister Tony Benn—latterly reinvented as an avuncular mainstream leftie—emitted the sort of apologias for USSR policy that gave him a decidedly sinister sheen. Not all of the people who felt a domestic military intervention was inevitable or necessary were right-wing extremists—although it was usually the latter who were to be found on weekend maneuvers with private armies of small businessmen and retired bank managers preparing for Albion's own Armageddon. This atmosphere clearly fed into and inspired the second track on *Give 'em Enough Rope*, even if there is a knowing hyperbole to "English Civil War."

That the song is an updating and Anglicization of American Civil War folk song "When Johnny Comes Marching Home" would suggest a paucity of composing ideas in the Clash camp were it not now known that the band had stockpiled songs but failed to include them on this LP. Not that it matters. Although undoubtedly trite is the comparison between the body-strewn horrors of the War Between the States and the irritants of living in what was merely the most unsettled of the Western democracies, the track is thrilling, from the predictable drama of Strummer's vocal through Jones's sparkling overlapping guitar solos to the final verse speed-up (and ominous, sudden closing slow-down). Jones's cooing harmonies deftly prevent the concoction from being overloaded with harsh noises, while Headon keeps things rolling with some of his best work on the record, his accents and rolls niftily accentuating Strummer's wide-eyed enunciation of the tale of Johnny returning "by bus or underground" to a vista of paranoia and horror.

Mention of terrorism today immediately leads to thoughts of Al-Qaeda and Islamic fundamentalism. Terrorism in the Seventies, however, was synonymous with left-wing ideology.

The West German Baader-Meinhof gang, aka Red Army Faction, was the most famous of the Western organizations that put themselves in opposition to the self-concern of the "me decade" by promoting their Sixties-rooted social causes via violent direct action. Other well-known organizations of this stripe included Italy's Brigate Rosse and the United States's Weathermen and Symbionese Liberation Army (abductors of heiress Patty Hearst).

The main trouble posed to the radical aims of such organizations was that the ever-increasing wealth of the Western proletariat meant that the ground was constantly shifting under them. While the inhabitants of Western countries were receptive to liberal social reform—especially younger ones, for whom the iniquity of being at the mercy of the value systems of parents and teachers is always still fresh and raw—economic revolution was not something in which they were interested. The Seventies had troubles that could superficially make capitalism appear to be in terminal crisis, but desire for the sort of overthrow of state aimed for—if in rather vague terms—by such organizations was somewhat limited in households that could see that, by any yardstick, they were better off than their parents. The cause of anti-imperialism, meanwhile, could never be more than an abstract to such people, especially if they spent their waking hours doing jobs they didn't particularly enjoy and sought nothing but intellectual escape in their leisure hours. Moreover, the very phrase "Marxist-Leninism"—the ideology to which many such organizations were adherents—sent a shiver down the spine of a public who saw the grimness of Soviet life on their television screens and in their newspapers on a regular basis. Such lack of receptivity often engendered fury in radicals, who were disgusted at the way they felt that the social consciences of the poor were easily bought by consumer durables. This itself could make direct action organizations feel more inclined to commit violent acts so as to shake people out of their apathy, something which in turn antagonized further those whose liberation they sought.

Yet while it was true that, in most of the First World, violence was never going to lead to anything but repugnance, at one point an opinion poll found a quarter of young West Germans expressing sympathy for the aims of the Baader-Meinhof gang. Even in countries without the unique past of West Germany—where there was widespread disgust that many ex-Nazis were prominent in civic and industrial life—there were pockets of approval for paramilitary activity with a leftist bent. The notion of the urban guerrilla was glamorous to some—including those who delighted in shocking their parents and/or friends by espousing causes they in their heart of hearts felt to be unjustifiable. That latter set of complicated motives is presumably not too distant from the impetus for Joe Strummer in the late Seventies to sport a T-shirt that put together the name of Brigate Rosse with the machine-gun-and-acronym logo of the Red Army Faction. (One also suspects the agitprop friendly hand of Bernie Rhodes in the decision; as a Jew, Rhodes no doubt drew the line at the Swastika-adorned armbands and T-shirts in which Malcolm McLaren swathed The Sex Pistols, and this was the most palatable equivalent.)

Certainly, Strummer's fashion choice didn't withstand intellectual scrutiny. In a toe-curling section of the motion picture *Rude Boy*—a pseudo-documentary on The Clash interspersed with drama released in 1980—Strummer is seen washing his Brigate Rosse T-shirt in a hotel room sink. In this improvised scene, Ray Gange, who plays a Clash fan–cum-roadie, is cued to ask him about it. Strummer patently had little idea of what the groups stood for, and little interest beyond the purpose of a vaguely anti-establishment piece of inflammatory sloganeering. Gange asks if the RAF are communists. When Strummer shrugs, "I don't know. They can't be if they shoot communists," he is not being merely cavalier about his own ignorance but by extension the human lives snuffed out by these groups.

That being the case, it's surprising what a thoughtful song is "Tommy Gun." The third track on *Give 'em Enough Rope* was automatically assumed by some to be an irresponsible glorification of a terrorist. Whereas it might be assumed that a condemnation of terrorism would necessarily employ a slow, mournful arrangement, "Tommy Gun" possesses a thunderous power right from its opening military-tattoo-and-power-chord combination, a sonic showboating which can't help but suggest a gesture of approval. Sections of the lyric acknowledge the frisson of nobility and altruism surrounding people who style themselves freedom fighters (after all, one of the demands of Patty Hearst's kidnappers was the distribution of food to the poor). One verse of the song directed at the terrorist—whose name seems to be, in an implausible occasion of poetic coincidence, the same as the titular weapon—finds the narrator veritably drooling over the subject as he cuts out a front-page picture of a man who is a hero in an age of none. Another verse in which the subject is stripping his weapon down for a customs run rings with the glamour of drama and a depth of knowledge suggested by use of jargon.

Despite all this, and the vocal refrain "Whatever you want, you're gonna get it," the song is a total repudiation of the terrorist's methods. The disciple who views Tommy Gun as a hero is clearly being mocked, not least because he is depicted as planning to pledge allegiance to the terrorist's cause only after he has obtained his style of jacket. The lyric asks Tommy Gun if he really has to mow down people and suggests to him that if his war is ever won, he will by then be one of the dead. In the final verse, the narrator states that if death is so cheap to the terrorist, so must be life. Said verse precedes another military tattoo/chord crash that brings the proceedings to an explosive climax.

Just as ambiguity and condemnation undermine the expectation of approval, so the track is provided musical reprieve. This is no lumpen heavy-metal exercise, courtesy of Jones's adroit high harmonies and piercing staccato guitar work (the closest a Gibson has ever come to sounding like a radio signal).

The Clash's flirtation with terrorist chic—which encompassed a Strummer "H-block" T-shirt in reference to the prison cells especially built for terrorists in Northern Ireland and a comment in an interview that terrorists were people "laying their lives on the line for the rest of the human race"—came to an end in mid-1979. It was at that point that the band were rudely apprised of the difference between game playing and reality. A "Riot Wing" party manifesto which Strummer wrote for the *NME* included the "policy" "Troops and Britain out of Northern Ireland." It inspired a death threat from Red Hand Commando, a Northern Ireland group loyal to the crown and opposed to secession.

In March 1978, a British judge handed down to seventeen people combined prison sentences of 120 years for a conspiracy to manufacture and market LSD. The trial was the result of a police undercover investigation named Operation Julie after one of its female staff. The news story felt like a dispatch from another era. Speed (amphetamine sulphate) was the intoxicant of the age ushered in by the New Wave. While the punks, just like all their drug-oriented peers, were also not averse to a bit of grass, acid trips seemed as antiquated as long hair and love beads.

Strummer notes in the lyric that the sentences are so long it will enable the convicted to count all of their hair. Contrary to his assertion of fourteen-, nineteen-, and twenty-five-year terms, nobody got sent down for more than thirteen years. However, these were savage sentences at a time when heroin distributors were getting eight years. He seems less angry by this, though, than amused. There was nothing untoward about Operation Julie in the sense of police malpractice, even if they would seem to have over-egged the pudding with the press. It's also difficult to read into the lyric an attitude that the state pursuing the manufacturers and distributors of a dangerous and illegal drug is a symptom of oppression. LSD is potentially harmful even in its pure form, as opposed to narcotics like heroin, which—overdosing aside—become dangerous via the adulterants added by suppliers. The Clash would have known this as much as anyone by dint of rock's roll call of acid casualties: Fleetwood Mac's Peter Green, Pink Floyd's Syd Barrett, and The Beach Boys's Brian Wilson were all by now known to have had their talents and mental well-being severely depleted by LSD usage. The Clash don't even exploit the opportunity to take a pop at hippies, for whom LSD was a supposed path to revolutionary enlightenment that, for punks, transpired to be a cul-de-sac of self-indulgence. The song, then, has no ideological message. So why write it?

Strummer has said he was amused by the idea of undercover cops in Operation Julie having to don far-out garb to gather evidence, but that doesn't strike one as an explanation of creative impetus. "Julie's Been Working for the Drug Squad" seems to be the first major example of The Clash groping for subject matter as a consequence of their success taking them out of the milieu that had supplied the material for their previous recordings. This problem would increase exponentially as the years progressed.

Although the band were never truly well-off until the success of 1982's *Combat Rock*—before then, despite a judicious publishing deal struck by Rhodes, their insistence on low ticket and album prices compromised their earning potential so severely that it had the effect of keeping them at an income level not wildly dissimilar to that of their audience—they were unquestionably no longer in the position they had been during the writing of *The Clash*, when they were subsisting on £9.70 a week Unemployment Benefit, and the homeless Joe Strummer was sleeping on the floor of the group's rehearsal space. It went deeper than that, though. However affectedly rebellious they continued to be in the company of record company executives, media interviewers, gig promoters, or customs officials, the fact was that the presence in The Clash's lives of such figures of authority or quasi-authority was the measure of a rarefied existence. Their songs did not spring any longer from being caught up in riots or being suffocated by the boredom of inner-city life, and nor could they ever be again. A return to their roots for purposes of observation might generate song ideas, but could only ever be slumming for a group of young men who were now living the stuff of many people's fantasies. Although The Clash's social conscience remained intact, increasingly they now had to turn it outward. In the long term, this meant transforming their art from local-color canvases to travelogue paintings. In the short term, they were sometimes reduced to almost desperate measures to come up with a lyric.

In the case of "Julie's Been Working for the Drug Squad," they appear to have chosen their subject because its tableau of alternative types in conflict with the forces of the Establishment gave it a patina of social relevance. The result, however, is essentially empty. The somewhat generic honky-tonk piano work of Blue Oyster Cult's Allen Lanier only emphasizes the lack of substance, as well as providing another alarming sign, for those inclined to fret over such things, that the band were losing their punk edge.

The peculiar thing is, so engaging is the recording that you can't find it in your heart to mind any of its shortcomings. Apart from the lazy line "They arrested every drug that had ever been made," the lyric boasts neat rhymes and twinkle-eyed humor, while the melody is jaunty, the arrangement sprightly, and the piano easy on the ear. Whatever else it suggested, "Julie's Been Working for the Drug Squad" proved that even punks are capable of—entitled to—whimsy with no ambition other than to cause three minutes to pass pleasantly.

In complete contest to the (listenable) vacuity of the previous track, "Last Gang in Town" is suffused with relevance, a song torn from the nation's headlines, and furthermore of specific topicality to the group's audience.

Youth culture had been a part of British life since the early 1950s. Although post-war austerity still prevailed, the welfare state had created the first generation both with money in their pockets and a sense of identity. The upshot was Teddy Boys, so called because their preferred fashion was long drape-coats last popular during the reign of King Edward VII in the first decade of the twentieth century. Although like all images it took some time to evolve, the archetypal "Ted" look also ultimately involved frilled shirts, bootlace ties, drainpipe trousers, and thick-soled brothel creeper shoes. The classic Ted hairstyle was an elaborate Brylcremed quiff with long, wide sideburns. When rock 'n' roll arrived, its primitive beat and sloganeering lyrics seemed tailor-made for this new, bellicose, disobedient, and narcissistic social group. Teds became synonymous with violence and disorder, if on a level that would be considered pussycat by even the standards of the Seventies, let alone today.

Although Teds continued to exist, by the Sixties there was a variant called the Rocker, who adopted a look and lifestyle similar to the leather-jacketed roadster rebel depicted by Marlon Brando in *The Wild One*. Their nemesis was famously the Mods, short for Modernists, who favored smartly cut suits over leather and denim, and current soul and pop over Fifties rock 'n' roll. One might imagine that said differences were hardly such a yawning chasm in values as to provoke violent conflict, but the pitched battles between the two factions at British coastal towns on bank holidays became famous.

Come the late Seventies, there occurred another youth war, one that made the tabloid papers exclaim that it was "mods and rockers all over again" (the first time many teenagers of the day had ever heard those terms). On one side was the Teds (a new generation rather than the original vintage, even if a remarkable number of first-time Teds had retained the fashion style of their youth into undignified middle age). On the other, punks. Those people who had seen Mods-versus-Rockers disorder as another yardstick of the decline and fall of civilization may have been amused that the antipathy toward the punks on the part of the Teds—for it was that way around: for all the provocativeness of their appearances, punks were largely peaceable—was one based on a certain snobbery. Teddy Boys were genuinely disgusted by punk, which seemed to them a pretend youth culture. That may, to some extent, have been the point: punk always had a strain of being anti-everything rather than pro-anything, and the repudiation of many social phenomena implicit in their all-pervading negativity naturally included previous youth cults. However, to Teds who were forever preeningly pulling a comb through their hair, the deliberate debasement of the self involved in the ugly punk look was incomprehensible and contemptible. So too was the pogo, the punk scene's dance style, which involved simply jumping up and down on the spot: Teds were nifty on the dance floor, their jiving involving quite complicated and athletic moves.

On April 2, 1977, Joe Strummer was to be found claiming in the *NME* that he had been beaten up by a Ted. In an example of the irresponsible bravado to be found in several early Clash features, he told Tony Parsons, "I had a knife with me, and I shoulda stuck it in him, right? But when it came to it I remember vaguely thinking that it wasn't really worth it, 'cos although he was battering me about the floor, I was too drunk for it to hurt that much and if I stuck my knife in him I'd probably have to do a few years." Happily, Strummer the songwriter was usually a more humane and temperate persona than Strummer the interviewee. In "Last Gang in Town," he takes the position that the battles between the "crops" (skinheads), "stiffs" (non-aligned/straights), "spikes" (punks), "quiffs" (Teddy Boys), soul rebels, ska punks, and Rastafarians all amounted to "young blood flowing down the drain." Although not stated as such, his denouncement of this bloodshed would have been read by his audience as an exhortation to put aside their differences to form a common allegiance with the aim of taking on the system that kept them down. While this social program may be simplistic and barely more coherent than Sham 69's deathless 1978 manifesto "If the Kids Are United," the song's touching sorrow and compassion lend it a gravitas.

In the last verse, Strummer throws in a youth cult of his own invention, a high-rise dwelling bunch with no definable fashion style. This is the "last gang" of the title, for whom all the other youth cults are looking but who disdain violence themselves. According to Strummer, it was a form of self-mockery, but The Clash had already demonstrated a penchant for self-mythologizing, and the title seems to vaingloriously allude to the fact of The Sex Pistols having split, even if the preference of this superior, messianic breed for zydeco and Cajun music is a biographical red herring.

The musical setting for this thoughtful song is a mid-tempo affair with doom-laden, syncopated choruses. The track has a twanging rockabilly bottom-end through which Jones's extended guitar lines snake sinuously. Mick flashily brings the track to a close with a penetrating series of notes worthy of any Sixties guitar god.

Had he lived, Strummer may have taken comfort from the fact that there is now little occasion for the sort of violence this composition laments, simply because youth cults now barely exist in Britain. Aside from tiny isolated pockets, the Teds, the Mods, the rockers, the punks, the soul boys, the Rastas, the skinheads, and all the other tribes that once served to divide teens and twentysomethings have disappeared from the streets. Goth is just about the last standard bearer for the phenomenon of the kid who wants to make himself look different to the mainstream. Instead, youth culture has been swamped by its own mainstream, with the paradoxical uniformity of tracksuit culture now having held sway over those kids who fancy themselves as different to straights for an astonishing quarter of a century.

In the introduction to "Guns on the Roof," Strummer declares that he will tell the whole truth and nothing but. He then proceeds to come out with a pack of lies. Those not aware of The Clash's story might take this track (whose composition is credited to all four Clash members) at face value, even if that face value is nebulous: a condemnation of mercenaries, possibly, or terrorism, or perhaps simply war. The enemy is defined merely as "they," the blood-soaked scenarios against which

Strummer impassionedly rails explained only in terms of the slaughter of the innocent by some vague, wicked power.

Even despite the unimaginative (and not even first in the Clash canon) co-opting of The Who's "I Can't Explain" riff, Jones's musical intelligence shines through, him bringing a new intensity to even such a hackneyed riff, and additionally deploying more of those urgency-evoking radio-signal-esque guitar beeps. However, once *au fait* with the incident which gave rise to the song, statements like the one in the couplet about a system built by the sweat of the many creating assassins to kill off the few become truly contemptible.

Strummer was clearly inspired to write the lyric by an incident in March 1978 in which Paul Simonon, Nick Headon, and three friends were arrested by armed police after climbing onto a roof to test out an air pistol and an air rifle by firing them at some pigeons. Said creatures turned out to be homing pigeons belonging to a nearby resident, who was understandably distraught. Simonon and Headon were charged and fined (hence the buffoonish oath opening). That Strummer should want to extrapolate this rather shameful incident into some sort of fatuous protest song rather than forget about it as quickly as possible brings into question not just his sense of proportion but his very concept of justice. (Why not a song on behalf of pigeon fanciers whose pets are murdered by bully-boy rockers?) It demonstrates how easily the self-aggrandizement of rock—let alone the heightened self-righteousness of punk— could so easily tip over into a slightly disturbing conviction of being perennially in the right, the type that can make someone assume that an official rebuke of any kind in any circumstances amounts to "Ree-preessh-uun!" The Clash would have done better to abandon this track and include "Pressure Drop," a reggae cover recorded at the *Rope* sessions whose inclusion would have given the album the equivalent of the first LP's "Police & Thieves."

As if The Clash had had second thoughts about the incident that gave rise to the song—even, God forbid, become ashamed of it—when the lyric of "Guns on the Roof" was reproduced in The Clash's *Second Songbook* (1979), it was given the parenthesized (and meaningless) subtitle "Of the World."

"Guns on the Roof" happens to be sequenced next to the album's other substandard song, although the issue with "Drug Stabbing Time" is not the words—which are mildly clever—but its sonics.

This is the track where accusations of the album being relentless almost to the point of cacophony are on their strongest ground. Admittedly, its bludgeoning instrumentation would in isolation make "Guns on the Roof" exciting, but the fact of it being the seventh cut in succession to exhibit an all-out commitment to volume and histrionics calls to attention the fact that its melody is the weakest present, with the effect of the listener suddenly realizing he's a bit weary. As if in recognition of the danger of that, a sax solo by Stan Bronstein of Elephant's Memory is thrown into the mix.

However, it's not that leavening which provides the track its major salvation but Strummer's lyric and his delivery thereof (even if he and Jones—who sings much of the song with him—sometimes perilously skirt American accents in pronouncing "time" as "ta-a-me" and "answer" as "ann-ser"). The lyric—written in the second person—is a scathing depiction of the wretched and paranoid life of a smack addict who is working on the Ford assembly line in Dagenham in order to pay off a big fine, presumably for possession. In a semi-spoken-word, double-time climax, Strummer amusingly relates a drug bust as seen through the blurry vision of the "wasted."

The track is most interesting for dedicated Clash fans for the insight it provides into the impetus for the band's sacking of Nick (by then better known as Topper) Headon in 1982. Although the debilitating effects on Headon of his heroin use had been insinuated in print by journalists as far back as 1980, some were surprised that Strummer— who was known to be a prodigious consumer of marijuana and who worked alongside Jones, a cokehead—should seek to get moralistic about drug use. However, this song goes some way to proving that Strummer's high-minded viewpoint on heroin—and his stance that it was distinct from drugs which did not impede the ability to perform music—was present from the beginning, and long before Headon began using.

Strummer had always loved The Rolling Stones right back to his youth, but the junkie chic radiated by songs of theirs like "Brown Sugar" and "Coming Down Again" clearly held no sway with him. Where others garlanded Keith Richards with accolades like "World's Most Elegantly Wasted Human Being" and exulted in his topping a magazine poll to find the rock star most likely to die in the near future, Strummer was heard to be opining in interview that the Stones were responsible for killing people by writing songs that suggested drugs were cool. The first manifestation in The Clash's career of Strummer's anti-heroin opinions would seem to be "Deny." Anti-heroin sentiments would continue to appear in his lyrics ("Hateful" on *London Calling*, "Junkie Slip" on *Sandinista!*, "Ghetto Defendant" on *Combat Rock*). Moreover, music journalist and onetime junkie Nick Kent has related that back in the days of the 101'ers, Strummer would stare coldly at addicts like him arriving to score off a dealer who lived in the building next door to his squat.

By 1982, Strummer had begun to feel that Headon's behavior and "habit" was making a mockery of his lyrics, thus forcing his hand. This all makes particularly startling verse two of "Drug Stabbing Time," where Strummer spits that, as nobody wants either a user or a loser, the subject's song must be kicked out the door, which should no longer be answered to him. This almost exactly describes Headon's exit, four years in advance.

Fortunately for a flagging album, the following track is among the most melodically and lyrically enjoyable offerings of the record. Over the years, Strummer would increasingly give his more emotional songs to Jones to sing. It was either out of embarrassment or a belief that Jones's higher-pitched, sometimes quasi-hysterical, vocal style lent itself more to such material. Either way, him being the lead vocalist on a certain stripe of Clash offering—"Gates of the West," "Lost in the Supermarket," "I'm Not Down," "Somebody Got Murdered"—created a misapprehension that Jones specialized in penning heart-tugging lyrics. However, "Stay Free"—sung and written almost exclusively by Jones—is one example of Mick actually being responsible for the sweet-natured composition he trilled.

On one level, "Stay Free" is simply the ultimate proof of Jones's love of Mott The Hoople. This soaring, self-mythologizing anthem could have come from their acclaimed 1973 LP *Mott*. When Mott unknowingly passed the anthemic baton to Jones, his preferred subject was a composition that details the separate paths bequeathed by fate to two childhood friends.

With punk's compromise-o-meter permanently set to "high," and emotionality consequently in danger of being dismissed as sentimentality, "Stay Free" was the closest The Clash could come at this point to proffering a love song. (Unless we count space-filling, Clash-predating

B-side "1-2 Crush on You.") Its pair of protagonists are a petty thief who ends up in prison and a kid who chooses a fork in the road involving studious practice which eventually leads to rock 'n' roll stardom.

The rocker is, of course, Jones. His unfortunate mate is Robin Crocker, who attended Strand Grammar School with Jones but ended up banged up at Her Majesty's Pleasure (although not in Brixton Prison as the song suggests). Whatever the liberties Jones takes with the truth, both the song's tune and its human drama are glorious. The lyric is the epitome of street poetry. Jones may stud them with local landmarks, colloquialisms, double negatives, and obscenities (one couplet is soaringly completed by the phrase "We'll burn it faakin' dahn!"), but the songwords have a smooth-flowing grace. They're also witty: when he asks his jailbird friend in a letter if the screws are too tight in Butlins, Jones is sarcastically comparing prison to a seaside holiday resort while playing on a slang word for prison warders.

In the final verse, Jones expresses his joy at Crocker's release from 'nick' but then whisperingly cautions the title phrase. It is blush-making stuff. Crocker, naturally, was moved when Jones played the song to him on acoustic guitar one evening between the release of the first and second Clash albums. "Unfortunately, I didn't Stay Free," he told Dave Simpson of the *Guardian* newspaper on December 13, 2008. "I did a wages snatch in Stockholm and got banged up again." After a spell as a journalist, Crocker ultimately settled down into a straight life as voice-over artist, drolly-styled Robin Banks.

Listening to "Cheapskates," one is struck by the sheer lack of proportion of punks. Part of the punk ethos was the assertion of an integrity in counterpoint to previous musical acts. Part of the punk experience was enduring hostility from the mainstream media and resistance from the music establishment. The combination of these things prompted New Wavers to compose self-referential anthems almost as a matter of course, whether it be The Sex Pistols's "EMI (Unlimited Supply)," Stiff Little Fingers's "Rough Trade," The Adverts's "One Chord Wonders," The Nosebleeds's "Ain't Bin to No Music School," or Generation X's "Your Generation." Ironically, these broadsides against record companies, old-guard music critics, or older recording artists created a sense of self-mythologizing supposedly inimical to punks' anti-star ethos.

As a band who had started mythologizing themselves before their first record was out by writing "Garageland," The Clash were hardly the type to agonize about that paradox. They were at it again on "Cheap-skates," a snarling riposte to the British music press who had begun to make The Clash their whipping boys. The backing to this lyric is thunderous widescreen drums emphasizing swirling and growling guitars. Yet it's quite sobering to realize when listening to all this Sturm und Drang that The Clash were far from household names and could walk down any street safe in the knowledge that almost no one would recognize them. Contrast that to the number of self-mythologizing anthems written by The Beatles, a band not only vastly more famous than they but uniquely important on a sociopolitical level: none.

When one has a public platform, however, it's difficult to resist hitting back when subjected to criticism in either the press or the street, and such is the nature of anger that a sense of proportion—and even rationality—can be the last thing on one's mind when doing so. Marry that to the self-aggrandizement infused in punk's DNA and you end up with an orgy of self-absorption like "Cheapskates," where Strummer lashes out at every irritant in his and his colleagues' lives: people who approach him in pubs and clubs who are amazed almost to the point of contempt that a star should frequent the same venue as they; music journalists who have decided to join in a Clash backlash because they think the band are no longer the golden boys; talentless nobodies who insufferably assume a sense of superiority over them because they are laboring under the delusion that they will also one day be successful.

Strummer's objection to band critics accusing them of sniffing coke and dating model girls is somewhat undermined by the fact that certain members of the band were publicly known to be doing precisely those things. Meanwhile, the lyric has internal faults not dependent on this knowledge: how can Strummer complain about the critics abandoning them like rats fleeing a sinking ship when, in the next couplet, he tells the same critics not to give him the benefit of the doubt because he'll just spit it back at them?

Yet one doesn't particularly feel inclined to raise such caveats, nor point out the absurdity of the martyrdom of such a bunch of (in the global scheme of things) nobodies. This is because one is swept up in the fury. One of Jones's most melodramatic melodies and richest arrangements is graced by one of Strummer's most glittering pieces of rough-hewn poetry: Joe effortlessly rolls with the swells and lulls of the tune as he peels off elongated colloquial lines like "Just because we're in a group, you all think we're stinking rich." It all leaves the listener inclined to stand shoulder-to-shoulder with the band.

"All the Young Punks (New Boots and Contracts)," the closing track of *Give 'em Enough Rope*, is almost ridiculously suffused with rock culture references and allusions. In its delineation of the supposedly bleak prospects for anyone who doesn't ride the train to rock 'n' roll stardom, it's like an embittered, slightly inverted cousin of the songs on *Mott*. Said album was a brilliant collection of tracks celebrating popular culture and lamenting the vicissitudes of the rock industry. The autobiographical elements of "All the Young Punks" also suggest the influence of Mott The Hoople's two theme songs "Ballad of Mott The Hoople" and "Saturday Gigs." For good measure, the title of the same band's "All the Young Dudes" (written by David Bowie) is co-opted. The cut is posited as a companion piece to the similarly self-mythologizing closer on the last Clash album, right down to the parenthesized subtitle's nod to the part of the lyric of "Garageland" in which Strummer talked of his newly signed punk musician friends now being able to afford new boots. The new song's subtitle also alludes to the title of Ian Dury and the Blockhead's 1977 debut album, *New Boots and Panties*.

Leaving aside such Pavlovian stuff, "All the Young Punks" rather impressively creates an epic vista of tragedy predicated on precepts that are questionable but become difficult to argue with.

We are being manipulated every step of the way: the opening winding guitar figures give way to Jones enunciating emotion-molding, elongated "Aaahs." This leads us into an opening verse in which Strummer is explaining how the band coalesced after a meeting in a market, but it's immediately noticeable that this self-mythologizing doesn't have the defiant or aggressive tone one might ordinarily expect, but instead a timbre of sadness. We are then into a chorus (like all of them, it deftly rhymes "punks" with "cunts"—Epic must have been on the brink of an embolism) in which Strummer advises punks to plunge headfirst into the limited pleasure their existences offer them: they should laugh their lives because there is nothing for which to cry; furthermore, "Live your lives, there ain't much to die for."

Following a second verse in which he indulges in a little self-pity by comparing the contract the band signed to enable them to become recording artists to contracts put out on murder victims by the Mafia, Strummer acknowledges in the bridge and the final verse that the band's fans have it much worse: by dint of their musical career, the Clash members have been saved from a lifetime spent in soul-destroying unskilled labor and economic poverty. The final verse also questions whether the brave new world offered by punk is going to be realized. Even Jones's ringing, rising guitar solo can't offset the despondency.

It's a genuinely affecting song, and its absolutist message—no different to that of "No Future," the original title of The Sex Pistols's "God Save the Queen," or those of The Clash's own "Career Opportunities" and "Cheat"—was no doubt believed implicitly by the band's fans.

Many of those young Clash fans who supposedly had nothing for which to live will have since gone on to gainful, even fulfilling, employment, even those lacking educational qualifications. Many of them will have lived happy lives. Very few of them will have done the thing most logical after taking to heart a message about the unrelieved grimness of their existence: committed suicide. Thus, these now middle-aged fans will have learned via the simple warp and weft of life that the conspiracy against them to keep them in their place articulated in "All the Young Punks" doesn't reflect the nuances of the picture, or even necessarily the truth. Not everybody, of course, can be a rock star, but that is not the same thing as being denied the chance for betterment. However, believing that one has been denied those opportunities is perversely pleasurable when one is young: it is more attractive and less discomforting than acknowledging a more complicated situation which doesn't allow one to pluck from it a victim status.

Released fourteen days after the appearance of *Give 'em Enough Rope*, "Tommy Gun" ended The Clash's policy of stand-alone singles. This act of compromise was compounded for many by the fact that the record—which reached no. 19 in the UK—had a B-side that gave ammunition to those who complained of The Clash having "gone all American."

Although attributed to Strummer/Jones, "1-2 Crush on You" is a Jones composition from his days with pre-Clash group The London SS. It often featured as a Clash live encore. However, whereas "Protex Blue" transcended its pre-punk origins because its tone and subject matter happened to chime with punk sensibilities, this number was immediately recognizable as emanating from the pre-'76 Mobius Strip. Its school canteen milieu, teenage soap opera vocabulary ("I wanna get serious right away"), moon-in-June lyric, and incrementally rising doo-wop vocal introduction (the melody line of which is a nod to The Beatles's version of "Twist and Shout") all give "1-2 Crush on You" the whiff of the year before Year Zero. Only a blast of scabby guitar at the end suggests punk's edge.

These days, it seems a competently executed piece of hackwork—even mildly enjoyable, especially the sweet sax solo from Gary Barnacle—but in 1978 could be viewed only as flimsy and/or laughable and/or contemptible. On top of the fact that it seemed a catalog of the kind of Americanisms and romantic clichés of which British musicians had been prisoners before bands like The Clash liberated them, Jones was unashamedly singing in an American accent. It was just the bleedin' limit.

Or perhaps that state was reached on February 23, 1979, when insult was added to the injury of the ending of The Clash's stand-alone single policy by the release of a second 45 from *Give 'em Enough Rope* in the shape of "English Civil War." That it climbed as high as no. 25 in the UK chart at a point where every Clash fan had surely already bought the parent album was presumably the consequence of it, like the previous single, having an otherwise unavailable song on its flip (opinions divided over whether this constituted cynically forcing their fans to buy a song they already owned or a gesture of generosity by the group).

Said B-side was "Pressure Drop," a cover of a Maytals single from 1969. The Maytals were the group who provided a new form of music a name via their 1968 record "Do the Reggay" [sic]. The Clash members almost certainly encountered "Pressure Drop" either in the 1972 film *The Harder They Come* or on its sound track album. Both movie and record were highly influential on some of The Clash's generation of musicians. A compilation of mostly previously released reggae singles, some of them very well known in Jamaica, the sound track provided a hard-core view of an exotic type of music that had penetrated the UK and U.S. singles charts in sweeter manifestations. "Rivers of Babylon" by The Melodians, for instance, was a glimpse of a type of religiosity highly prevalent in Jamaica which was oriented much more around the Old Testament than was Western Christianity and whose adherents possessed extremely in-depth knowledge of arcane biblical passages and phrases. (This made it all the more bizarre that, in 1978, it became a UK no. 1 for lightweight pop act Boney M.)

The album was also heavy with imagery of outlawdom ("Johnny Too Bad" by The Slickers, Jimmy Cliff's title track) and oppression ("Many Rivers to Cross" by Cliff, "007 [Shanty Town]" by Desmond Dekker). This, and their high quality, made both movie and record cult items for the more alternative-minded early-Seventies would-be rocker even as a certain level of mainstream success gave *The Harder They Come* the status of an entrée to reggae for the uninitiated parts of the wider public.

The influence of the film and sound track on The Clash is not just evident in them covering "Pressure Drop." They wittily inserted Johnny Too Bad into "The Prisoner" as a putative sparring partner for Johnny B. Goode from Chuck Berry land. They also co-opted the phrase "Rudie Can't Fail" from the lyric of "007 (Shanty Town)" for a song of their own of that title.

In the case of "Pressure Drop," The Clash, as with their cover of "Police & Thieves," took a subdued original and gave it punk muscle. However, whereas their "Police & Thieves" retained the original's sensuality, their version of "Pressure Drop" sounds a little ham-fisted compared to its antecedent. It's good, slick stuff nonetheless, and in its use of resounding piano notes and parts where Strummer's promise of the titular pressure ("You're gonna FEEL it!") is hammered home with a gigantic crash of instruments, it even turns its very lack of subtlety into a virtue.

3

REINVENTING PUNK

May 11, 1979, saw the release of The Clash's second EP. If their first, *Capital Radio*, raised some eyebrows by only qualifying for the status of Extended Play through the inclusion of a song fragment and an interview, *The Cost of Living* can have left no one feeling disappointed. It boasted four full-blown songs, all of a very high standard, not to mention witty, deluxe packaging (a gatefold sleeve whose front was made up to look like a packet of washing powder, a picture of a scattering of coins amusingly hidden inside the pocket holding the record and a raised middle digit obscuring its barcode). It felt like half a brand-new album.

Furthermore, the record pointed a way forward from the aural blast of *Give 'em Enough Rope* to a more melodic but nonetheless powerful extrapolation of the original punk idea. It certainly gave an accurate indication of where The Clash would go on their next album, *London Calling*, not least in the slick, widescreen mixing-desk work of Bill Price, who shares production credit with the band as a whole. Price only further cemented the Clash–Mott The Hoople connection: he had been the engineer on *Mott*.

The EP was actually recorded on the sly, The Clash using time paid for by the producers of *Rude Boy* at London's Wessex Studios in January 1979. These sessions were intended for the purpose of overdubbing Clash live performances in said film. The EP was not released in the United States but reached no. 22 on the UK singles chart. Although its contents were aesthetically unimpeachable, sonically it suffered from its appearance coming a few years before the fashion for 12-inch singles. The tracks sound better on CD than they did on the original vinyl, where grooves had to be scrunched up to accommodate double the normal number of songs for a 7-inch disc.

It goes without saying that there were naysayers about The Clash's new record. In the case of the lead track, it has to be conceded that the doubters had some sort of a point. It went beyond the simple fact that, in deciding to record a cover of the Bobby Fuller Four's 1966 U.S. top-tenner "I Fought the Law" (no. 33 in the UK) and placing it at the start of the record, the group seemed to be shamelessly attempting to garner the sort of airplay that their own more provincial compositions were largely unable to. Moreover, this recording suggested something later borne out by events: that it marked the point where The Clash began moving into the realms of a generalized rebellion, a stylized rock 'n' roll bad boy aura. This involved almost inevitably a crossover with the Americana supposedly anathema to them. "I Fought the Law" was the perfect example of a process which, though perhaps inevitable, unavoidably had the smack of compromise.

Although the Bobby Fuller Four made the song famous, it has an interesting and little-known backstory. It was first recorded by The Crickets in their post–Buddy Holly incarnation, written by one of Holly's replacements, Sonny Curtis. One would imagine that if The Crickets were to have a viable recording career without Holly, this would have been the song to effect that, but in 1960 it was squandered as a B-side. Others saw more fully the song's potential, and it had acquired more than one cover version before Bobby Fuller issued two separate takes on it. His second had an elongated, trebly riff as infectious as its title vocal refrain and its singular percussive effects.

That the song is a wonderful outlaw anthem can't be disputed. It also can't even be accused of the sort of irresponsible crime-chic which can be alleged of Clash songs like "White Riot" and "What's My Name": as the second line of every chorus makes clear, the law won the fight. However, it is a quintessentially *American* outlaw anthem, its tableaux of six-gun hold-ups and rock-breaking chain-gang prisoners being far removed from the somewhat less larger-than-life crime-and-punishment scenarios to be found in the UK. Additionally, references to the jailed criminal being separated from his "baby" are not things in the vocabulary of the Briton.

All of that being true doesn't mean that the Clash version is not very enjoyable. They completely punkify "I Fought the Law," turning the strummed, trebly riff into a wailing, plucked affair, throwing in accompanying crunching rhythm guitar work, and providing an additional level of excitement via a blistering drum track. The word "and" is left hanging in the repeat of each chorus, with the original's repetition of the line about the law winning replaced, in almost a parody of punk's intensity, by even more crunching guitar.

Curtis also wrote (with Jerry Allison) the more gentle-natured "More Than I Can Say," a hit for both Bobby Vee and Leo Sayer. Fuller's fate was less pleasant: he was dead within only a few months of his biggest hit, an ostensible suicide considered by some to be a murder.

It barely matters from this end of history, but for the sake of their credibility The Clash might have been better advised to make "Groovy Times" the opening track on the EP. Not only is its subject indisputably British, but it is the most important cut on the record in marking a way forward for the punk movement. It stylishly blew a gigantic hole in the notion that the spirit of punk could only be manifested in high decibel levels, minimalist chord progressions, or even guitars that were amplified.

By 1979, both punk musicians and their fans were beginning to tire of thrash, which was a semi-pejorative term to describe British punk's studied freneticism and minimalism long before it became a designation for a genre of music. Even if the punk bands hadn't begun to feel that they'd made their point about the rock aristocracy's self-indulgent virtuosity, the artist's natural quest for new horizons would have provided the impetus for change in any event. Seventy-nine was the year punk rockers showed themselves to be less embarrassed about more melodic sounds and higher production values. In fact, it could be said that The Jam had beaten The Clash to it on this score: their 1978 album *All Mod Cons* had audaciously mixed the spirit of punk with the sonics of R&B-inflected pop. However, "Groovy Times" takes the process of evolution even further.

The track is propelled by strummed acoustic guitar, admittedly mixed up to unusually high levels but still a shocking departure into gentleness compared to everything else yet released by the group. The soundscape is decorated by toots of mouth harp, tasteful flecks of electric guitar, and speckles of classical guitar. Headon heralds the instrumental break with a pattering roll across the full span of his kit almost as if to give the listener time to prepare for a surprise. The mellifluous, delicate, acoustic guitar solo which follows is certainly that, as well as delectable.

Despite the quasi middle-of-the-road arrangement, "Groovy Times" has a grim tone. The chorus—consisting of the repeated title phrase—is singalong, but sarcastically so, for this is a composition drenched in blood. The song arose from Strummer's dismay at the way British soccer fans were beginning to be fenced in at stadia to prevent pitch invasions. It was a trend that had started after an infamous incident in April 1974 when First Division side Manchester United went a goal down to local rivals Manchester City in a match that could doom them to division relegation after an unbroken thirty-six years in football's top flight. Pitch invasions were something of a tradition, but had previously had a generally benign quality, such as the famous jamboree attending a spectacular goal scored by Ronnie Radford of minnows Hereford United against glamour club Newcastle United in a 1972 FA Cup tie. The pitch invasion at Manchester United's Old Trafford ground was a deliberate attempt to cause the match to be abandoned so as to make the result void. It also had a malevolent tinge that raised the issue of players being in physical danger by dint of it confirming hooliganism's graduation from the terraces to the pitch. By the next season, Manchester United supporters were—in tabloid newspaper parlance—"caged." Other clubs began to follow suit.

One can debate whether the move was right or wrong: it certainly seemed an unfortunate necessity at the time, although did ultimately result in the 1989 Hillsborough disaster when ninety-six Liverpool Football Club fans lost their lives because the fences meant they couldn't escape the crush of an overcrowded terrace. In any case, the lyric is the usual scattershot Clash concoction, moving from a first verse that pretty accurately summarizes the vistas of boarded-up shops and heavy police presence that were becoming depressingly familiar in the streets around football grounds on match day, to a second verse in which Strummer melodramatically talks of police gunshots and dead bodies (fatalities were, in fact, rare at football), to a non sequitur of a third verse about a TV presenter who has abandoned his former values. Counterpointed with all this bleakness is the rosy insistence of house-wives (possibly fictional ones in commercials) and the media that times are good.

"Gates of the West" is the second song on *The Cost of Living* to indicate a way out of punk's stylistic cul-de-sac without sacrificing its values. Although not predominantly acoustic like "Groovy Times," it delivers its own surprise in being rendered in an effervescent soul style. It's a novel type of soul, however: Jones sings this example of a genre born and developed in Detroit and Memphis in his London accent.

Moreover, "Gates of the West" finds The Clash for the first time acknowledging the emotion of happiness. "Stay Free" was almost their first life-affirming song, but its emotionality and tenderness is too rooted in the ungenerous supposition that the narrator and the subject are the wise ones in a world comprised of fools to qualify. In contrast, although "Gates of the West" finds the band immodestly acknowledging that many people think they are great artists, the track also boasts a humility and big-heartedness. In fact, it's big-hearted enough to be able to concede that whatever the misgivings that the group expressed about cultural imperialism in "I'm So Bored with the U.S.A.," America remained a land of awe and wonder for them.

"Gates of the West" details Strummer and Jones's thoughts on the United States and their band's growing stature in the music industry, prompted by their trip over the Atlantic to finish *Give 'em Enough Rope*, at whose sessions they worked on a version of the song, which they were then calling "Rusted Chrome."

Whatever the nationalist self-assertion involved in the punk movement, the extremity of its anti-Americanism was no more genuine than its disavowal of the achievements of past rock acts. Just as the punk generation's disgust with the increasing irrelevance and flatulence of established rock artists couldn't wipe away boyhoods spent fantasizing about being their musical heroes, nor could it make them forget the fact that many of those heroes—as well as rock per se—hailed from across the Atlantic. While the American dreck bought from American networks by the British Broadcasting Corporation and Independent Television (ITV) may have been irritating, the inhabitants of the British living rooms into which so many hoary episodes of *Kojak* and *The Six Million Dollar Man* were broadcast would still all jump at the chance to visit the States. America remained a land of myth and glamour, of Elvis Presley, Marilyn Monroe, cowboys and Indians, yellow taxicabs, soaring skyscrapers, gleaming Cadillacs, hamburgers, Coca-Cola, and other such phenomena impossible to imagine happening or originating in gray, drizzly, low-key, low-waged Britain.

It wasn't just this that gave America a mythical status, however. It was then a land far more distant to Britons than it is now. Few of The Clash's generation had had the opportunity to see it firsthand because up until September 1977, when Laker Skytrain began offering round-trip tickets to the States for £118, the cost of transatlantic flight was so high that it was primarily restricted to businessmen and the rich.

And, of course, rock stars. The Clash (airfares paid by their record company) naturally exulted in the privilege of being in a country only recently completely beyond their reach, a privilege by which all their mates and relatives would also naturally be mightily impressed. The lyric of "Gates of the West" marvels that they have relocated from usual climes like North London's Camden Town Station to 44th and 8th in New York. "I should be jumping, shouting that I made it all this way," it says, with the chorus positing a receptive American audience in the form of characters it calls Eastside Jimmy and Southside Sue. However, a note of ambiguity is injected, with The Clash communicating that it's difficult to get too carried away at their hot status considering all the injustice and suffering they see around them in the Home of the Brave.

It was a canny move to allow Jones to take the vocal. Jones is a hugely underrated vocalist whose intense emotionality can lift a song from the realms of the very good to the great. This is a case in point. He audibly takes an almost blush-making delight in bringing his music to the birthplace of rock 'n' roll.

As if The Clash's development hadn't been underlined enough by *The Cost of Living*, the EP closes with a re-recording of "Capital Radio" that constitutes a handy—and astounding—barometer of their progress in the twenty-five months since they first laid down the song.

The motivation for the revisit was actually the band's dismay that their fans were having to shell out extortionate sums for the *NME* EP, which had already become a collector's item. However, the souped-up, broadened-out, better-played, more clearly sung version of that scrag-gly original coincidentally served to illustrate that this band were developing at a lightning pace and not sacrificing an iota of beef in the process.

It starts almost tauntingly with a piece of noodling on acoustic guitar before one of Jones's trademark "one-two-free-fours!" unleashes, what might be termed these days, a re-imagining. The pace is faster, Jones peels off guitar-hero runs of which he would not have been capable in 1977, and a new humorous, spoken-word section features some superb blurred drum work from Headon.

Of course, the conscientious gesture by The Clash in providing a new version of this song in no way reduced the silly-money prices being fetched by the *NME* EP: the whole point of completists is that they want every different recording. The original "Capital Radio" is now freely available on CD, where it has been renamed "Capital Radio One" to differentiate it from the *Cost of Living* version (a confusing re-titling for Britons, as it looks like a conflation of the names of radio stations Capital Radio and Radio One, plus it can cause a muddle with 1981 Clash B-side "Radio One"). "Capital Radio Two"—as the re-recording is now known—soon began to have its own rarity status because the *Cost of Living* EP was quickly deleted, with its tracks remaining uncollected on album ironically long past the point where the first "Capital Radio" had been made fairly widely available on American rarities album *Black Market Clash*.

A 48-second mock advertisement closes *The Cost of Living* wherein Strummer in a cod Jamaican accent proclaims to the backing of "I Fought the Law" the EP's availability. Because it was ignored when Clash compilations were assembled, this mini-track became even more rare than either version of "Capital Radio" ever was. These days, of course, the Internet has made obsolete the very idea of a piece of music being rare (as opposed to the disc on which it was issued).

When Epic Records refused to release The Clash's debut album in 1977 on the grounds of it being too abrasive for American ears, it made many wonder whether the world had moved on in any way in the birthplace of rock 'n' roll in the more than a decade since The Who's classic single "My Generation" had been greeted with incomprehension by a U.S. label who thought the iconic feedback was a mastering error. Ordinary Americans—always more intelligent than countrymen who have power over them—responded by simply buying *The Clash* on import. Its sales of 100,000 copies are reputed to have made it the most successful import in history up to then. In July 1979, Epic—probably mindful of the fact that all the profits from those imports were going to CBS in Britain—finally gave in. With follow-up *Give 'em Enough Rope* having long been available Stateside and with The Clash's third album actually not far off, the label agreed to a domestic release for *The Clash*—albeit on their own terms.

For the U.S. version of *The Clash*, Epic jettisoned—apparently arbitrarily—"Deny," "Cheat," "Protex Blue," and "48 Hours" to make room for singles and B-sides. (The album version of "White Riot" was additionally replaced by the single version.) As those singles hadn't been released in America, no extra sales would have been conferred—except perhaps from those who had bought the import and who could now be expected to purchase the new edition to get hold of the hard-to-find 45s. The completely anachronistic "I Fought the Law" was also tossed in, while the running order was shuffled. In an apparent final declaration of no faith in the product, the label added a free single containing "Groovy Times" and "Gates of the West."

It was an American record company behaving in a way to which British groups were long used. Everybody knew that Beatles and Stones albums up to 1967 were "buggered about with" by the "Yanks." Just about every other member of the so-called British Invasion also found their long-playing artistic vision traduced via the dropping of cuts (a means of enabling the creation of additional albums), the jumbling of running orders, the throwing on of tracks that in their homeland had only ever been intended as singles, B-sides, and EP tracks, and—worst of all—the deployment of an artificial stereo processing which rendered previously raw and powerful music antiseptic and thin. Although by 1979 the "rechanneled stereo" issue no longer existed in an industry that had left mono behind, The Clash's art had otherwise been subjected by Epic to quintessentially American record label philistinism.

Yet it has to be admitted that the American version of *The Clash*—the cover of which featured the same image as on the UK issue but with a blue instead of green border—was not completely bereft of thoughtfulness. How else is one to describe the sequencing of "Complete Control" after "Remote Control"? Or the fact that "White Riot" is followed by "(White Man) in Hammersmith Palais"? Some even detected a similar inter-track dialogue in the other pairings on the original vinyl side one: "Clash City Rockers"/"I'm So Bored with the U.S.A." and "London's Burning"/"I Fought the Law."

However, it wasn't this revealed understanding of the band's music that mollified Strummer about the U.S. version of the album. "It was a relief to see it go out 'cos they didn't want it released in the first place," he told this author in 2002. "If you've never heard of the group before, it's kind of a good bunch of tunes really. It wasn't the days or the time for concept albums. Punk was quite throwaway so we didn't sit around sniveling because the track order was changed . . . Punk was more about getting a message out rather than worrying about the details. We felt that we had our say on the tunes and we got sick of arguing with them."

The "good bunch of tunes really" attitude held sway with the public: the American *The Clash* reached no. 126 on the U.S. chart, two places higher than *Give 'em Enough Rope*. We will never know how much higher it would have gone had the U.S. version and import-copy sales been combined, but it was still a handy way-paver for their third album. It was also a hit with critics: in Robert Christgau's *Village Voice* review, he gushed, "Cut for cut, this may be the greatest rock and roll album . . . ever manufactured in the U.S. . . ."

The third Clash album would, like its predecessor, bequeath a single.

Those inclined to cry "sellout" were probably not mollified that "London Calling" was the album's sole spin-off 45 and had an otherwise unavailable B-side. Nor that it was technically itself otherwise unavailable when it appeared—that status only lasted the seven days before the release of its identically titled parent album in the UK. However, such issues lacked potency this time around, for, courtesy of a deal struck by the band with their label which had a delightful element of getting one over on a corporation, *London Calling* was a double set retailing for the price of a single album.

"London Calling" is a song rooted in political debates which now seem quaint and antediluvian. In 1979, the Cold War was still raging and—come the following year and the ascension of the hawkish Ronald Reagan to the American presidency—was soon to reach its zenith. That the Americans and Russians were so antagonistic was disturbing to say the least: they had missiles trained on each other in various parts of the globe that could destroy all life on the planet many times over. With the word "nuclear" therefore possessing for many pejorative connotations, it only made more disturbing the accident at Three Mile Island, Harrisburg, in March 1979. Although the partial meltdown at a civilian power

plant was ultimately not considered to have caused major health or
environmental damage, it occurred in the very month of the release of
The China Syndrome. Not only did this motion picture portray safety
failures and cover-ups thereof at a nuclear power plant, but said fictional power plant was located in Pennsylvania, the American state in which
Three Mile Island was situated. For all these reasons, the last year of
the Seventies was one in which both nuclear weapons (synonymous
with the phrase Mutually Assured Destruction, with its 'nuff-said, be-
yond-parody acronym) and nuclear power (the waste from which was
known to remain toxic for thousands of years) had reputations which
stank to high heaven.

When Joe Strummer's romantic partner suggested a song based on
nuclear issues, the result was something that rather disproves those who
accuse The Clash of being an overtly agitprop band. While the group of
course leaned in that direction, Jones's and (especially) Strummer's
intelligence militated against manifestos. In the hands of The Tom Robinson Band or even The Jam, the issues of nuclear weapons and nuclear
power would have led to sloganeering and/or preaching. Strummer's
song (unusually, he was the prime mover behind the melody as well as
the lyric) is a somewhat more humorous and opaque take on the issue.

Although Strummer stirs unease with references to a nuclear error
and the breakout of a war that unleashes the terrifying prospects of
engines ceasing to run, thinning wheat crops, a flaring sun, and a burgeoning ice age, he also can't stop cracking jokes, if morbid ones. Using
the conceit of a BBC World Service transmission—"This is London
Calling" was broadcast in Received Pronunciation across the globe by
the corporation at the start of radio programs—his narrator warns not to
look to the capital: London no longer swings except for the police trun-
cheons whistling down. He also warns against looking to rock idols for
salvation.

The Campaign for Nuclear Disarmament was a major political organization in Britain at the time of the composition and release of
"London Calling." It has since withered on the vine, testament to the
fact that the public's anxiety about nuclear weapons all but evaporated
once the Soviet Union began to break up in the late Eighties and its
constituent parts became allies of a sort of the NATO countries. Nuclear power to some extent also ceased to be an issue, not because disturbing accidents stopped happening but because it became less popular

among governments as a means of generating a way to keep the lights on. Even the song's references to the possibility of London being submerged are antiquated. The Thames flooding the capital was a background fear in Britain for many decades—as prevalent as the dreaded prospect of the Big One in California today—but was finally put to rest in 1982 with the completion of the Thames Barrier. "London Calling" is therefore now absolutely bereft of its once cutting-edge topicality. Moreover, judged on paper, parts of the lyric are whimsical, even risible. There are non sequiturs like references to a drug-addled friend nodding off, Strummer's own recent hepatitis infection, and even zombies. The sense of an arbitrary stream-of-consciousness is added to by Strummer's statement that the fact that London is drowning doesn't bother him because he lives by the river, a reasoning that has no logic and is only thrown in because in real life he was currently domiciled along the path of the Thames. Yet, the track feels denuded of power neither by its irrelevance or its quirkiness. Part of the reason for this is that enough time has passed since the end of the nuclear era for its status to have made a transition from embarrassingly dated to accurate snapshot of a bygone time. Part of it is the sheer excellence of the lyric, whatever its whimsicality: it's both insistent (to which, of course, Strummer's emphatic, impassioned vocals contribute) and highly colloquial ("And you know what they said? Well, some of it was true!").

Mostly it's due to the symbiotic relationship between the biting songwords and the intense music. It's as though no other subject could be married to this instrumentation. Instantly catchy from the moment one hears its incredibly sustained synchronized, two-note guitar lick, "London Calling" shortly moves toward utterly haunting. Mick Jones's continual ghostly vocal echoing of the title phrase and the ominous rumbling bass runs are the perfect accompaniment to Strummer's breathless recounting of catastrophe. The groove of the song is so tense that it feels ready to blow up at any moment. Headon maintains a pitilessly fast clip throughout. The instrumental break finds Strummer cawing dementedly and guitars squalling as if in imitation. The instruments are pared back for an ominously subdued final section. When proceedings end, it's in the ultimate, literal sense. Jones enunciates one last desperate radio ID but there is nobody left to hear: the entire population of the world has disappeared in the shadow cast by the mushroom cloud to end them all, and Strummer's warbling of a line from Guy Mitchell's/Tommy Steele's hit "Singing the Blues" is cut off in mid-stream.

Despite the apocalyptic subject matter ostensibly rendering it chart-unfriendly, its sheer, compelling power ensured that "London Calling" achieved the band's highest placing on the UK chart while they were still extant. However, rather than no. 11, it could conceivably have made pole position. Certainly, it's rather interesting to learn the identity of the record that did top the chart in the late-December/early-January time frame that the Clash record's release date made the obvious juncture for such an eventuality. If Pink Floyd's "Another Brick in the Wall"—a brooding chant about the iniquities of the British education system—could be the nation's Christmas number one, there is no reason to believe that, in other circumstances, "London Calling" couldn't.

That the Clash never had a UK top ten single in their lifetime, let alone a chart-topper, was a consequence of one of the principled stands they were wont to take. This particular one would cause them serious commercial problems in their homeland over the entire course of their career: their refusal to accept invitations to appear on *Top of the Pops*.

That the power then held by the BBC's Thursday night TV chart program was inexplicable to non-Britons was summed up by comments made by American Roy Thomas Baker to John Tobler and Stuart Grundy for their 1982 BBC radio series about his profession, *The Record Producers*: "One of the minor gripes I have about England . . . is that you can't have a hit in England, unless it's played on *Top of the Pops* . . . Now if people don't like it, that's fine . . . but what annoys me is if they don't get the chance to hear it. One of the reasons that the first Queen album was a hit over here but not in England, was that over here the FM/rock stations played 'Keep Yourself Alive' on the radio . . . It wasn't a hit in England basically because it wasn't on *Top of the Pops*, and that's the bottom line to it."

That *Top of the Pops*—with odd exceptions—only featured records that had already made it into the charts was hardly contemptible: it had outlasted all other television pop shows since its arrival in January 1964 specifically because of its populism. The problem arose because of the concentration of power in the British media. Once a record had generated sufficient sales through word of mouth and/or radio play to make it into the charts, and therefore become eligible for inclusion on *Top of the Pops* via a studio appearance or the playing of a promotional film, the record was guaranteed to do even better. Because *Top of the Pops* was the only regular program dedicated to popular music on any of the nation's three television channels, the entirety of the country's pop demographic watched it. A record's sales would therefore skyrocket after just one appearance. Records which hadn't appeared on the program were not debarred from the charts either formally or informally, but that virtuous circle of exposure meant that the upper reaches of the charts inevitably tended to be dominated by records that had been heard and seen on *Top of the Pops*.

The opportunity of an appearance on *Top of the Pops* was therefore a privilege that no musical artist could afford to turn down. Nor would many want to: so ingrained was the program in the nation's psyche, and so much was a *Top of the Pops* appearance a barometer of success, that it was every aspiring musician's dream to be seen on it. The only people who declined were members of the rock aristocracy who were too dignified, rich, or possessed of an albums-oriented fanbase to feel the need to bother anymore. Until punk. There was never any question of either The Sex Pistols or The Clash agreeing to turn up at the BBC's famous circular building in White City, London, to promote their latest product. As the enemies of society, the very idea of the Pistols peddling "Pretty Vacant"—the first of their opening trio of singles the corporation did not ban—on an inane, mainstream show like *Top of the Pops* was absurd. As for The Clash, Strummer explained their hostility to the program in a Clash mini-biography given to journalists with their second LP: ". . . they refused to appear on 'Top of the Pops', considering it an old pop TV show left over from the 1960s, which requires performers to mime along as their record is played at a low volume somewhere in the distance."

It should be clarified that this did not mean that either group's music was not represented on the program at all. Sex Pistols fare was seen and heard on *Top of the Pops* via promotional films (or videos, as they would increasingly be known). While The Clash were so absolutist as to even ban their "promos" being aired on *Top of the Pops* (they got into a tussle with CBS about the label wanting to supply the corporation a clip of "Tommy Gun"), this meant that they were running the risk of the show's resident scantily clad dance troupe Legs & Co. (successors to the mantle of Pan's People, disbanded in 1976) performing one of their famously literal, inevitably demeaning interpretations of their art as it played over the monitors. This very fate befell The Clash's "Bankrob-ber" in 1980: the sexy dancers appeared behind jail-type bars in leotards striped to resemble a cartoon burglar's top, bandanas across their faces, hurling money into the air and holding up a sign reading "This is a stick-up." Not that this happened often: any musical act known to not cur-rently be aboard who declined to make a *Top of the Pops* studio appear-ance would—as much as such was possible while maintaining the show's validity—be punished in the form of their record not being represented except by a title card in the chart rundown.

The Pistols's and The Clash's problem was not with—as has often been erroneously reported—miming per se. After all, they pretended to sing and play unplugged instruments in promos. Rather it was the whole cheesy aura of the show, which as well as Legs & Co. (whose decorative function some found sexist) featured unctuous presenters (all, incestuously, BBC radio DJs), banal banter, garish backdrops, and fatuous screen effects. The musicians didn't even mime to their actual records. In another example of the disproportionate power of the trade unions of the era, Musicians Union rules dictated that the BBC oblige the acts to lip-synch to a re-recording of the single made in their repre-sentative's sight, one whose one-day turnaround made a mockery of the care invested in the laying down of the record over weeks or even months. Meanwhile, the show's title was so familiar that nobody thought about it anymore, but even that was steeped in old fartdom: Britons had stopped referring to the charts as the "pops" long before its first broadcast. In short, The Clash didn't like *Top of the Pops* because it catered not to rock culture but show business sensibilities. Not only was it not cool, it was in no way interested in being so.

Yet in declining to make *Top of the Pops* appearances, The Clash were cutting their own throats. (The fact that the Pistols cut their own throats by unraveling in all but brand name would shortly make their non-appearance policy moot.) Every musical act, no matter how edgy, uncompromising, or alternative, wants an audience. The Clash were shutting themselves off from large parts of their potential demographic. Of course they might be inclined to assert that in getting to the cusp of the top ten without consenting to a *Top of the Pops* performance repre-sented a triumph in itself, but The Clash were always speaking in inter-views of their desire to convert unenlightened music lovers to their music and beliefs.

Other New Wave groups who considered themselves to have an anti-showbiz attitude distinct from previous generations of artists were happy to appear on the program. Among them numbered The Adverts, The Boomtown Rats, Generation X, The Jam, Sham 69, The Rezillos, Stiff Little Fingers, The Stranglers, and X-Ray Spex. Their oft-repeated rationale that they were taking on the system from the inside was not without validity. Few would claim after witnessing their glowering and/ or frenzied performances that lip-synching on crassly decorated sets before bopping teenagers had somehow robbed them of their integrity. (Yes, not even when Jimmy Pursey took to prefacing Sham 69's appearances with a variant of " 'allo, mum! 'oo's on *Top of the Pops*, then?")

The most significant of the aforementioned artists are The Jam. The Woking band had by 1979 become almost synonymous with The Clash, so similar on one level were the two groups' styles and philosophies. By rejecting the chance to put their wares before the widest public possible, The Clash had to sit and watch as The Jam achieved the dream The Clash had always harbored but which their ethics had denied them: racking up number-one hit singles with records combining hard-hitting music and lyrics of social protest.

In June 1979, Strummer told the *NME*'s Charles Shaar Murray that the refusal to appear on *Top of the Pops* was "tough shit for us now, because all we get is 22 or 23 in the chart, but in the long run it's gonna be for the best." It was a not untypical Strummer admission of regret coupled with a meaningless addendum of defiance. The Clash were not, individually, men who found it easy to admit they were wrong. Their group identity was so steeped in declarations of integrity as to virtually make a refusal to back down a badge of honor. With them having nailed their colors so firmly to the mast of their contempt for *Top of the Pops*, they could never make a U-turn. If they were ever so inclined, of course, they would have been conscious of the fact that there were plenty of journalists on, and correspondents to, the music press who would be ready to denounce their betrayal of values. So they stuck to their guns, even as they did other things which signified they were losing touch with their original ideals—for instance, the way that Strummer for promotional purposes became increasingly close to *The Sun*, a British tabloid whose pro-Thatcherite values were the quintessence of most everything he despised.

The Clash would continue to have minor British hits until they expired, but there is no getting away from the fact that being *Top of the
Pops* "refuseniks" robbed them of the large audience the quality of their
music deserved.

Quite remarkably, the B-side of the "London Calling" single boasted
a track every bit as good as the A-Side. "Armagideon Time" is a sensu-
ous reggae first recorded by Willie Williams in 1978, although it began
life as an instrumental variously known as "Real Rock" and "Reel Rock"
by a group variously known as the Soul Vendors and Sound Dimension.
The Jamaican music industry tradition of recording new vocals over old
tracks has ensured that there has been some rancor over the song's
publishing. Although the composition of "Real"/"Reel Rock" was originally partly credited to Coxsone Dodds—owner of the studio in which it
was recorded—The Clash credited it to Williams. It is now attributed to
Williams and Jackie Mittoo, a musician who was influential on the day
of the recording by the Soul Vendors/Sound Dimension.

Although packed with motifs alluding to the Old Testament that will
only fully make sense to Jamaican Rastafarians of the era (not least the
play on words in the title), it also has a haunting, apparently socially
conscious vocal refrain—"A lot of people won't get no supper tonight,"
with the "supper" replaced by "justice" in its repeat—tailor-made for
The Clash.

The Clash's version is—as you would expect from them at this
stage—heavier and faster than the original, but it is no musical hybrid
like "Police & Thieves," "(White Man) in Hammersmith Palais," or
"Safe European Home." Instead, it is the group's first authentic reggae.
It also enriches and broadens the source. A spiky flourish of a guitar
riff—counterpointed by organ warbles—and a pulsating bottom-end
are built on to create an extraordinarily opulent arrangement. An additional, vaguely oriental guitar riff is replicated on tubular bells. Fire-
work sound effects complete a brooding impression of trouble about to
kick off at any moment.

The track also reveals that Strummer is truly beginning to come into
his own as a vocalist. The man at whom the old guard had always
laughed for his muffled and sibilant delivery was learning to overcome
the impediments created by his broken front teeth via an absolute commitment to the material, one that was on a higher level than such things
as his inarticulate loss of control in the final verse of the album version

of "White Riot." What is remarkable about his emoting here is that it doesn't feel like artifice, the feelings-to-order standard for a singer in front of a microphone, but instead a spontaneous welling-up of genuine compassion and anger.

And then there are instances of brilliance that are down to serendipity rather than planning and application. At around the three-minute mark of "Armagideon Time," a voice suddenly intrudes on the proceedings, demanding "Alright, time's up. Let's have you out of there!" The band break off, with Strummer insisting that the owner of the voice not push them when they're hot. Then as if on a signal from him—indeed on the very word "hot!"—they launch back into the song, which continues—exquisitely—for a further three quarters of a minute.

The intruding voice belongs to sharp-dressing Clash aide Kosmo Vinyl who, before the recording, opined that all the great singles in history had lasted no longer than 2:58. It was a silly piece of absolutism, the type of which is often heard from music lovers of his pose-adoring, rock-myth-loving generation. Both he and Strummer would have been perfectly *au fait* with the fact that such a rationale dismissed "The House of the Rising Sun" by The Animals, "Like a Rolling Stone" by Bob Dylan, "Hey Jude" by The Beatles, and sundry other titanic rock classics. However, something about the assertion appealed to the rock 'n' roll romantic in Strummer, possibly because it stirred fond memories of all the sub–three minute rock classics that proliferated in his boyhood, as well as provoked bad memories of the fashion for the bloated epics purveyed by the likes of Genesis, Emerson, Lake & Palmer, and Yes that punk had insisted was a case of Emperor's-New-Clothes elaboration without improvement. Accordingly, Strummer told Vinyl to stop the band when they had reached that crucial point beyond which there were supposedly only diminishing returns. When Vinyl did that, though, Strummer rebuffed him because he had concluded that the group were on fire.

Instead of ruining the take, the interruption ratchets up its power. It makes the listener jump on the first listen, as well as on those subsequent occasions when he isn't prepared for it. It feels like an organic part of the record, like some piece of verbal interplay inserted to heighten the drama: the enunciated words and their tone have the smack of the loud-hailer barking of a police officer at a street demonstration. Adding to an air of serendipity-verging-on-miracle is the fact that Simonon maintains his throbbing bassline throughout Vinyl's intrusion, almost as though he is keeping intact the thread of the music for a full-scale resumption he always knew was going to occur.

"London Calling" was the subject of the first-ever Clash 12-inch single. For a brief moment in the early to mid-Eighties, the 12-inch looked like the future of music. A single that was the same size as an album was a concept that sounded strange at first, but the wider dynamic range conferred by a 12-inch disc containing only one or two tracks was a revelation.

However, 12-inch singles quickly became a source of mild controversy. Conscious of the need to persuade consumers that it was worth shelling out the extra money for the new format, record companies and artists began to throw on enticements. They usually did so in the easiest and cheapest way possible: extended mixes and remixes—artificially lengthened or differentiated versions of the A- or B-sides or both. The sound effects and looping integral to this process had the upshot of compounding what was already a grand sense of pointlessness with buffoonishness. That sense of tomfoolery was underlined by the fact that extended mixes and remixes were often given fatuous parenthesized subtitles like "Day Mix" and "Night Mix." This entire phenomenon was profoundly depressing to people beginning to get agitated by an increasing mechanization of music, whether it be via the growing prevalence of synthesizers or the creeping spiritual insipidness of a medium that (punk notwithstanding) had been losing its sociopolitical timbre for the best part of a decade. Although 12-inch singles could occasionally generate worthy records—New Order took advantage of the medium to purvey "Blue Monday," a groundbreaking piece of electropop of 7½ minutes' duration, which they refused to release on 7-inch because it would have been either brutally cut or muffled—the overwhelming impression about them was of an adjunct to an artist's canon that could be entirely disregarded. Some artists seemed to be embarrassed by the issue. The sleeve of one 12-inch single by Eighties UK pop act ABC bore a sticker carrying an almost defiant statement that the contents were exactly the same as the 7-inch and that the purchaser had the choice of which to buy according to his own preferences.

The vogue for 12-inch mixes—and indeed vinyl itself—was brought to an end by the advent of the age of the CD, where sound quality (and disc size) was uniform. However, the half decade or so in which 12-inch singles flourished has ensured that all recording artists active in that era have discographies littered with aesthetically negligible variants of songs in their core canon. The multiplicity of versions of the same song and the similar titles given them often bring about confusion. For instance, many is The Clash expert who can unhesitatingly reel off the band's corpus up to the 1981 12-inch single "This Is Radio Clash," whose additional tracks, "Radio Clash," "Outside Broadcast," and "Radio Five," invariably cause them to stumble in their litany. Even The Clash get confused by these four variations of the same song: the single's tracks have been known to be given incorrect titles on compilations.

The onetime prevalence of 12-inch singles created an additional problem when the phenomenon of box sets took off. Many music fans are adamant that those box sets that come attached with a claim of comprehensiveness should live up literally to it by rounding up everything commercially released by the relevant act: B-sides, original tracks from multi-artist compilations, cuts from promo-only releases, and all other forms of rarity, including mixes which only nominally make a track different to its template. Some Clash fans were therefore dismayed when *Sound System*, the massive twelve-disc Clash box set of 2013, omitted—as well as "Outside Broadcast" and "Radio Five"—alternate mixes of "Armagideon Time" ("Justice Tonight" and "Kick It Over"), "Bankrobber" ("Robber Dub"), and "Rock the Casbah" ("Mustapha Dance"). Yet despite their apoplexy, it's unlikely that many of them would profess to enjoy listening to any of the omitted tracks, which may be an indictment of completist fans but is indubitably also an indictment of the very invention of 12-inch mixes and remixes.

Having said all of that, The Clash thought laterally when it came time for their first 12-inch mix. "Justice Tonight" and "Kick It Over"—versions of "Armagideon Time" of a cumulative length of nine minutes that appeared on the B-side of the 12-inch single of "London Calling" (the A-side of which featured the same versions of "London Calling" and "Armagideon Time" as on either side of the 7-inch)—were an immersion into a style of musical experimentalism in which the group were already deeply interested: dub. "Dubwise stylee," to use the Jamaican vernacular, is a reggae tradition dating from the late Sixties. It involves removing a record's vocal track and manipulating elements of its instrumentation, typically by echo, delay, drop-out, repetition, and extension. Often the only songwords will be snippets of the excised vocal track that are made to skitter weirdly across the soundscape. (The very titles "Justice Tonight" and "Kick It Over" constitute an allusion to this, being phrases lifted from the lyric of "Armagideon Time.") Some conventional (mostly First World) musicians find this process ridiculous. Others think good dub has a mesmeric, dreamlike quality.

As reggae enthusiasts, The Clash could be expected to have an affinity for the dub medium. Admittedly, the results were qualitatively not too dissimilar to the more modern technique of the extended mix, but "Justice Tonight" and "Kick It Over" could at least be said to have a motivation more elevated than the usual arbitrary and half-interested impetuses behind a 12-inch mix. Sure enough, there would be many more dub versions of Clash songs after this. Nor was this restricted to locations synonymous with musical afterthoughts such as 12-inch singles or B-sides of 7-inch singles: almost a sixth of their triple *Sandinista!* album is comprised of dubs.

The Clash initially toyed with calling their new album *The Last Testament*, but—possibly concluding that this would be a case of self-mythologizing a conceited step too far—instead made *London Calling*, released on December 14, 1979, the only Clash album, then or now, named after one of its songs.

They began recording the long-playing follow-up to *Give 'em Enough Rope* at Wessex Studios in late August 1979. That the album had been worked through in a rehearsal space beforehand was probably crucial to its quality, circumventing those problems faced by bands who effectively "rehearse" their first albums in live settings and are then surprised that subsequent albums—recorded when they aren't so readily able to hone new material—are less assured. Bar the mixing, the album was finished a month later.

The rehearsal space was Vanilla Rehearsal Studios in Pimlico, southwest London. Their previous Camden Town base, Rehearsals Rehearsals, was no longer available to the band because *London Calling* was the first Clash album not recorded with Bernard Rhodes at the group's management helm. The Svengali figure who had to some extent molded their image, attitude, and even song subjects had been sacked in October 1978 over his dictatorial approach. Mick Jones's cocaine hauteur had lately been both irritating his colleagues and making them doubt his commitment to the punk ethos, but Rhodes's suggested solution of ousting him in favor of Sex Pistol Steve Jones was going too far. Simonon's girlfriend, Caroline Coon, managed their affairs for a brief period after that. Although technically Blackhill Enterprises were their new managers, The Clash always seemed slightly discomforted by the fact of their affairs being overseen by a mainstream team whose other clients had included Pink Floyd, no doubt partly because of the inevitable sarky comments from music journalists.

Perhaps recruiting Guy Stevens as their new album's producer was a response to this, as though the band were seeking to replace one eccentric-verging-on-demented true believer in the multi-faceted power of rock with another. As well as having overseen the demos The Clash cut for Polydor, Stevens was yet another link to Mott The Hoople, having been the manager of Mick Jones's heroes.

However, although Stevens is credited as producer of *London Calling*, eyewitnesses seem to agree that his quasi-psychosis reduced his real role to merely that of cheerleader, and even sometimes obstacle. Jones and Bill Price appear to have been the real producers, with Price in the subservient role. Price told Marcus Gray in his exhaustive/exhausting book on the album, *Route 19 Revisited*, that Jones's dominance even extended—following The Clash's departure of the studio for an American tour with the mixing process not yet begun—to transatlantic phone instructions. Despite the guitarist's undoubted maestro position, the resulting album has Price's sonic stamp: *London Calling* possesses the same widescreen, larger-than-life attributes as *Mott*, also engineered by Price. Whoever is mainly responsible, *London Calling* is one of the best-produced albums of all time, so rich, layered, and slick as to impact on the listener's senses to almost dizzying effect. That and the often joyous tone to the songs make it easily the most accessible thing The Clash released in their career.

To which the response of many detractors was, "That, sir, is your charge"—or its, no doubt, profane punk equivalent. A significant number of critics thought *London Calling* an atrocious betrayal of principles. This wasn't so much represented in the reviews—although Garry Bushell of *Sounds* dismissed it in precisely those terms—but in asides in features on and reviews of other groups over the following months:

the on-going low-level warfare then made possible by the multiplicity and frequency of British music papers.

To The Clash, the brickbats must have been bewildering. Not only were they on the crest of an artistic wave, but by intricate maneuverings they had pulled off a coup that lived up to all their man-of-the-people rhetoric. The band had been annoyed that CBS had insisted on a retail price of £1.49 for *The Cost of Living* rather than the one pound that was their preference. They had requested of CBS that the new album feature a free single, and, once that objective had been secured, innocently suggested the single be in 12-inch format. In neglecting to stipulate a maximum content for the gratis single, CBS ensured that the band were free to include the same number of tracks on this second disc as one might expect to find on an LP. This, and the undertaking the band had secured that the album have a recommended retail price of £5, meant that The Clash were providing their fans a double album for the price of one, albeit a fairly short one (around 65 minutes, where a standard double-album length was approximately 80). Strummer described it to Chris Bohn in *Melody Maker* on December 29 that year as, "our first real victory over CBS."

However, those disgusted with the record were not about to be mollified by either value for money or patent aesthetic excellence. With the growing consensus that the musical definition of punk was becoming passé and a dead end in which nobody with any sense was going to stay, few expected The Clash to continue sounding like they had on their first album. The objection was that the album proved that The Clash had completed the "going bloody American" process allegedly begun by their second album.

There were certainly now nods in their music to American pop luminaries and stylings, from Phil Spector to Stax soul. The values of other U.S. hit-makers seemed implicitly embraced in keyboards, horns, an overall exuberant tone, and ultra-slick production methods. The leap in logic that critics and died-in-the-wool punks made, however, was that such things were the sole preserve of residents of the U.S.A. or those who aspired to their alleged values. The album had a considerable reggae element, which, while it didn't constitute an insistence on their Englishness (their accents and vernacular continued to serve that purpose), hardly suggested artists disdaining any music except commercially safe mainstream American rock. Moreover, in no sense did the album's American-set songs like "Koka Kola" or "The Right Profile" accept the assumptions of American supremacists. Even the Yankophilia of the cover "Brand New Cadillac" was partially an illusion: it was written by Vince Taylor, more transatlantic than American.

The record's exuberance seemed a sellout to some people because of the gushing ambience then surrounding American popular culture: it's less pronounced today, but in the Seventies, the United States seemed to be represented by the toothpaste smiles and smug homilies of television talking heads who seemed laughable compared to the more sarcastic presenters to whom Britons were used. Moreover, it somehow seemed wrong for a band born in the fires of punk—and who still claimed to adhere to its values—to sound happy.

The final confirmation of sellout for some was the cover artwork and album packaging. Pennie Smith's dramatic in-concert photo of Paul Simonon smashing his bass was reminiscent of The Who's Pete Townshend's stage shtick. The lapel-grabbing pink and green jagged lettering was deliberately redolent of the design of the first Elvis Presley album. While the jacket seemed to demonstrate an un-punk sense of being in thrall to rock antecedents, the album's format of two records contained in a single outer sleeve, with the discs inside housed in separate card sleeves bearing untidily hand-scrawled annotation, was very reminiscent of the design of The Rolling Stones's 1972 double set *Exile on Main St.* It felt as if not only were The Clash paying homage to one of the rock gods dethroned by punk, but they were also having the presumption to bracket their latest work with an acknowledged classic.

As with so many controversies stemming from the punk revolution, it seems absurd today that such things were ever issues, and as with so many problems afflicting The Clash it was partly their own fault, inevitable from the moment they wrote "I'm So Bored with the U.S.A." A stung Strummer was still complaining about the album's reception more than two years later when he told the *New Musical Express* of its genesis, "I never thought about beefburgers once, or Mickey Mouse, or the Statue of Liberty."

In the heated and uptight climate of the time, it was less easy to see that the album confirmed that The Clash had learned to harness the power of punk without needing to opt for either the sort of minimalism to be found on their first album or the crash-and-thunder evinced on *Give 'em Enough Rope*. On *London Calling*, The Clash reinvented the very concept of punk by demonstrating that it could be about a social and artistic conscience rather than a particular sound.

That their music was now glossy and melodic and their lyrics generous and warm was a function of the fact that they were leagues more proficient and leagues wiser than the group that had made *The Clash*. Their new album was life-affirming, but it was not the syrupy result of a success that had confined them to ivory towers. Their songs continued to acknowledge the harsh realities of the lives of their fans.

The *Exile on Main St.* similarities weren't superficial. The Clash did now undeniably sound like the early-Seventies Rolling Stones. However, it was in a punk-positive sense. They were what The Rolling Stones might have been if the Stones had come after punk rather than helped cause it: possessed of a "mateyness" and a tenderheartedness antithetical to those kings of hauteur, and displaying a rebelliousness not predicated on a belligerence that could as easily be rooted in self-aggrandizement as social conscience. And if the Clash were now a rock, rather than a punk, band, they were also the perfect rock band for the postpunk era.

The title track kicks off *London Calling* in dramatic fashion. Following its emphatic Englishness comes an unexpected journey into Americana, albeit one—as mentioned before—of less purity than might be assumed.

Just as old rockers enjoy only semi-seriously fostering absolutist myths such as maximum single length, so they have penchants for championing and ranking unacknowledged greatness. In The Clash's 1979 tour magazine *The Armagideon Times*, Headon called Vince Taylor's "Brand New Cadillac" "the first British rock 'n' roll song." In 1999, Strummer insisted to Kieron Tyler of *Mojo*, "Vince Taylor was the beginning of British rock 'n' roll. Before him there was nothing." The Clash's inclusion of "Brand New Cadillac" on *London Calling* was clearly partly a consequence of their romantic conclusion that Taylor had been the real thing unjustly neglected in favor of vanilla imposters like Cliff Richard.

However, it seems safe to assume that another part of their motivation was an additional romantic rocker's penchant: a love of beautiful losers and damaged psyches. As mentioned previously, Syd Barrett, Peter Green, and Brian Wilson were rock musicians whose talents were decimated to a greater or lesser extent by LSD. Vince Taylor can unquestionably be bracketed in the same sad category of acid casualty. However, in rock fandom one acquires cool by virtue of being *au fait* with the obscure. To invoke the name of Taylor—either in conversation or via the gesture of a cover version—was hipper than referencing Barrett, Green, or Wilson because fewer people knew about Taylor, who was also a more tragic figure because his decline was not cushioned by the sort of wealth possessed by the others.

In the Sixties, to express concern about the possible harmful effects of Lysergic Acid Diethylamide would have rendered one instantly unhip. Not that it was unknown that the drug produced ill effects: every "acidhead" had a story of a "bad trip." However, in that decade society was discarding an authoritarian approach where one's conduct, dress, and values were dictated by church, state, or employer. This often engendered a with-us-or-against-us climate that rendered one almost a figure of suspicion for raising the possibility of the potential long-term adverse side effects of recreational drugs favored by the young such as LSD. There was another kind of pressure (internal and external) against articulating doubts about acid: users adored it.

For a substance that has no odor, taste, or color, the effects of LSD are reported to be staggeringly vivid and powerful. The effect the drug has of suspending the "gatekeeping" part of the human brain leads to an avalanche of unfiltered impressions, or "sensory overload." This gets translated into surreal experience: thinking one can see for a thousand miles or feeling that the ticking of a wristwatch is deafeningly loud. Moreover, it's not only pleasure that is considered to be imparted by the drug, but wisdom too: many is the person who imagines that they have found on a trip the answer to life's mysteries. Or as enthusiast Ken Kesey once claimed, "LSD lets you in on something."

The vagueness of that endorsement will immediately arouse the suspicions of the skeptical—as will the fact that Kesey's own talent seemed to evaporate in a psychedelic haze. After, in the first half of the Sixties, producing two rapturously received novels in *One Flew Over The Cuckoo's Nest* and *Sometimes A Great Notion*, Kesey seemed to dry up, issuing works very infrequently and to little acclaim. It was difficult not to conclude that his precipitous decline was directly related to the LSD consumption he enthusiastically championed.

Vince Taylor technically had an American upbringing, but Britons can plausibly claim him as their own: he was born in the English county of Middlesex and raised there until the age of seven. Moreover, in the late-Fifties he moved back to Britain to further the rock 'n' roll career he'd begun in his adoptive America a few years earlier. There, he became part of the first wave of British rock 'n' roll stars alongside the likes of Tommy Steele, Cliff Richard, and Billy Fury. He didn't have the chart hits those recording artists could boast but did possess something possibly more valuable. Although British rock always had a slightly ersatz feel prior to The Beatles reimagining the medium and exporting it back to its homeland, Taylor's American accent, squared-jawed good looks, and redoubtable quiff gave him a greater air of authenticity than his new compatriots. That said, the only real semblance of gravitas in a recorded catalog dominated by covers of hoary old rock 'n' roll chestnuts and generic originals is Taylor's 1959 self-composed B-side "Brand New Cadillac." It seems significant that Taylor's main success was on continental Europe, where acclaim is afforded artists who would be considered negligible in Britain or America: the Lost in Translation syndrome.

Taylor might have been forgotten were it not for the tragic aura that ultimately hung over him. His recording career began dribbling away during the Sixties as drugs took their toll. He seems to have cottoned on to LSD before most in that era, and the legend is that a single acid trip left Taylor permanently mentally impaired and delusional. David Bowie met him several times in the mid-Sixties and recalled a very disturbed man with a messiah complex, babbling about UFOs and formulating plans to found a new Atlantis. Taylor's condition inspired one of rock's most famous concept works. Bowie told Paul Du Noyer in *Q* magazine in April 1990, ". . . he always stayed in my mind as an example of what can happen in rock 'n' roll. I'm not sure if I held him up as an idol or as something not to become . . . There was something very tempting about him going completely off the edge. Especially at my age, then, it seemed very appealing: Oh, I'd love to end up like that, totally nuts. Ha ha! And so he re-emerged in this Ziggy Stardust character."

Bowie's 1972 album about a doomed rock star, *The Rise and Fall of Ziggy Stardust and the Spiders from Mars*, was the only great piece of music associated with Taylor—until The Clash decided to record "Brand New Cadillac." The trouble was, the Taylor song they chose to cover was inevitably provocative for the music press and parts of their fanbase. Cars—let alone iconic and beautiful ones like Cadillacs—were never part of the UK rock landscape. In post-war Britain, austerity meant that it was all Teds could do to scrape together the cash for their fancy clothes, let alone wheels. Even when a youth cult generational change had occurred and an offshoot of Teds—rockers—inhabited a more prosperous society, they could still only afford motorbikes as a mode of transport. The standard of living in the UK remained so far behind that of the U.S.A. that, even into the late Seventies, cruising around in an example of the big-finned beauties seen in films and magazine features remained firmly outside the experience of most of British youth. Hence a song celebrating an example of such was doomed to ring false—especially coming from artists who insisted on Englishness and repudiation of phony Americana. In that context, it's easy to understand those who felt "Brand New Cadillac" both a retrograde step and talismanic of a loss of principles.

Once again, a dichotomy was eating at The Clash: they might disdain rock star excess, rock archetypes rooted in artifice, and the vulgarity of American culture, but they wouldn't be rock fans if they didn't also love those things. The attraction of the rock 'n' roll dream—the path from poverty to riches and the sort of hedonistic extravagance recently summed up by Ian Dury as "Sex and drugs and rock 'n' roll"—was lodged in the soul of every musician of their generation. Leather clothing and quiffs were synonymous with America, but few looked cooler in leather trousers at this juncture than Mick Jones, and few pulled off a quiff better than the increasingly Adonis-like Paul Simonon. And who the hell was going to celebrate the glories of a Ford Cortina over a Cadillac? (Well, actually The Tom Robinson Band, but that is another reason why TRB were never destined to capture the public imagination the way The Clash did.)

Just as clues to the Clash members' love for the bulk of the back catalogs of the rock aristocracy had inevitably and increasingly begun seeping into their art—it's difficult to play rock for very long without falling into line with the classic forms which created its appeal—so it must have occurred to The Clash that it would be increasingly silly to continue pointedly ignoring the points of reference of rock, many of which were American consumer durables. It's true that The Jam—the yardstick against whom The Clash would increasingly be measured— would never write or record a song about such a thing as a Cadillac, but it's almost certainly for that very reason of glum purism that The Jam's music—however excellent it often was—rarely achieved the grandeur and excitement of which The Clash were capable.

There is also the proof-in-the-pudding argument. As with much The Clash touched at this juncture, their version of "Brand New Cadillac" is sublime. Vince Taylor and his Playboys' original may not be great but is a high quality record: the whirling guitar riff is dramatic and flashy, the song has a blues element unusual for rockabilly (down to the first line of each verse being repeated), and the track almost daringly turns gender assumptions on their head (it's the girl behind the wheel of the titular vehicle, and the guy getting dumped).

When Mick Jones plays the distinctive riff, his attempts to make it more dramatic than the original's end up causing it to sound almost like a mockery of an archetype, something that Neil Hefti might have rejected as too outrageously over-the-top for even the *Batman* TV theme. It gives the track a comedic tinge, which can also be misinterpreted as defensive, as in "See? We're not really serious about this Yank stuff." Despite that element of the comic, as with "I Fought the Law"—their previous cover version that was allegedly a sellout to the Americans—The Clash beef up the song. Strummer executes brutal downstrokes on rhythm guitar, and the track has an overall greasy, dirty ambience, one that feels apposite in the context of discussion of a vehicle that will not have been a stranger to oil pits and dirty rags. This particularly applies to Jones's sparks-raising lead guitar, a menacing presence throughout. Comic or serious or both, it would be a real safety-pinned curmudgeon who didn't conclude that the whole thing is great fun.

Perhaps it is in deference to such types that Strummer (who undeniably sings in an American accent) attempts to provide the track punk credibility by throwing into the lyric "balls" and "Jesus Christ"—epithets Taylor would never have dared put into his original.

The danger with a band whose art is oriented around social commentary is to assume that their every song has political import. It's naturally understood that the very small smattering of tracks in The Clash's corpus that could be described as love songs have no social commentary content. However, with the rest, the listener automatically searches for a meaning in the sense of formal protest even where it seems elusive. "Jimmy Jazz" is a case in point. The opening line of this vista of street life states that police have raided a joint looking for a fellow called Jimmy Jazz. This, the use of the Ethiopian phrase "Satta massa gana" and the fact that Strummer sings in a semblance of patois, all lead to the natural conclusion that the story being told is about a Rastafarian facing harassment from the police, something strengthened by a reference to someone called Jimmy Dread, "dread" being a common word with multiple meanings among Jamaicans. At the time, this subject being explored by a British band would more than likely involve a denunciation of stop-and-search tactics employed by police forces. Known colloquially as SUS ("sussed out" being slang for "found out"), they allegedly unfairly targeted young black men.

Yet not even the staunchest critics of London's Metropolitan Police would have suggested that any West Indian youth was ever subjected by them to the fate detailed for Mr. Dread: his ears and head being lopped off. Contemplating that fact, it becomes evident that "Jimmy Jazz" is merely a *demi monde* vignette of no ideological bent or profound import—or even linear logic. "A piece of nonsense" is how Strummer described the lyric to the *Melody Maker*'s Chris Bohn in 1979. (Aside from "Train in Vain" and the cover versions, Strummer wrote all of the lyrics on *London Calling*.) Strummer—as self-deprecating about his own work as he was self-aggrandizing about The Clash's significance—was being unfair on himself. It's more accurate to say that "Jimmy Jazz" is no less a piece of whimsy than "Julie's Been Working for the Drug Squad." The difference is that it's on a far higher musical plane than that *Give 'em Enough Rope* throwaway, even perhaps The Clash's most sophisticated creation up to this point.

Three tracks in, it is becoming clear just how remarkable a leap forward is this album: in 1977, The Clash would not even have been able to think about what they pull off, apparently effortlessly, here: a brass-augmented quasi-swing number. The track begins in muted but remarkable fashion with Jones effecting for several bars a pastiche of the languid style of legendary jazz guitarist Django Reinhardt. Although the pace picks up, everything is unfamiliar: whistling sounds, strangulated, understated electric guitar, thrumming bass patterns, skittering drums, isolated downstrokes on acoustic guitar, and a horn section. The latter crop up on five other cuts, and their presence is always welcome, often blissful—not least in this track's central section, where they and Headon strut proudly together into the instrumental break.

The brass section was facetiously credited as "The Irish Horns" in the album sleeve notes. They were in fact three-quarters of The Ru-

mour Brass, a former adjunct of Graham Parker's backing band: bari-
tone/tenor saxophonist John Earle, tenor saxophonist Ray Beavis, and
trumpeter Dick Hanson. (The group's Chris Gower was not booked
because The Clash were aiming for the sort of brass aggregation heard
on Stax records, whose soul styling didn't usually incorporate trom-
bone.) All their work was recorded in one three-hour session wherein
Strummer and Jones hummed the parts they envisaged sitting in the
gaps they had left (instructions which The Rumour Brass apparently
treated as suggestions only). Astoundingly considering this, the Brass's
contributions at no time sound like either an afterthought or an intrusion, always feeling like an integral part of the soundscape.

Toward the end of the track, we are treated to the sort of aural
eventfulness that characterizes many parts of this album and which
demonstrates the way that *London Calling*'s instrumentation and production are very much intertwined. The nonsensical phrase "And then
it sucks!" is, as if on cue, followed by an avalanche of strummed and
percussive noise. In all likelihood, Strummer was singing over an already completed track and was merely creating the impression of inter-
acting with the players, but it—clearly deliberately—has the effect of a
form of call-and-response. Strummer would convey this idea of the
vocalist as a godlike figure—the instrumentation at his verbal command—in several other tracks, to bewitching effect.

Such is the aesthetic quality and aural richness of *London Calling*'s
opening three numbers that it's almost a relief to encounter a slight
track. However, it has to be admitted that, with "Hateful," those who
complain of *London Calling* being guilty of tunelessness and cacophony
are on relatively solid ground.

When the album appeared, there were people to be found complaining of it being "all just the same old chords." In a literal sense, that
accusation against such a melodically sophisticated and varied record
was patent nonsense. However, the Clash fan was also uncomfortably
aware of at least a glimmer of justification to the criticism. Half a dozen
tracks on *London Calling* are untuneful in whole or in part: "Hateful,"
"Koka Kola," "Spanish Bombs," "Clampdown," and "Death or Glory" all
have sections of melody that are unimaginative and/or monotonous,
while "Four Horsemen" has a bridge which clumsily drags on a line or
two too long.

Around a third of an album's tracks having melodic weaknesses hardly seems to warrant the aforementioned charge, not least because of the sky-high quality of those parts of *London Calling* that are good, and the redeeming humanity and high production values of even the songs with dubious musical content. However, the impression of tunelessness was exaggerated in people's minds by a couple of factors. One was the hectoring and/or complaining tone of a lot of the album's lyrics: ears chafing at music they find unpleasurable will be further antagonized by someone bellowing at them grievances about which they may or may not care. The other is a values gap. Those music lovers not steeped in punk—which did not necessarily mean people older than the average Clash fan—were often slightly antipathetic to the New Wave and its traits. That *London Calling*'s social commentary was not leavened with much romance, that its main vocalist had a conventionally inadequate delivery technique, even the fact that musicians who called themselves punks only a couple of years back were now having the presumption to adopt classic popular musical styles, all played a part in the upturned noses of a certain sector of the record-buying public. To such people, any inelegant sections of music here represented not an inevitable bad-to-good ratio but a manifestation of the naïveté and presumption of musicians who'd decided they'd had enough of that punk stuff but didn't really know how to play "proper" music. It's all yet another nuance of the musical debates of the time now disappearing into the folds of history.

In terms of "Hateful" specifically, the cut is probably not helped by following something so opaque as "Jimmy Jazz": whimsy giving way to mediocrity. Although the frantic narrator of "Hateful" never explicitly cites drugs as his problem, the details of his pitiful condition are commonly associated with heroin, while the phraseology will be familiar to anyone who has heard The Velvet Underground's "I'm Waiting for the Man" and "Heroin" or has read the likes of William Burroughs's *Junky*. It's tempting to view the presence on the second Clash album in succession of an unsympathetic depiction of a heroin user as some sort of manifestation of band frustration with Headon, but the drummer has stated that his smack addiction dated from the run-up to the following album, *Sandinista!*

The lyric is well observed, capturing the simultaneous defiance and self-loathing of the addict, and a relationship with dealers that resembles Stockholm Syndrome, wherein a kidnap victim begins to relate to the person at whose mercy he finds himself. The lyric's lines artfully resemble a junkie's disordered mind. This reaches its apotheosis in the last verse, as phrases declaring a drug-induced loss of memory and of mind barge into each other and overlap.

However the lyric can also be ungainly. For instance, when Strummer sings that what his dealer gives him is not free, it should logically be followed by "It's paid for," but that line is deferred until the title description is enunciated. This is all carried on something that is either a chant or a rhythm but is not a tune. The track seeks to ape the shuffling sonic trademark of Bo Diddley. As the latter had been The Clash's support act in January–February 1979 during their inaugural American jaunt (the drolly titled Pearl Harbour Tour) it might constitute a nice sentimental tribute, but it's a disjointed noise. Moreover, the cawing vocal interplay between Strummer and Jones in the verses is oafish. All combine to leave this a negligible cut.

At the end of "Safe European Home," Mick Jones can be heard adopting a Jamaican accent to declaim one of the half-sung, half-spoken postscripts—something between a speech and a rant—frequently to be found on Clash recordings. One of the phrases that pops up in this postscript is "Rudie can't fail." The band then turned the phrase into a song, which closed the first vinyl side of *London Calling*. Those *au fait* with the work of Desmond Dekker would have recognized the phrase as a line from his 1967 single "007 (Shanty Town)."

Rudie was a slang word for rude boy, essentially the Jamaican equivalent of what in the 1950s in the West was called a "Juvenile Delinquent" and—like the latter—a term adopted to describe a disturbing new social phenomenon considered to contain the seeds of societal devastation insofar as it suggested on the part of the younger generation debased, or even non-existent, values. The difference was that whereas American delinquency seemed rooted in affluence—unprecedentedly rich American parents being over-indulgent with their offspring, financially and morally—rude boy behavior was spawned of poverty. During a recession in the first half of the Sixties, waves of young men emigrated from the Jamaican countryside to the capital, Kingston. They then turned to crime when they found there weren't even sufficient jobs for those already resident. The phrase "rude boy" refers to the unsophistication that, from the perspective of the city dweller, goes with rural origins. As their arrival roughly coincided with a metamorphosis of the upbeat ska to the laidback rock-steady and thence reggae, and as there were many songs (pro and anti) released to cash in on the rude boy phenomenon, rude boys became synonymous with a musical form. That process was accelerated by the movie *The Harder They Come*: Jimmy Cliff's character Ivan Martin—whose misadventures are sound-tracked by reggae songs—could be posited as an über-rude boy.

More than a decade after Jamaica's rude boy phenomenon, British musical groups The Specials, Madness, and The Selecter, along with their label Two-Tone, adopted rude boy as a motif vaguely encompassing youth culture-based rebellious attitudes as well as a philosophy of racial harmony. At the end of the Seventies, "rude boy" and "rudie" were phrases therefore very much in the air in the UK, especially among musicians. In late 1979, The Specials even had a hit with a cover of one of those Jamaican rude boy anthems, "A Message to You Rudy." (The B-side of their next hit was a self-generated rude boy anthem, "Rude Boys Outta Jail.")

As The Clash's catalog was already pocked with Jamaican songs, influences, and references, they could plead not guilty to jumping on the bandwagon with "Rudie Can't Fail." (Indeed, it has even been suggested in some quarters that the fertilization went the other way, at least in one respect: the entire natty-dressing, pork pie hat–sporting British rude boy look has been claimed to be based on Paul Simonon's dress sense of the time.) Nonetheless, the suspicion was in the air because The Specials supported the Clash on a mid-1978 UK tour and were then briefly part of Bernard Rhodes's management stable.

"Rudie Can't Fail" was written for the sound track of the film *Rude Boy*, and thereby gave the film its name. (An instrumental version of "Revolution Rock," also on *London Calling*, is used as incidental music in the same film.) All the evidence suggests that it was composed as a sort of anthem for the film's main actor/character, who shared the name Ray Gange. However, just as Desmond Dekker's "007 (Shanty Town)," The Slickers's "Johnny Too Bad," and several other rude boy hymns were not the unambiguous celebration for which many took them, so "Rudie Can't Fail" slips in some digs at the rudie's expense. In fact, it takes the ambiguity a step further by representing both sides of the argument, its lyric being a dialogue between a rude boy and a disapproving (implicitly older) person. The critic condemns the youngster as rude, crude, reckless, and feckless and tells him his salvation lies in calming down and scanning the newspapers for a job. The rude boy responds that he understands his lifestyle makes the man nervous, but "I tell you I can't live in service." He further states that he is like a doctor born for a purpose. This reference to reggae record "Born for a Purpose" by Dr. Alimantado (1977), although rather contrived, integrates surprisingly well. The evenhandedness is rather spoiled in the "outro" by a gratuitous mocking of British rude boys for imagining they look pretty hot.

Musically, "Rudie Can't Fail" is a smorgasbord of different musical styles: reggae, rock, jazz, the Bo Diddley shave-and-a-haircut-two-bits rhythm, and even a tinge of calypso can be discerned in its hugely attractive instrumentation, which is propelled by a spiky, twining, fat guitar riff and flarings of brass, and culminates in a closing third that has the ambience of a celebration. Jones on vocals (frequently prompted and shadowed by Strummer) is alternately indolent and defiant.

By 1979, the Spanish Civil War had been over for precisely forty years. However, it still held an allure for leftists. That it was a conflict that the left unequivocally lost was an element all the better for socialists with a romantic penchant for martyr-strewn tragedy. "Spanish Bombs," the song which opened side two of *London Calling*, was partly spawned by contemporaneous news reports of Basque terrorist bombings of tourism spots in Spain, which Strummer posits as an "echo" of the conflict of the Spanish Civil War. However, the song also tackles romance of a different sort.

Joe Strummer had such an affinity with Spain that there is now a square named after him in Granada. Perhaps significantly, it was Spain to which he fled when he lost confidence in the final Clash album, *Cut the Crap*, and decided not to promote it. The affinity was partly the consequence of his relationship in the mid-Seventies with future member of feminist punk band The Slits, Paloma Romero. Romero—jollily rechristened Palmolive by Paul Simonon after the name of a brand of soap—shared a squat with Strummer, her sister Esperanza, and Esperanza's boyfriend, 101'ers drummer Richard Dudanski. Strummer wrote his first song about Palmolive, "Keys to Your Heart."

The latter was a lovely tribute—and an impressive writing entrée—but also the sort of thing Bernard Rhodes deemed out of the question for The Clash. Only on *London Calling*—with Rhodes now no longer in the picture—were the group free to explore the field of romance. "Spanish Bombs" was, in part, a love song and, again, about Palmolive. It wasn't, though, set in the present: she and Strummer had long since split, and Strummer was now involved in what would be a fourteen-year relationship with Gaby Salter, which would result in two daughters. Jones would also take advantage of newfound post-Rhodes freedom to contribute a love song to the album—one that, coincidentally enough, was also about a former girlfriend who became a member of The Slits (in his case Viv Albertine). Jones's "Train in Vain," however, followed far more conventional lines than Strummer's return to the territory of the love song. So much so that most people who have been enjoying it for a third of a century are probably unaware that "Spanish Bombs" is anything other than political commentary.

"Spanish Bombs" certainly has plenty of the imagery and references one would expect of a song with such a title, including Andalucía, Granada, Federico Lorca, the Guardia Civil, freedom fighters dying on a hill, red and black flags, trenches full of poets, and a ragged army attaching its bayonets. However, in the choruses, a very different message is being conveyed. As though in embarrassment, Strummer doesn't render it in English, but in what he later termed "Clash Spannish" [sic]. As this means there is not sufficient accuracy in the Spanish to make an exact conversion to English, it doesn't seem unfair to proffer Google Translate's deciphering: "I love you infinity, oh I remember you my heart."

That politics and love were all wrapped up in the same song wasn't unrepresentative of Strummer and Palmolive's relationship. The latter told Chris Salewicz in *Redemption Song*, ". . . part of our courting was about the Spanish Civil War. The fight for freedom really interested him."

Regardless of the interplay in "Spanish Bombs" between romance and social commentary, one album previously The Clash would have devised a thunderous accompaniment for this song. Now, they came up with instrumentation that, although taken at a fast clip, employs the smooth-rolling, refined attributes of soft rock. It's an almost shockingly middle-of-the-road ambience for a band with The Clash's hinterland, especially the tasteful, almost effete, drumrolls that begin and end proceedings. The melody is a trifle repetitive. Strummer and (especially) Jones sound slightly silly when they sing some sections in Spanish (some might uncharitably be inclined to suggest they master English first). That Strummer lazily rhymes "hill" with itself at one point is also grating.

These, though, are jarring notes in a recording that is otherwise sumptuous, the most pleasing aspects of which are Jones's sleepy lead guitar lines and a huge span of sound framed in either speaker by matching acoustic guitars.

Guy Stevens's one significant contribution to *London Calling* (apart from overruling the band's misgivings about the way "Brand New Cadillac" speeds up) seems to have been in persuading Joe Strummer to read a biography of movie actor Montgomery Clift, whose right profile was the only one seen on-screen after the left side of his face was paralyzed in a car crash.

"The Right Profile" is another track where the mind can't help reaching for sociopolitical import that is not intended. A condemnation of Hollywood artifice? Some sort of denunciation of Clift for an element of his private life that taste forbids Strummer repeating? It's neither of these things. It is, though, quintessentially punk. Before punk, nobody would have written a song about a movie star's decline that wasn't couched in terms of sentimentality or tragedy. Punk introduced non-judgmental observation to popular music. It also introduced non-romantic callousness. Although Strummer evocatively describes Clift's sweaty, dependent state in the years following the crash ("Nembutol numbs it all"), the song is ultimately not only whimsy but uncharitable whimsy (at the close, Strummer seems to imitate what he imagines to be Clift's death rattle). Moreover, "The Right Profile" can't proffer the redeemingly delightful instrumentation that "Jimmy Jazz" can.

Not that elements of the music aren't enjoyable. There is a nicely sleazy sax solo, while the tension-building combination of undulating piano and ride cymbal, that precedes said sax solo, is one of those moments that you simply sit through a recording waiting for. However, the doubled-up horn riff is too shrill, the "New York, New York" cooing underlining the mention of that city unnecessary, the crashing piano glissandos dotted throughout unwelcome, and the electric guitar pluckings too prevalent. Moreover, cumulatively these elements—which, as so often with music, take on human characteristics—somehow serve to unappetizingly suggest jeering rubber-neckers at the site of Clift's accident.

"The Right Profile," more than any other track, is emblematic of a fault that occasionally afflicts *London Calling*: overkill. The richness of *London Calling* is part of its appeal. It's not just a matter of the multi-layering common to very "produced" albums, but the fact that every little nook seems crammed with surprises: squiggles of instrumentation or vocals which unexpectedly counterpoint the main musical motifs. Usually, it's delightful. Sometimes—chiefly "The Right Profile," but also "Clampdown," "Death or Glory," and "Koka Kola"—it tips over into exhausting and claustrophobic.

In writing "Lost in the Supermarket," Strummer illustrated a drawback with such a politically committed movement as punk: a feeling of an obligation to find cause for complaint where little or none existed. As the title suggests, Strummer uses the supermarket as a metaphor for urban alienation. It's a well-worn theme. The glaring lights, exclamatory enticements, bland muzak, and depersonalized atmospheres of such places have often caused offense to those of a poetic and/or leftist bent. However, such offense always seems a little manufactured, not just because it seems such a triviality over which to brood when there are so many real horrors and injustices in the world, but because of the fact of the low prices in supermarkets. The discounts such outlets are able to offer their customers by passing on to them the benefits accrued from their purchasing in bulk are a godsend for the cash-strapped. The average working-class mum will have little sympathy for the idea of the supermarket as a source of her oppression. Accordingly, a sense of wide-of-the-target pseudo-protest suffuses "Lost in the Supermarket."

Strummer has noted in interviews that the song was inspired by the supermarket attached to the World's End Estate in Chelsea, southwest London, in which he and his girlfriend were domiciled at the time that The Clash were rehearsing and recording *London Calling*. The name "World's End" often sounds to those unfamiliar with it like a handle elaborately intended to convey dread, like something from an old-fashioned horror movie. It actually derives from an adjacent pub, itself named after an antiquated method of demarcation of town boundaries. However, it certainly turned out to be appropriate for the council estate completed in 1977 (into which residents began moving in 1975). While some fans of architecture have waxed lyrical about its properties ("What we have at World's End is the extraordinary efflorescence at the summits of the towers, where the flats are cantilevered out and piled up into an irregular skyline of great romantic appeal," gushed James Dunnet in *BD Magazine*, November 2008), those who had to live in it often styled it a "shithole." Along with Battersea Power Station—visible from some of its flats—the World's End Estate is one of London's ugliest landmarks. An above-ground rabbit warren in red brick, including seven tower blocks, it doesn't seem to bode well for those contemplating entry. Nor does it exactly chime with the refined reputation of the King's Road on which it sits, even if at the juncture where the King's Road becomes the New King's Road, the addition which takes the traveler from upscale Chelsea into less smart Fulham and Putney.

Like most council estates (British equivalent of what Americans know as project housing), the World's End Estate has been improved in recent decades by the sorts of measures that never occurred to planners and architects at the time of its construction: entry systems and a general conscientiousness about environmental health. Residents being given the opportunity to buy their flats has also created an improved atmosphere. However, it had at the time of Strummer's residency a terrible reputation for anti-social behavior, vandalism, and violence. As with many such places, it was victim of the sort of vicious circle mentioned previously: its bad name made people unwilling to live in it, which meant the local council (Kensington & Chelsea) had little option but to use it as a dumping ground for those tenants whose previous behavior or rent arrears gave them reduced choice about the properties they were offered. The combination of this and the high number of tenants—up to three thousand on what was originally the largest municipal estate in Western Europe—meant that the problems traditionally associated with council estates were significantly magnified.

Knowing Strummer's partiality to such notions as the nobility of the working class and the need to suffer to make great art, there's little doubt that part of him reveled in being located in such a place. That romantic streak would have been further tickled had he been *au fait* at the time with the fact that Edith Grove—the turning off King's Road which stood below his front room window—was the location of the early-Sixties flat share of Mick Jagger, Keith Richards, and Brian Jones of his beloved Rolling Stones. (He only found out later.) He would unquestionably have been aware that the road running parallel to the World's End Estate on the river side—Cheyne Walk—was the location of Jagger and Richards's current London homes. Completing the clus-

ter of rock 'n' roll landmarks, across the King's Road from the estate—
and again visible from some of its windows—was Seditionaries. Formerly known as Sex (and before that Too Fast To Live, Too Young To
Die; and before that—as part of Paradise Garage—Let It Rock), it was
the clothing shop in which a few years previously Malcolm McLaren
gathered around him the group that became known as The Sex Pistols.

Strummer's domicile explains the reference to the 19 bus in "Rudie
Can't Fail": it was the number of the double-decker he would catch to
take him to Wessex Studios. (It wouldn't have been much good for
rehearsals at Vanilla as it turned left, away from Pimlico, at the Sloane
Square end of the King's Road to follow a path to the West End. Having
said that, the punks who treated the King's Road as a punk Mecca—and
who would do so until they were worn down by the council's removal of
benches in the second half of the Eighties specifically to prevent their
loitering—would have made that journey a mild hassle on foot.)

One of the few things the World's End Estate did have going for it
was its own supermarket. It sat at its base and its red brick made it look
integrated into the estate. Although of course open to anyone, not just
the estate's residents, its convenience meant that residents would not
have announced that they were going "down the road" for a pint of milk
or a packet of cigarettes, but "downstairs." As well as convenient, the
shop was also quite compact, and certainly not the sort of place where
any but the youngest of children could find themselves "lost." Joe
Strummer, though, ignores the positives and the problematic facts and
writes of it only in the negative.

Some have posited the lyric as possibly Strummer's most autobiographical. However, this seems restricted to a verse about living in the
suburbs as a child. The following verse about having heard at that time
the disturbing sound of the people who "lived" on the ceiling screaming
and fighting tallies neither with the social caste of Strummer's family
nor his talk of his parents owning a bungalow. However, meshing autobiography and fiction to convey an ambiance is, for the artist, less cheat-
ing than tried-and-tested methodology, as proven by the verisimilitude
in the detailing of the narrator's journey from the soporific suburbs to a
no-less-alienating high-rise: when he talks of the noises made by kids in
corridors and of pipes in walls as his only company, he is evoking quite
superbly tower block isolation. Furthermore, the cutting of discount

coupons from teabag packets that is also mentioned is precisely the sort of compensatory activity engaged in by the friend- and money-poor.

Although this sort of skillful detail lends an illusion of value to a lyric based on a contrived premise, it's the music which finally makes the falsity irrelevant. Like "Spanish Bombs," "Lost in the Supermarket" is axle-greased, air-brushed soft rock. If the funky bass throughout is the only semblance of grit in a track dominated by measured guitar lines and stately drums, that's not a demerit. The quasi-blandness is actually thematically apposite for a track alluding to identical rows of garish packaging beneath neon strip lighting.

The track is another exemplar of the album's rich, playful production: the way that the understated guitar break cheekily sneaks from one speaker to another, briefly lingers, and then dashes back is delightful.

Once again, Strummer's decision to hand his composition to Jones to sing is well judged: Mick's less coarse voice feels right in the context of such instrumental smoothness and discussion of superficiality. Over and above that, though, Jones's vocal performance (rendered in almost a baritone that is very unexpected from him) is restrained and polished. When he enunciates the line "Long distance callers make long distance ca-a-alls," The Clash's new melodic sophistication and Jones's increased authority as a singer come together in a moment of gilded melancholia.

According to Clash roadie Johnny Green, the impetus for Joe Strummer writing "Clampdown"—an apocalyptical depiction of a society collapsing into fascism—was rather mundane. Said Green in his 1997 Clash memoir *A Riot of Our Own*, "At Vanilla, Joe told me 'Clampdown' was about parking clamps."

Some have suspected this to be a joke by either Strummer or Green, both of whom were known for a mischievous sense of humor. Moreover, wheel clamping was a scourge yet to hit Strummer's home country. (They were first used on the streets of London in May 1983.) However, as a now-seasoned traveler, Strummer would have seen wheel clamps or heard about them: in the States, they had been around since the mid-Fifties. Moreover, it wouldn't have been the first time that a relatively trivial irritant spun off a Clash song soaked with a grand sense of injustice whose lyric chiefly concerned burgeoning totalitarianism: as we've seen, just such a description applies to "Remote Control."

In the case of the song from The Clash's long-playing debut, the disproportionate power of local councilors to close down concerts because they didn't like the cut of performers' jibs was extrapolated on by Jones in an anthem in which he posited the entire country "under heavy manners" (to use a reggae phrase to be found stenciled on Strummer's clothes in the early days of the band). With "Clampdown," Strummer would seem to have used an even more mundane starting point for a flight of fancy incorporating an even more outlandish prophecy, one whose first verse details a disquieting scene wherein a man is having the turban wrenched from his head by somebody demanding to know whether he is a Jew. The instigators of such acts are stated as being blue-eyed—a clear allusion to the Aryan ideal—and to be working for something called a clampdown, implicitly a campaign of oppression based on racialist principles.

The second verse finds somebody kicking against these values, defying a judge who is in the process of handing him down a prison sentence for—again implicitly—declining to follow the clampdown's edicts. Said person launches into a speech calling for a nationwide rebellion. In the bridge—which is urgent and smooth-following where the verses are staccato—a second-person point of view describes a man fleeing people who are in charge of what is termed a factory. Some have posited this as a slip into the mundane—a typical Clash call to jack in two-bit employment as in "Clash City Rockers" et al.—but that seems an overly literal interpretation of a word that is not necessarily out of place here: concentration camps have certainly often been likened to death factories.

The following verse traces a trajectory of compromise, as the rebel grows up and calms down, dons a uniform, starts feeling important, and drifts into his first murder in the name of a cause he once denounced. The final two verses—performed at half speed—rather lose focus, being almost asides from Strummer about recently toppled dictators and containing another reference to the accident at Three Mile Island, the latter something Strummer acknowledged in interview as also being an influence on the song.

The one thing that Strummer doesn't seem to have cited as a spur to his writing "Clampdown," but which almost certainly was, is the growing support among the British public in the late Seventies for the National Front. A far-right party opposed to immigration, it had alarmed some with its electoral advances and growing media profile. In truth, the NF's potential was limited by first-past-the-post: the Labour-Conservative-Liberal three-party hegemony engendered by a system not predicated on proportional representation made it destined to never gain a seat in parliament, let alone one on a government's cabinet. Nonetheless, the party's rhetoric so disturbed and repulsed some that movements like the Anti-Nazi League and Rock Against Racism sprang up to combat it. (Some organizations also exploited anti-NF sentiment for their own undeclared purposes: a scene in *Rude Boy* discusses groups which propounded anti-fascist beliefs without revealing their broader hard-left agendas.) In one of the earliest Clash interviews (the *NME*, December 11, 1976), Strummer said, "I think people ought to know that we're anti-fascist, we're anti-violence, we're anti-racist and we're pro-creative. We're against ignorance." The Front aren't mentioned, but in the climate of the times, it was axiomatically the case that they were the main target of his declaration. The Clash also famously played the Rock Against Racism concert in April 1978 in London's Victoria Park, the sort of event at which the air would resound with the demo marcher's chant, "The National Front is a Nazi front/Smash the National Front!"

As well as the final two verses, there are other clumsy passages to the lyric of "Clampdown," such as the description of the colors of the clampdown merchants' uniform as blue and brown: no self-respecting fascist would be seen in something so effete, and the colors were clearly chosen to make the line rhyme and scan. However, parts of the songwords are high quality. The duologue between the judge and the rebel manages to be pithy, evocative, and syncopated all at once. Meanwhile, in having the rebel declare, "Let fury have the hour," Strummer manages to devise a phrase so poetic that it sounds centuries old even though clearly of his own invention.

Despite its grave subject, the lyric is not without humor. The opening line would have been familiar to any Briton who was an aficionado of the zany and post-modern wit of Spike Milligan, a former member of the Goons comedy team whose BBC solo shows often featured him ending a sketch via the lazy/ingenious method of repeating with his fellow cast members the line "What are we gonna do now?" while advancing in stages toward the camera lens.

"Clampdown" has a great melodic bridge (whose quality is further enhanced by the fact that it's sung by Jones, thus providing a contrast of vocal tones). It also boasts a fine introduction whose brooding, rolling texture and not-quite-decipherable but urgent spoken words have the dark menace of gathering storm clouds. Yet the remainder is disjointed: the song's riffs and chorus don't quite inspire the air-punching response for which they aim, and the whole exercise has a feeling, sonically, of running on the spot.

That the music is far more of a mixed bag than the lyric is the biggest surprise about "Clampdown." Throughout this album The Clash prove so adept at every new musical form they tackle that it comes as a bit of a shock that this attempt at the sort of hard rock anthem of which they had so often proven themselves masters doesn't come off.

Brooding reggae "The Guns of Brixton"—the final song on side two of *London Calling*—was Paul Simonon's inaugural compositional attempt and vocal performance. Much has been made of Simonon's lack of musical ability. Headon, his partner in the band's rhythm section, told this author in 2008, "Mick taught him how to play the bass and that's all he did. He didn't improvise. He wasn't what I would call very musical . . . Paul's role in the band was mainly onstage and in charge of the artwork and the look of the band." Headon also admitted that Jones played bass on "a hell of a lot" of Clash recordings. Although firsthand witnesses attest Simonon was by no means absent on Clash tracks, from *London Calling* onward his role in the studio would seem to have been what one might term a secondary bassist, providing a sonic bed while Jones dealt with the more fluid and virtuoso bass parts. However, there is no dispute that the menacing bass riff that runs throughout "The Guns of Brixton" and gives it much of its dark power was both devised and played by Simonon.

Simonon had moved to Notting Hill by the time he wrote the song but had spent large and formative parts of his life in Brixton. The latter, though, probably wasn't the reason he chose the south London district as the location of his first composition. Brixton is a name synonymous with crime, black culture, and riots, the British equivalent of Harlem or the South Side of Chicago. Consequently, it has both a menace and a romance.

In the second-person lyric of "The Guns of Brixton," someone is being asked whether, when the police bang on his door, he will come out with his hands on his head or on the trigger of a gun. It would be like a scenario from *The Harder They Come* transplanted to SW2 even without that film's name directly enunciated elsewhere in the lyric and the song's lead character being named Ivan. Of course, it's another example of silly and irresponsible Clash bravado, one which this time confuses reality with celluloid. Guns were so uncommon in Britain at the time as to make their mention almost fantastic, nor had there been anything resembling a Death Row (the stated possible fate of one of the characters) since capital punishment was abolished in 1969. (That Simonon had been watching too many movies was also suggested by the *Guns of Navarone*–style title, although it may have been a nod to the reggae record and UK hit of the same name by The Skatalites.) However, in broad terms the sort of confrontation and sentiment depicted is not that unrepresentative of Brixton, then or now.

The song's drama is slightly undermined by almost comedic "boing" sound effects, but this is compensated for by the unexpected expressiveness of Simonon's singing.

"Wrong 'em Boyo," the cover version which opened side three of *London Calling*, is actually a medley. That it has a fake false start in the form of a snatch of "Stagger Lee"—a transatlantic late-Fifties hit for Lloyd Price—is reflective of the way that, in a less copyright-conscious age, Jamaican music would on occasion merrily incorporate slices of well-known hits. In this case, it seems to have been done as a means to mock glorification of outlawdom.

"Stagger Lee," like many other marginally differentiated songs, was inspired by a real-life late-nineteenth-century St. Louis murder made all the more awful by the facts of it being over nothing more important than a card game and by it taking place on Christmas Day. Clive Alphanso composed songs for (but was not a member of) obscure ska merchants The Rulers. His "Wrong Emboyo" [sic] was another rude boy song, this one anti. After using the "Stagger Lee" snatch in an almost Pavlovian way, he then torments listeners salivating for bloodshed by having the lead vocalist call off the band and start all over again with a lecture against bad behavior to a totally different melody: "Don't you know it was wrong to cheat a trying man?"

Strummer changes the "was" to "is" but makes more profound alterations as well, adding some couplets of his own, for which, as was usual, he doesn't take any credit or publishing money. His invention extends to his singing: this track evinces more of his omniscient vocalist "thang": in a moment of silence prior to a rattle of drums, his "Hup!" makes it sound like he is giving the nod to Headon to restart proceedings (that, or gleefully following the trajectory of a leaping frog). When he emits "Yay!" at another juncture, it's as though he is carried away by the musical jamboree going on around him, rather than simulating pleasure at the pre-recorded activities coming through his headphones.

The Rulers's 1967 original is a rather downbeat affair. The Clash's version is breakneck. It's also incongruously joyous, in large part due to Mickey Gallagher. The keyboardist's career had begun in 1965 as a temporary replacement for Alan Price in The Animals and was currently ticking over nicely with a berth in Ian Dury and the Blockheads, one of the bands of the moment. He was the additional man in The Clash's touring party when they mounted their again drolly titled Clash Take the Fifth Tour of the United States in September and October 1979. He pops up in several places on *London Calling*. Here, his organ provides smooth-gliding castors—to which Strummer's rollicking "pianner" (as the sleeve notes would have it) is an earthy contrast. Headon's nimble drumming and percussive effects tease us delightfully with pauses, drop-outs, speed-ups, and delayed re-starts, all cheered on by Strummer. Guitar is barely evident, but it matters little when The Irish Horns are on particularly impressive form. The track ends in a welter of warbling organ, cheek-puffed sax, and extended vocal cooing that is all gloriously self-mocking.

Because it is a non-original and devoid of a sociopolitical message, one rather suspects that this track was initially little more than a fuck-you to CBS, i.e., that The Clash were knocking out a cover to fill up the 12-inch "single" they had hoodwinked their label into including with their new album. If so, rarely has such a gesture of contempt had such pleasurable consequences.

While the brickbats attracted by "The Guns of Brixton" for glorifying violence and outlawdom were reasonable, criticisms leveled at "Death or Glory" were anything but. There are other tracks on *London Calling* which fit the description of self-mythologizing, but "Death or Glory" isn't—as some claimed—one of them.

The conclusion was always puzzling to anyone who listened closely. Although Strummer's enunciation could, as ever, hardly be said to be clear, the track's lyric—like that of almost all of the songs—was printed inside. The most cursory perusal of it reveals the fact that—despite its apparently defiant motto of a title, and contrary to its anthemic, blam-blam choruses—it is the complete reversal of rebel rock posturing. Rather, "Death or Glory" finds The Clash ganging up with the critics on themselves.

Strummer's superb lyric exposes the way youthful idealism and No Compromise stances are inevitably eroded by the exigencies of life. The first verse depicts the pathetic mundane domestic situation of a former rebel whose only surviving vestiges of youthful fire are the "LOVE" and "HATE" tattoos on his knuckles. Those knuckles frequently connect with his children's faces as he takes out his lack of fulfilment on them. It's like a heart-wrenching scene from a classic British Kitchen Sink film.

The chorus declares that bravado such as the title phrase becomes, in the end, just another story. The second verse focuses its merciless glare on The Clash themselves and concedes that their own anti-sellout mantra is doomed to failure. Not that the band is named, but of whom else could Strummer be speaking when he states that every "yob" mining rock 'n' roll for gold asserts he'll die before he's sold? "He who fucks nuns will later join the church," is his brutal part-Confucian, part-punk dismissal of that ideal. A sort of coda in which Strummer mordantly recites to a different melody a promise to march a long way and raise hell can only be interpreted as sarcasm, a mocking of the halcyon declarations of rebels everywhere.

Its rough-hewn poetry and naked, self-lacerating honesty mark out "Death or Glory" as one of the best lyrics Strummer ever wrote. The more one thinks about it, the more shocking a self-demystification and expression of doubt it appears. The surprising resistance by critics to the idea of the song being self-effacing rather than self-aggrandizing meant that he never really got full credit for it.

The sonics of "Death or Glory" would have a hard task matching up to its words. It's pretty good, nonetheless, with the enunciation of the title phrase rousing in spite of the way it's consciously undermined by the lyric. However, not for the first time on this album, one is struck by the fact that anthemic hard rock doesn't seem to be where The Clash are currently most inspired. The main riff—like that of "Clampdown"—is too harshly metallic to be attractive. The most impressive musical aspect of the recording is an understated, leisurely introduction consisting of strummed acoustic guitar, delicate electric guitar, nimble drums and almost lachrymose bass.

That "Koka Kola" combines lyrical banality with melodic mediocrity makes it probably the weakest track on *London Calling*. It's a view of Madison Avenue culture by someone who has never experienced it firsthand, one so inchoate that, in talking of people jumping from skyscraper windows, Strummer seems to confuse New York's advertising district with Wall Street, its financial quarter. Meanwhile, while discussion of a snubnose .44 might be a reference to a drug-induced hallucination—conflating Coca-Cola with cocaine is one of the song's hardly impressive conceits—it also feels like a classic element of an Englishman's movie-oriented misperception of American daily life. Lines like "Executive decision, a clinical precision" might have a pleasing rhythm, but are empty slogans. The whole thing could be considered a companion piece to The Jam's similarly secondhand and uninformed depiction of British boardroom life, "Smithers-Jones," released as a B-side earlier in 1979. Only a snort-inducing comment that someone's alligator suit and snakeskin boots require a vet rather than a launderette gives a glimpse of Strummer's usual cleverness.

What is most objectionable about the track, however, is the same problem afflicting "Lost in the Supermarket": it is pseudo-protest, a song that tackles a subject not because the writer is genuinely concerned about it but because he thinks he should be. Advertising, like supermarkets, is one of those things with pejorative connotations for leftists, some of whom seem to feel obliged to then make the jump into casting it as an active evil, an allegation which never quite convinces. Advertising may be frequently simplistic, loud, and, in extreme examples, misleading, but would life be better without it? Does it not serve a useful purpose in alerting people to products which they might find desirable or useful? And what about the consumerism with which advertising is entwined, also perceived as evil by some leftists (and, to be fair, religiously minded right-wingers)? Would the members of The Clash have been without their Les Pauls, Fender Telecasters, leather jackets, and record collections? Modestly waged and ostentatiously men-of-the-people The Clash might have been, but that was not the same thing as rejecting capitalism for a Spartan life.

Strummer retrospectively implied that the song was more anti-cocaine than anything else. If true, it would only make the song worse.

Why not, after all, a song condemning cocaine use among rock stars, where it has always been just as, or more, prevalent than in advertising? That of course takes us down the awkward path that is the public knowledge that all four Clash members—but Jones and Headon, especially—had at one time or another problems with the drug.

Its music is the death knell for "Koka Kola." Although one of the fastest—certainly the most breathless—of the album's cuts, it's in no way exciting. Apart from its bridge, it is tuneless. Even that bridge—a dreamy affair where Jones's surreal harmony vocals nicely complement Strummer's vista of a stroll down Broadway in the rain—is let down by the way it untidily throws in a non-rhyming reference to Manhattan at the end as though as an afterthought. Mercifully, "Koka Kola" is, at 1:47, the shortest track on *London Calling* by more than a minute.

More than any other track, "The Card Cheat" confirms The Clash's philosophical and musical shifts. The lyric is heartrending: the tale of a man who tries to acquire prosperity through devious means but—fatally—doesn't realize he is out of his depth in the sinister circles in which he is operating. It seems at times like a companion piece to "Wrong 'em Boyo," but there is also evidence of Strummer having viewed Bergman's *The Seventh Seal*, with its famous chess scene fought for the prize of life. The music is orchestral although there is no orchestra present: standard rock instruments were used but double-tracked to create a pomp associated with the Wall of Sound methods of producer Phil Spector. The cherry on this rich cake is Jones's singing, suffused with such empathy as to be goose bump–inducing.

"Lover's Rock," which opened side four of *London Calling*, is another Clash song whose title testifies to how confusing can be the Jamaican term "Rock." It is not used here to allude to rock 'n' roll but as a designation of a musical style, just as was "rockers" in "Clash City Rockers." Lover's rock was a laid-back reggae subgenre popular at the time. Strummer and Jones—singing mostly in harmony—ridicule the style's overt romanticism with some saucy songwords which, among other things, endorse oral sex as a means to prevent unwanted pregnancy.

The track has been accused of sexism but is really merely ribald. Jones exploits an opportunity to prove he's not just a hard rocker with some molten guitar lines which lend the track a blissful, summery air that suggests the band were fonder of lover's rock than they let on and that this may not be the "mickey take" it's widely assumed to be.

The title of "Four Horsemen" does not refer to the legendary quartet associated with the Apocalypse but that linked to, erm, the Westway. Yes, it's another Clash song about The Clash. This one is a potted history of the band, but unlike the last one, "All The Young Punks," is underpinned by positivism—although it must be noted that that positivism is rooted in the kind of bravado that "Death or Glory" so honestly exposed as a sham. The bridge, meanwhile, refers to a "you" that might be the listener: it's certainly seems in the distasteful Clash tradition of saying "boo-hoo" to people in less fulfilling circumstances than they, and moreover with another unintended Thatcherite subtext (Strummer tells someone that his life being bad is the price he has to pay for lazing around). Other than those caveats, the lyric is witty and clever, and ingeniously gives Terry Chimes a footnote in the band's growing body of self-mythology as a hiker who "didn't want a lift from the Horsemen."

Musically, it's bitty: there is some exciting grinding guitar work, but the bridge—by going on a couple of lines too long—becomes a drone. A kind of triumph is snatched right at the death: the way the track segues into the following one is sublimely dramatic and enhances both numbers.

It's a quite astonishing fact that *London Calling*'s keynote song, tucked away on side four, is rarely remarked on by critics and was barely played live by the band. That "I'm Not Down" is both a stupendously powerful piece of music and a moving affirmation of life in the face of adversity makes it a miniature of the entire album. For many years it was assumed to be a Jones confessional in the tradition of "Stay Free," not least because it alludes to a rough upbringing and the same recent traumas referenced in "Train in Vain" two tracks later. In fact, it was another of these instances where Strummer would appear to have used a Mick vocal as a shield. Jones, however, acquits himself beautifully, emotionally detailing, over an uptempo backing, various vicissitudes that have afflicted him before insisting in a rousing chorus that he won't be demoralized ("I've been beat up, I've been thrown out, but I'm not down!"). The streetwise language (including phrases like "Shown up" and being "done" that may be confusing to non-Britons) add an additional grittiness.

The arrangement is almost dizzying: hooks abound among broiling verses, pugnacious choruses and galloping interregnums. The bridge is simply astounding in its onomatopoeic qualities: descending when

Jones refers to sinking further and further into depression, and spiraling, in stages, skyward as Jones describes incrementally bursting out of that depression.

In any artist's catalog there is a moment constituting perfection, a magical confluence whereby a lyrical, spiritual, and musical peak is reached at the same instant and where an additional layer of craft ensures those elements combining to optimum effect. "I'm Not Down" is that moment for The Clash.

With "Revolution Rock"—into which "I'm Not Down" segues—it's Strummer's turn to prove he can "choke you up."

The song was originally a 1976 Jamaican release by Jackie Edwards, composer of the Spencer Davis Group hits "Keep On Running" and "Somebody Help Me." It was then known as "Get Up." In the aforementioned jackdaw tradition of Jamaican music, Danny Ray retooled it later that year as "Revolution Rock." Following in that tradition, Strummer and company play fast and loose with Ray's record, turning a basic idea to their own devices. Unlike in the tradition of Jamaican music, however, they engaged in no intellectual property squabble, happy not to take a publishing credit despite the fact that their tweaks immeasurably improved the song: it remains credited to Edwards and Ray.

In The Clash's hands, the song is transformed from a relatively banal celebration of partying into a call for a revolution, although one of attitude, not burning barricades: in a crackling, witty, syncopated lyric, Strummer aims his ire at the base-level duckers and divers of life, the small-time hoods and the smack dealers who make conditions worse for those already enduring penury. The band hit a fine skank-able groove with loping bass, sinuous lead guitar, and a wide array of percussion, all ably assisted by staccato horn charts and a production which discreetly employs reggae delay and echo technique. Once more, Strummer uses his voice almost as an instrument in the way he cleverly manufactures the illusion of call-and-response routines with already recorded instruments, the most delightful example of which is a moment where the organ sounds some tentative notes and then springs into life when his cry "The organ—play!" seems to give it permission to do so.

However, lest we get the impression from this playful and mischievous tone that there is not a serious message here, Strummer leaves us in no doubt about that in a final verse in which he castigates the rockhearted, cruel-toned Kingston gangsters who make the already unenviable lot of the poor unbearable. His anguish is clear when he talks of the despair of poverty leading to the sight of "talent thrown away," and when he describes people dying of malnutrition while cargo food goes rolling by, his voice cracks with emotion.

Those who bought *London Calling* in its first British pressing remember that it contained a final track not listed on the sleeve. It was more than surprising. Hidden tracks would not be a feature of the music industry until the CD age, and that this was still very much the vinyl age is demonstrated by the fact that, initially, the only billing for the song came in the form of a message carved into that vinyl side's run-off groove: "Track 5 is 'Train in Vain.' "

Some must have been unsure whether that title was a joke. Leaving aside the vague comedy inherent in it rhyming, those words didn't appear within the song. In the absence of a publishing credit, some would also have assumed that the song was a cover: its soul groove and lovelorn lyric made it of an archetypical bent like nothing ever essayed by The Clash previously, with the sole exception of "1-2 Crush on You." Adding to a general air of outside origination was the fact that part of its refrain contained the same words as that in Ben E. King's hit "Stand by Me," while another line was redolent of Tammy Wynette's "Stand By Your Man." Because of a combination of the above, some will even have concluded that the track wasn't listed because the band were ashamed of it.

Everything soon became clear via Clash explanations in music press interviews. "Train in Vain" was indeed the song's true title, and a way of avoiding confusion with King's song: the exact meaning has never been explained but Robert Johnson's "Love in Vain," with its train/departure/affair-ending motif, has been theorized as the derivation. It was originally intended to be featured on a disc provided free with the *NME*, not a send-away offer like the *Capital Radio* EP, but a flexidisc attached to every cover of one edition. It was unlisted because it was added to the album after the sleeves had gone to the printers.

What the band didn't reveal was that, as it featured the playing only of Jones and Headon, "Train in Vain" technically wasn't a Clash track. It had been devised too late for Simonon to be taught the bass part, while Strummer simply refused to appear on anything so soft. Moreover, the band's explanation for why it was released through the aegis of CBS rather than the *NME* has been called into question: rather than publisher IPC refusing permission for a flexidisc giveaway as was originally claimed, Jones appears to have decided to "bagsy" it for *London Calling* when he apprehended the unexpected quality of a cut put together (albeit probably over an already partially completed basic track) in the space of twenty-four hours.

A serendipity was attached to that process of "It's too good to waste." "Train in Vain (Stand by Me)"—as Epic re-christened it—would become The Clash's first American hit, making no. 23 in Spring 1980. It was just the right kind of Clash song for the U.S. market: something that wouldn't alienate radio programmers with social commentary and whose traditional subject would appeal to the mainstream record purchaser.

Yet steeped as it might have been in archetype and even sentimentality (Strummer continued to be disparaging about the song in concert), "Train in Vain" is, in its own way, groundbreaking.

Before the late Seventies, with a few exceptions like Ray Davies of The Kinks, the only British rock musicians who didn't affect an American drawl at the microphone were doing so for comedic purposes. This changed with the advent of punk for reasons that were a combination of practicality and credibility. As Strummer said to Caroline Coon in the *Melody Maker*, November 13, 1976, "It's the music of now. And it's in English. We sing in English, not mimicking some American rock singer's accent. That's just pretending to be something you ain't." However, while it may have been logical to deliver "Towerblock Rock" in a recognizably English voice, because punk was not a medium in which love songs played a large part the issue of how its musicians were to deliver songs based around romance hadn't much come up. In The Damned's debut—and love song—"New Rose," vocalist Dave Vanian trod a middle ground, not emphasizing his national origins, but not going full-out with the Americanisms. The Jam delivered those parts of their repertoires that were love songs in, broadly speaking, American accents even as they insisted on Estuary English for political material. Even when they recorded songs called "London Girl" (1977) and "English Rose" (1978), their hands remained surprisingly unforced as those creations happened to not contain words that would create the dilemma of singing naturally (their own accents) or conventionally/bogusly (American accents), although they did employ "Mum" rather than "Mom" in the former. The Buzzcocks were always more relationships- than politics-oriented in song subject, and singer Pete Shelley certainly declined to Americanize his Mancunian voice.

However, although Mick Jones couldn't claim to be the first person in the rock era to sing a love song in an unashamedly English voice, when he opted to tackle "Train in Vain"—a recording whose musical style was quintessentially American—in his natural brogue, it was a seismic moment. Hitherto, such a decision might be considered to be "taking the piss," as patently and deliberately absurd as when Peter Sellers had rendered the modernistic pop lyric of The Beatles's "A Hard Day's Night" in histrionic Shakespearian. By singing a soul ballad London-stylee, and doing so very movingly, Jones ensured that no Briton need ever again be scared that performing a love song in the accent of his hometown would sound ridiculous. The whole debate might seem absurd to non-Britons, but this was genuinely revolutionary. It's certainly interesting that Paul Weller of The Jam went unabashedly English in his love songs from here on.

The song also constitutes another breakthrough, although one limited to The Clash themselves. With the qualified exceptions of "Deny," "Spanish Bombs," and "1-2 Crush on You" (that track whose release seems to be proven as misbegotten by it cropping up in this text mainly as an exception to one Clash trait or another), "Train in Vain" was the first Clash song about a relationship. It was destined to be one of the few such creatures in the Clash's canon, ultimately sharing the status only with the above three tracks and "Should I Stay or Should I Go." (A case can be made for including "Long Time Jerk" in that category, but only a tenuous one.)

The second song on the album about a member of The Slits was inspired by Jones's recent split with guitarist Viv Albertine. It may also have been inspired by the Slits song "Typical Girls." If so, Mick would seem to be living up to the feminist complaint of men who don't listen properly: in said song, Albertine is mocking women who stand by their man, thus stating the opposite of Jones's allegation here that she had said she would stick with her man and then didn't. However, the composition comes across as anything but bone-headed. Jones's voice trembles and whimpers as he enunciates sentiments like "I remember these things the most."

There are other autobiographical elements in the song: Mick's statement that his job doesn't pay and he needs somewhere to stay would seem an elliptical reference to the fact that this rock 'n' roll star had recently had to briefly but humiliatingly move back into his nan's flat after a traumatic burglary at his home. That he rattles off the line about needing somewhere to stay with a stylized quasi-machismo of which any Stax vocalist would be proud, however, demonstrates that Jones is not all hysteria.

His following assertion that he doesn't give a damn about having a place to stay or money to spend as long as he has his departed lover around is affecting. None of this, of course, would mean anything to the average listener who didn't take an interest in Clash members' private lives, and Jones wisely keeps things universal by couching the song in classical soul language, that familiar stand-by-me refrain being only the half of it. His talk of heartaches, tumbling dreams, wolves that need to be kept at bay, and explanations necessary from his fickle lover mean that Otis Redding would in no way have found this a foreign lexicon.

For a cut whose completion was rushed and whose personnel is a skeleton crew, the music of "Train in Vain" is amazingly assured and full-bodied. A track whose stylings make it tailor-made for brass doesn't have any: the Irish Horns's brief visit to the studio was long in the past. Jones, though, adroitly creates the illusion of brass via harmonica and double-tracking. His main guitar riff is reverb-treated to sound epic. He also throws in the occasional rumbling piano line. Naturally, he handles bass duties, too. The only other musician present, meanwhile, is in his element. A son of a headmaster and a teacher, and a veteran of an act that had opened for The Temptations, middle-class soul-boy Headon had always used punk as a flag of convenience, even if his personality ("nutter" and "psycho" were the flavor of the descriptions flying around) in no way made him out of place in the movement. Probably unable to believe his luck at finding himself back on familiar and much-loved territory, he produces a crisp, hi-hat-heavy performance that creates a fine groove. The fact that the track fades in—making for an equivalent to a drumroll—only adds to a grandeur that the recording has no right to possess.

There was another strand of serendipity to the track's last-minute inclusion on *London Calling*: it transpires to be the perfect album closer. After Jones and Strummer have successively broken our hearts with the previous two numbers, the mellow ambience of "Train in Vain" acts like a soothing balm on our exhausted, wracked emotions.

On July 26, 1980, The Clash secured a significant victory in their end-less quest to prove that they hadn't been corrupted by their success. As was often the case, it took the form of being seen to get one over on their record company.

The band had decided to embark on a singles campaign. Their inten-tion was to release a 45 every month, rushing out a new one whenever the previous one started dropping out of the charts. These would obvi-ously be new songs: the policy would hardly be remarkable—indeed, would be seen as contemptible—if based around milking albums. Their audacious plan may have been partly prompted by them being buoyed by their unprecedented chart success with the "London Calling" single, but it was no doubt also due to a penchant for yet another rock 'n' roll myth: that the best recordings in history are to be found on 7-inch discs.

The campaign would have been one the likes of which there had never been. Even before the turn of the Seventies, when the album became more significant than the single as a means of consuming mu-sic, artists restricted themselves to one single every two to three months. Yet the strategy was not completely unreasonable: 1979 had been the best year ever for singles sales in the UK, proving that the non-album market was one record labels ignored at their peril. Not only might the strategy have worked, but with a band of The Clash's political bent it could have also transformed the purpose of a 45: The Clash were exactly the group to make the single a state-of-the-nation address and to use it to respond to current events almost with the topicality of a news-paper.

Unfortunately, the plan fell at the first hurdle. When The Clash presented CBS with their proposed follow-up to "London Calling," the label refused to release it. It was almost certainly because "Bankrobber" was the biggest non sequitur imaginable to the instantly arresting, up-tempo "London Calling": a mid-paced, gloomy reggae, and furthermore not a rock-reggae hybrid but the purest reggae they had yet produced. On that level, the label's stance can be understood. The job of CBS was to make money, and this change in direction just when it appeared that The Clash were becoming as mainstream an act as a band like them could ever be must have been dismaying.

Although no doubt gutted by it, the rejection gave The Clash the type of opportunity they rarely spurned: to portray themselves as martyrs for their art and ideals. It also gave them a chance to do something that wasn't so easily achieved: score a victory over the record company. The Clash went on strike over the non-release, refusing to do any more work on album tracks they had recently recorded in New York. However, it doesn't seem to have been this that made CBS climb down so much as something exactly analogous to the way that Epic's decision not to release the first Clash album had to be reversed because of the embarrassingly high level of import sales. The Clash stable contrived in June 1980 to sneak out "Bankrobber" as a B-side to the Dutch "Train in Vain" single. Alerted to the availability of a Clash song they didn't have, the British fanbase bought the Dutch record in such numbers that, by July, CBS had consented to a UK release. Quite astoundingly, considering both the fact that so many Clash fans already owned an import copy and the fact of its hard-core reggae nature, "Bankrobber" proceeded to become the second most successful UK Clash single while the band were extant, reaching no. 12.

Again, the single would probably have marched into that top ten territory that would forever be unknown to The Clash during their lifetime had they only been prepared to promote it on *Top of the Pops* rather than leave it to the mercies of Gill, Lulu, Patti, Pauline, Rosie, and Sue. Although Legs & Co. were perfectly good—and perfectly beautiful—dancers, a less appropriate backdrop for their gyrations than "Bankrobber" is difficult to imagine. It's the mordant anthem of a man who opts out of the rat race via the felonious appropriation of the property of others (although never with violence). Strummer evokes with superb economy the misery of the petty-rule dominated workplace that the bankrobber sidesteps ("Break your back to earn your pay and don't forget to grovel"). It's not only with lyrics that he is improving in leaps and bounds: "That was a song Joe wrote on his own," Jones said in *Redemption Song*. Although the melody features changes that verge on generic, it's also highly hummable.

The group made doubly sure that this would be real-McCoy reggae by recruiting Jamaican producer Michael Campbell, better known as Mikey Dread. Dread supplies a dark, rich, booming, effects-pocked, ultra-authentic mix across the back of which drifts a disembodied, extremely catchy "Aaah-aaah" vocal refrain. Although the viewpoint in Strummer's lyric that life is necessarily tragic for society's unskilled is, as discussed, questionable, he and his colleagues are, as ever, adept at injecting it with pathos: "Bankrobber" is simultaneously proud and sad.

"Rockers Galore . . . UK Tour," the flip side of "Bankrobber," was actually the backing track of the A-side with Mikey Dread "toasting" on top, hence the publishing attribution "Strummer/Jones/Campbell." It's delivered in such heavy patois as to make it difficult to understand, but even if that weren't the case it would be unlikely to be considered a masterpiece.

In October 1980 came the release in North America of *Black Market Clash*, a 10-inch album containing an assortment of rarities and unissued material. This peculiar product was the first Clash compilation of any kind, and indeed the only one of The Clash's lifetime.

It was no banal best-of, however. Usefully for American fans, it collected tracks that were on the UK version of the debut album but not the doctored American one. To those, it added three tracks from the *Cost of Living* EP, some British B-sides, and "Bankrobber" in a new mix. It also included the then-very-rare first version of "Capital Radio." Even more intriguingly, it included the never previously heard "Robber Dub," "Time Is Tight," and a version of "Pressure Drop" which differed to the one heard on the B-side of "English Civil War" by virtue of horns. "Time Is Tight" is a cover of a percolating Booker T and the MG's instrumental. The observant will notice that its riff inspired the intro to The Clash's "Gates of the West." "Robber Dub" was intended for a 12-inch version of the "Bankrobber" single that was ultimately never released. With Mikey Dread at the controls, it's a superior example of the controversial form of dub.

Super Black Market Clash was an expanded version of *Black Market Clash* released in 1993, long after the band were dead and gone and when—one would imagine—such gimmicks as 10-inch records cynically designed as collector's items were as much a part of history as vinyl itself. However, the original *Black Market Clash* continued to have a desirability for Clash completists because of the fact that some of its mixes and edits remained unique to it. For instance, on *Black Market Clash*, "Justice Tonight"/ "Kick It Over" are segued and shortened by two minutes compared to the 12-inch "London Calling" single.

At the time of its release, *Black Market Clash* was not just a desirable product in the North American market for which it was intended.

That it both purveyed new material and rounded up tracks otherwise scattered across only singles and EPs ensured there was a demand for import copies in the UK. Its desirability was additionally enhanced by the fact that some thought had clearly gone into the package. The cover was striking: it bore a photograph—in dramatic negative—of a lone Rasta (Clash friend Don Letts) strolling across a backdrop of an ominous-looking line of police officers at the same 1976 Notting Hill riot that inspired The Clash's debut single. The triple-meaning of the title was witty, alluding to the cover photograph, the quasi-contraband air possessed by a collection of rarities, and the predominance of reggae on the record.

4

IN THE SHADOW OF THE JAM

With the singles blitz abandoned, the next British Clash 45 after "Bankrobber" didn't appear until November 21, 1980, and when it did was merely—aside from its exclusive B-side—a taster for their next album, *Sandinista!*

The single marked the end of the "Strummer/Jones" songwriting credit, at least on Clash product. The composition of both A-side "The Call Up" and its flip "Stop the World" was ascribed to "Clash," a publishing attribution which would remain until the post-Headon, post-Jones Clash album *Cut the Crap*. The change was the result of Strummer and Jones turning their righteous fire inward and finding themselves wanting. Strummer explained in interview his contempt for Jagger and Richards taking all the writing credit and publishing royalties for Rolling Stones music and paying their colleagues "a pittance."

The single also marked another end. With "The Call Up," the group squandered all the chart momentum they had secured with "London Calling" and "Bankrobber." It also started another sort of rot. The Clash's commercial freefall and reputational decline among ordinary punters in their home country began here.

This is not because "The Call Up" is in any way a bad record. It's a mid-paced number which spurns the usual Clash anthemic approach for a sad ambience in which the option of avoiding an army call-up is acknowledged but no more so than the inevitability of sanctions for doing so. More poetic lament than rallying call ("There is a rose that I want to live for"), this is a far cry from previous Clash exhortations to heedless defiance. Headon plays enjoyably imaginative patterns. The elegant rhythm guitar (possibly by ex-Voidoid Ivan Julian, who guests on this song) sounds a little like oriental chimes as it pinwheels along quite exquisitely. The peak UK chart position of this thoroughly worthwhile concoction was a miserable no. 40, the group's lowest so far, with the sole exception of the unauthorized and un-promoted "Remote Control" single. That it was a mistake for The Clash to release "The Call Up" as the taster for *Sandinista!* in Britain was not restricted to the fact that 5:25 (by far their longest single to date) was more than most radio stations felt comfortable with. Whatever its qualities, "The Call Up" was symptomatic of a growing problem with The Clash: their evident distance from, even irrelevance to, their compatriots.

Over the previous year, all those people who had said upon the release of *London Calling* that The Clash were going American had, unexpectedly, seemed to be proven right. The group recorded their new album in Electric Lady in New York. Unlike with the additional America-based work on *Give 'em Enough Rope*, this couldn't be put down to a producer or record label forcing the group to travel to foreign climes: Mick Jones was now living in that city on a seemingly permanent basis. Apparently, rehearsal spaces in Pimlico, recording studios in Highbury, and squats in Marylebone (let alone the servants' quarters of mansions in Regent's Park) weren't good enough for The Clash anymore. Nor, apparently, English women: Jones's U.S. domicile was the consequence of his relationship with glamorous U.S. chanteuse Ellen Foley.

British music lovers don't like abandonment. Only a half-decade previously, Slade had made a concerted, prolonged attempt to crack America. The consequence as far as their British fans were concerned was that they seemed to disappear off the face of the earth. The consequence for the previously mega-successful Slade was that when they returned to Blighty, after failing to convert the States, they found they weren't wanted anymore. For The Clash, their own absence created more problems than just the fact of their fans' attention wandering to new idols. "I'm So Bored with the U.S.A." was a long-standing point of awkwardness, but it was now giving rise to a grievance with real legitimacy. The Clash working a lot in the United States despite their anti-U.S. cultural imperialism beliefs was arguably just an irony of life. Unarguably, The Clash were now losing touch, a potentially fatal fact for artists whose entire image revolved around them knowing the score.

The subject of the military draft was currently a hot issue in America due to a 1980 presidential proclamation requiring all men born on or after January 1, 1960, to register with the Selective Service System. It created the prospect of unwilling souls being forced into fatigues in a national emergency and was causing dread memories of the Vietnam draft to re-enter the consciousness of a public that hadn't properly gotten over it. In a 1991 comment, Jones argued, "The registration for the draft affected a lot of our fans in America. I remember going to a demonstration on the Upper West Side." The Clash's concern about what affected their American fans was, of course, admirable, but its corollary was that they were less focused on what affected their UK fans, many of whom wouldn't have quite known even what "Upper West Side" meant. Britain was deep in recession and disputation. The Conservative administration of Margaret Thatcher that had assumed power in May 1979 was worsening that recession with public sector cuts consistent with its belief that Keynesian spending to defeat a downturn was no longer an option. And The Clash's response to this? To release a record of absolutely no relevance to a country where "National Service" had been abolished in 1960 and had no prospect of coming back.

Worse was to come, however, when it transpired that *Sandinista!* didn't merely commit the sin implied by its precursor single of turning the band's focus away from the UK toward American or global issues. Compounding that offense was that The Clash turned out to also still be writing London-set poverty tableaux. Objecting to this might seem paradoxical, but those latter songs inevitably invited juxtaposition with a lifestyle that may not have been technically jet-setting but might as well have been for the people still stuck in tower blocks in Notting Hill and factory jobs in Camden. The Clash were at this point in a real bind, one they arguably never escaped.

"Stop the World," the B-side to "The Call Up," saw The Clash expressing more anti-nuclear sentiment. The dragged beat and shifts in and out of focus create an ambience as ghostly as a nuclear corpse's "shadow," while the lyric is high-quality and evocative ("The panorama of the city is wrong"). Although not a great track, it is heaps better than much of the material that created the longueurs of *Sandinista!*

At the time, it seemed ludicrous beyond belief: a band with their roots in punk were to release a triple LP. Not only was undisciplined self-regard in music something to which punk was supposed to be a reaction, The Clash had gone one worse than the prog rockers synonymous with such preening releases by making their triple album a studio affair: three-LP sets by the likes of Yes and Emerson, Lake & Palmer tended to be live albums and were only so bloated because it was felt necessary to give purchasers as many of the act's most popular songs as possible.

The feeling that The Clash were becoming not just a joke but everything they'd once despised was deepened once people had the record on their turntables. That many of the songs explored foreign themes—as reflected by a title bewildering to Britons—felt incongruous for a band who had always emphasized their Britishness. Meanwhile, the record's sleeve confirmed that they were beginning to look ridiculous. The cover photo dripped with silly self-mythologizing and confused Americana, The Clash posing moodily in a bizarre jumble of styles which included leather jacket, biker's cap, GI helmet, fedora, sunglasses, and waistcoat.

Sandinista!—released on December 12, 1980—was selling for £5.99, only about a pound above the price of a single album, but the battle The Clash had fought with the record company to keep down the recommended retail price wasn't impressive this time around, not even when they revealed that, as a consequence, they would receive no royalties whatsoever on the first 200,000 copies sold in the UK: nobody in their right mind would have paid for this album's third disc.

Sandinista!'s unwanted abundance serves to diminish its good parts, creating an aura of material being cheap, as well as the distasteful whiff of the band thinking everything they did merited release. Strummer subsequently protested that the only reason they'd opted for a triple was as a kind of grandiose nose-thumb to fellow CBS artist Bruce Springsteen, who had appeared to copy the two albums/single outer sleeve/card inner sleeves format of *London Calling* with his 1980 *The River* LP. (The similarities were even more apparent when one listened to the music: in being a collection of anthemic, warmhearted songs detailing the tribulations of the working class and the oppressed, *The River* seemed like nothing so much as the transatlantic bookend to *London Calling*, even if Springsteen had been essaying similar subject matter—albeit in a more glum style—before The Clash first appeared on the scene.) Leaving aside that the fuck-you-Bruce defense hardly reflected well on The Clash, it was difficult to know whether to believe the explanation of men given to shaggy dog stories. In any case, if The Clash were determined to include a third disc, instead of filling it with dubs, doodles, and backward tracks as they did, they should surely have elected to make it a covers collection. That way, they could have ensured—à la David Bowie's *Pin Ups* or Guns N' Roses's *The Spaghetti Incident*—that much-needed royalties found their way to songwriters down on their luck.

Unsurprisingly, given its sprawling nature, *Sandinista!* was not recorded as an album but is the result of work in a variety of studios over a period of seven months, starting as an exercise to knock around ideas in New York's Power Station in March 1980. After being pleased with a version of Eddy Grant's "Police on My Back" laid down there, they shifted over to the same city's Electric Lady for three weeks. This was a recording period at which Paul Simonon was not present due to him attempting to start a career as a movie star by filming *Ladies And Gentlemen, The Fabulous Stains* in Vancouver. Norman Watt-Roy of the Blockheads deputized for him for the first five days, after which other members of The Clash laid down basslines. Simonon rejoined his colleagues at Jamaica's Channel One Studios, where only one track was recorded, supposedly due to demands for money with menaces that sent the band scuttling back to their safe European home and the familiar haven of Wessex Studios. Simonon replaced some of the band's (but not Watt-Roy's) bass work.

As a Clash album had for the first time mainly been written in the studio, and as he was often not present in the studio, Simonon could hardly be said to have been in all cases a co-composer. Although therefore he disproportionately benefited from the new egalitarian writing attribution, its supposed nobility is rather put into context by the fact that Watt-Roy and his Blockhead colleague Mickey Gallagher were shocked to receive no writing credits for their contributions to the LP.

The album's ham-fisted mix is implausibly credited to Bill Price. In fact, the cold, echoing feel—undoubtedly responsible for much of the negative critical reception—is the sonic trademark of Mick Jones, as proven by his later productions for artists like Ellen Foley and Theatre of Hate. It was a classic example of someone over-extending himself. Jones and The Clash would have been better advised to give way to

Price, whose mix did the band so proud on *London Calling*. Failing that, Mikey Dread would have been a good—and adventurous—choice: his shimmering mixes of a couple of *Sandinista!* tracks put the production on the surrounding material to shame. According to Dread in Kris Needs' *Joe Strummer and the Legend of The Clash* (2005) this eventuality didn't come to pass because Blackhill, feeling Dread was taking their clients down an uncommercial path, marginalized him during the sessions.

If it's the case that it is only possible to get a proper perspective on much of The Clash's recorded output once removed from the intense, purist scrutiny accompanying its release, this applies especially to *Sandinista!* As mentioned, it was an album that found them at an awkward stage in their career where they were destined to be perceived as in the wrong no matter what they did. A third of a century down the line, with punk's unwritten constitution a disintegrating memory and The Clash long scattered to the winds, people are free to acknowledge that the conclusions drawn in *Sandinista!*'s lyrics—regardless of whether they are impudent enough to address countries outside the UK, or impudent enough to address a UK they seemed to barely visit these days—do not in the main wither under scrutiny. Meanwhile, some of the music is extremely good.

What we are left with after all the fuss has now subsided into a quaint temperature of the times is an album that veers between great, good, and truly awful. There had never been truly awful material on Clash records before, but its presence here was not the signpost of an artistic downslide: as a single album, *Sandinista!* would have been a classic.

Criticized though their global gallivanting may have been, The Clash's tenure in the Big Apple ensured that they were present at the birth of a new musical form: in 1980, rap was in its infancy and barely known of in Britain.

"Rapper's Delight" by the Sugarhill Gang became the first hip-hop hit in 1979. Jones was enchanted by this new musical form, which emphasized rapid-fire and syncopated spoken-word lyrics. It's quite a leap from that, however, to decide to open *Sandinista!* with The Clash's take on this music. Leaving aside the potential for accusations of cultural imperialism, a lot of musicians at the time thought rap was a joke, a form practiced by those not talented enough to play "real" music.

"The Magnificent Seven" wasn't quite the first-ever rap recording by a white artist: Blondie's punningly titled "Rapture" appeared on their *Autoamerican* album a month before the release of *Sandinista!* Although "The Magnificent Seven" was the first white rap recording released as a single, its commercial performance (no. 34; U.S.: did not chart) was tepid compared to that of "Rapture," which upon its release on 45 was a U.S. no. 1 and UK top five. However, whereas "Rapture" was little more than bubblegum, "The Magnificent Seven" was the first example of rap being used for social commentary. As it preceded records like Grandmaster Flash's "The Message" by two years, it could even be suggested that without the example of "The Magnificent Seven," hip-hop would not have embraced the political content from which it is now indivisible.

Norman Watt-Roy told Salewicz in *Redemption Song* that Jones had approached him on the day of the recording of "The Magnificent Seven" and said, "We need something really funky, 'cos Joe says he wants to do a rap." While the musicians worked something up, Strummer devised the lyric. Two hours later, "The Magnificent Seven" was in the can. Considering its ad hoc genesis, it is astounding that "The Magnificent Seven" is one of The Clash's finest moments. Watt-Roy's funky bass riff was looped to provide a pulsating background to a Strummer lyric which riffed on a familiar Clash theme—the nine-to-five grind—but from a new, lateral angle. The rap format—whose conversationalism lent itself to playfulness—gave Strummer the chance to use slapstick humor and whimsy in order to condemn the seven hours (lunch hour excluded) of the working day. In a slang and abbreviation-packed affair, he has Karl Marx and Friedrich Engels visiting the 7-11(Engels bails out the financially embarrassed Marx at the checkout), Martin Luther King and Mahatma Gandhi attending a sports game together, and Socrates and Richard Nixon finding themselves going in the same direction. Despite the comedy, there is also an element of pathos, that aching sadness which Strummer habitually insists on attaching to the worker whose lack of skills supposedly gives him no prospect of self-improvement. Meanwhile, the catchy boss-worker "You lot!"/"What?" refrain in the choruses inevitably became a call-and-response routine between band and audience at Clash gigs.

Modern day hip-hop has a reputation for one-dimensionality, but the musical arrangement here is very rich. Watt-Roy's burbling bass is infectious, and its looped nature renders it in no way mechanical. Headon deserves kudos for fine, brisk drumming and percussive effects that create tension in the lead-up to his periodic drumrolls. Jones was notorious for playing loud and flashy onstage but, realizing guitar-hero stuff would be inappropriate here, he shows discipline by restricting himself to sinuous rhythm work.

It's interesting that the fresh, vibrant aura hanging over rap music in 1980 soon turned into something more sinister, even despicable. It wasn't long before it became a byword for misogyny, homophobia, anti-Semitism, and glorification of violence. It was understood that few of its practitioners were musicians in the conventional sense, but it actively seemed to attract types diametrically opposed to the classification "sensitive artist." By the 1990s, the violent content of hip-hop songs couldn't even be dismissed as bluster: the rap feud which sprang up between East Coast Bad Boy Records and West Coast Death Row Records was of palpable, murderous authenticity. It created a situation never previously imagined possible even by all those doomsayers of the Fifties disgusted by rock 'n' roll's degeneracy: recording artists slaughtering each other like gangsters.

Perhaps it should come as little surprise, then, that history shows that rap music ultimately consumed both The Clash and rock itself. At first, Strummer had been enthusiastic about the new sounds Jones was bringing him. Strummer's enthusiasm began to wane as Jones's obsession with rap led to a not entirely complimentary nickname. "I was so gone with it," Jones admitted in the 2000 Clash documentary *Westway to the World*. "The others used to call me 'Whack Attack'. I'd walk around with a beatbox." While Jones's post-1980 songs can't be posited as being exclusively hip-hop, it is beyond dispute that, following his conversion to that music's merits, he was never again the true believer in rock 'n' roll he had hitherto been. With that conversion, his previous propensity for stirring anthems evaporated: he didn't want to sound like Mott The Hoople anymore. Strummer stated to Michael Goldberg of *Rolling Stone* magazine in May 1984 that the last demo Jones had made before he was sacked from the group "wasn't our music. He was playing around with beat boxes and synthesizers."

Meanwhile, rap, from its beginnings at the turn of the Eighties, took little more than twenty years to take over the world. In 2002, it was announced that hip-hop records now outsold rock releases. The idea was once unthinkable, and for very good reasons. Hip-hop artists did not play instruments, did not write songs in the traditional sense, did not even sing as such. They were reliant on rock, pop, and soul's rich history for their musical hooks, a jackdaw process that became known as sampling. Moreover, the rhythm-heavy sound necessitated by artists possessing no means of generating original melody and the cacophony that often resulted from shouted lyrics (many of which had an additional unpleasantly harsh layer due to the medium's frequent braggadocio) made the form seem destined for nothing but niche status. That it is rock which is now the niche music seems partly down to the fact that young people view its rhythms and iconography as old hat and partly because of hip-hop's perceived authenticity: the strutting of rock frontmen must seem a little phony when many rappers speak of blood-drenched ghettos from personal experience.

By 1980, the diversity and quick-moving nature of the UK charts had long been a source of amazement to Americans. In February of that year, however, something happened that amazed even British chart observers.

That was the month that *The Special AKA Live!* by a Midlands ska revivalist band later known as The Specials topped the chart. That it was an EP was remarkable enough: EPs were so much a Sixties relic that their own chart had been abolished as far back as 1967, and Demis Roussos's *The Roussos Phenomenon* from 1976 was the only previous EP to make the singles chart summit. That *The Special AKA Live!* was a live record was further remarkable: on the few occasions when in-concert recordings topped the UK singles charts, it was usually in the form of novelty songs like Lonnie Donegan's "My Old Man's a Dustman" and "My Ding-A-Ling" by Chuck Berry. The nature of the lead track, "Too Much Too Young", made the record even more remarkable. It was a song about young lives ruined by premature parenthood containing the line "Ain't you heard of contraception?" The BBC was obliged by its success to allow the record's presence on radio and TV airwaves at a juncture in history when they refused to permit their DJs to enunciate the first word of Marvin Gaye's UK no. 4 "(Sexual) Healing."

Most remarkable of all, though, was the fact that *The Special AKA Live!* had been released on independent label Two-Tone. That a record company without the promotional muscle of a "major" behind it could top the charts was simply counterintuitive. It was a good, catchy, and streetwise record, but finding an audience large enough to send it to the top was only part of the difficulty an "indie" faced, as demonstrated by the fact that it was later alleged that the no. 1 preceding the Special A.K.A.'s—The Pretenders's "Brass in Pocket"—was sent all the way to the top by dint of simple corruption.

The success of *The Special AKA Live!* and Two-Tone was, however, a sign of the times. The turn of the Eighties was a period when independents flourished in Great Britain due to a confluence of factors including proliferation (a trend is interesting and will attract attention) and quality (for a while it seemed that most of the interesting records being released were appearing on non-majors). Two-Tone was the most remarkable of the labels to achieve success at this point in history because the people running it a) were artists, and b) barely looked old enough to shave. However, they had been preceded by Stiff (home of The Damned, Elvis Costello, Ian Dury, and—following their departure from Two-Tone—Madness). Other famous indies of the time were Factory (Joy Division, New Order, Happy Mondays), Rough Trade (Cabaret Voltaire, Stiff Little Fingers, The Monochrome Set), and Small Wonder (Bauhaus, Crass, The Cure, Angelic Upstarts).

It was an exhilarating time for artists and would-be artists because it seemed that a revolution in the music industry was under way. Never again would bands have to dance to the tune of corporations who put commerce before art. Never again would the charts be effectively closed to those unable to afford to either mount a huge advertising campaign or send people out to chart return shops with fistfuls of fivers.

Unfortunately, the revolution was cancelled. It turned out, after all, that the minnows could not compete with the big boys and that their brief flourish of success was an accident of history. Before the end of the Eighties, music papers were regularly running stories about how this independent had decided to sell up to that major, usually accompanied by a statement from the about-to-be-subsumed indie about how they would retain full artistic control within their new home and how the move was a way to continue a legacy of which they were immensely proud. Some found this less than heartbreaking because it has to be said that, by then, the indie charts had become tediously synonymous with a formulaic mixture of minor chords and doomy lyrics. However, it was still depressing how quickly it became corporate business as usual.

Before that turnaround, The Clash celebrated in song a situation whose do-it-yourself nature and David-defeating-Goliath implications were right up punk's street. The result was "Hitsville UK," and little could less flatter its subject. The lyric starts by portraying the ascension of the indie in absurdly mythopoeic terms, talking of kids "up and down the land" crying tears, shedding fears, and stealing guitars. The boys and girls no longer feel alone, the lyric concludes. In between, there is some very ungainly stuff. "UK" is not given a definite article in the refrain, with the effect of making the songwords seem a childlike litany. There is a contrived roll call of British indie labels. Moreover, an assertion that successful indie acts weren't considered to even have the slightest hope of a thousand sales is delivered with the drama appropriate for a recounting of the parting of the Red Sea.

The music cements the fact of the triumphs and the tragedies of *Sandinista!* being summed up in the space of its opening two tracks. Whereas "The Magnificent Seven" shows a band able to assimilate a genre and practice it with complete authenticity, "Hitsville UK" is simply a musical style reduced to cliché. As Motown was known as "Hitsville U.S.A.," the choice of the track's musical style was logical. Unfortunately, while on the surface the band ape the Motown sound competently, they exude little of its spirit: where Four Tops or Supremes records were either exhilaratingly joyous or sumptuously sad, "Hitsville UK" is frigid. The pulsating bass is quite pleasurable, but the presence of glockenspiel silly. Matters are worsened by a production that is utterly bizarre. The track features a vocal from Ellen Foley intended to be backing—or perhaps harmony—to Mick Jones's voice but which is mixed up so high that she becomes the lead singer. This not only lacks logic but puts one uncomfortably in mind of the way that Roxy Music album sleeves once regularly featured Bryan Ferry's latest girlfriend.

"Junco Partner" was the only one of *Sandinista!*'s tracks recorded in Jamaica before the sessions were aborted. An anthem of low-life inebriates apparently first heard by Strummer in a New Orleans piano ballad version by James Booker, it had once been a feature of 101'ers live sets. Here, The Clash reggae-fy the song in a clunky and charmless performance. The idiotic blooping sound effects—telltale signs of a Mick Jones production—don't help.

Nick Headon was more than just an excellent drummer. The music of "Ivan Meets G. I. Joe" was his creation, hence his lead vocal (his one and only while in The Clash). The production doesn't do justice to some snazzy Pearl & Dean–style brass and some Space Invaders sound effects are distracting, but this is a good piece of mock-disco.

Strummer's lyric sardonically reduces the permanent standoff between the Cold War superpowers to showdowns on the dance floors of New York's Studio 54 and Paris's Le Palace. Despite the comedy, running through this song is a resentment then felt by many of the citizens of European NATO member countries. At a point in history where the two big guns of the U.S.A. and the USSR were perpetually staring at each other, few were those in either superpower who contemplated the position of the continent caught in the middle. Americans might have considered themselves the good guys in the Cold War, but to temperate Europeans both sides seemed to be cartoonishly belligerent. Moreover, recent blood-drenched Vietnamese and Latin American history gave the United States a villainous air not too dissimilar to the Russians. The average American would have been horrified, had he only known, by how many Europeans thought the two superpowers just as bad as each other.

"The Leader" is a short, brisk, and somewhat characterless examination of the intrigue and kinky sex surrounding the Profumo scandal of 1963, which culminated in the ruination of a British government minister and the suicide of an alleged traitor.

The point of the song is unclear. The chorus line "You've gotta give the people something good to read on a Sunday" suggests a disapproval of the trivia with which Britain's tabloid newspapers fill their pages, but the Profumo scandal was far from inconsequential. The song is another that smacks of a feeling of a pressure felt by The Clash to make their every creation a protest song regardless of whether there is anything to protest about.

One critic described "Something about England" as being as precious as a Jethro Tull number—one of the worst insults that could be hurled at musicians forged in the punk revolution. In fact, mustering the willpower to see past the atrocious choirboy singing by Jones in the second verse and the fact that the track suffers more than most from the lunar chill that smothers the entire album, one can see that this is the only track on what was the first vinyl side of the album to come close to the quality of "The Magnificent Seven."

In this downbeat (in all senses of the word) composition, Jones plays the part of a young man who engages an elderly tramp in conversation. When the tramp—whose part is taken by Strummer—starts to recount the horrors of working-class life from the aftermath of World War I onward, the song assumes the mantle of something substantial. Strummer invests utter conviction in his persona, and the lyric is a superbly pithy evocation of an era when the proletariat was stricken with malnutrition while darling young things quaffed champagne at garden parties at which Britain's ownership of two-thirds of the world was roundly applauded.

In "Rebel Waltz," opening track of side two of *Sandinista!*, Strummer attempts to fuse what he felt to be the whitest form of music (waltz) with the blackest (reggae). The lyric is dramatic: the protagonist is part of an unspecified rebel army who sees his comrades' hopes dashed in a surprise military attack. Yet the exercise has a dreamlike quality, its lyric wafted on a gossamer melody and gentle instrumentation. An unusual and intriguing interlude.

"Look Here"—a 1964 Mose Allison composition—was the type of thing to infuriate those who saw this album as representing an arrogant assumption by a band only three years previously little more than competent on their instruments that they could now master any music to which they chose to address themselves.

One doesn't wish to keep harping on about the doltish mix, but the cavernous vocal here is what led many to dismiss this track as the efforts of those who were aping jazz without understanding it: its coldness is diametrically opposed to jazz's heat and grit. Mickey Gallagher's piano and Headon's double-time percussion are particularly impressive elements of a breathless and perfectly respectable recital.

Paul Simonon's vocal outing for this album is predictably in a song in his beloved reggae style, although Strummer, not he, wrote the lyric to "The Crooked Beat." As with "The Guns of Brixton," Simonon's bass riff is prominent, although not quite as compelling as the one which graced that earlier song. The mood is incongruously laid-back for a track suffused with an anxiety to party as a means of denying the fact of economic hardship. The lyric possesses at least one brilliant line: "Take a piece of cloth, a coin for thirst, for the sweat will start to run." The track segues into a dub mix that would presumably have been given its own billing had it not been decided to have exactly six tracks on each vinyl side.

"Somebody Got Murdered" was originally given to Jack Nitzsche for *Cruising*, the Al Pacino movie he was scoring, but it wasn't used. Although it has a Jones vocal, its lyric was written by Strummer and is another World's End–inspired creation: the car park attendant on Strummer's estate was murdered for small change.

Jones heightens the sadness of a fine lyric with one of his soaring anthemic melodies and a simpatico vocal that makes up for his embarrassing one in "Something about England." It's gratifying to see that although Strummer's natural inclination is to side with the "workers," he can perceive that poverty does not excuse callousness, particularly when directed at the fellow downtrodden. Or as he himself beautifully puts it in verse two, "I've been very hungry—but not enough to kill."

Right from the mesmeric opening notes of "One More Time," the listener can perceive the difference in quality of the mixing work to what has preceded it. Mikey Dread's adroit production techniques suffuse this anti-poverty reggae, making the instrumentation gleam and Strummer's rhetoric glow with authority. The band provide sensitive backing to the refrain of "One more time in the ghetto," which is repeated with grim insistence while disconnected piano chords and yelps from Dread flit in and out of the mix.

"One More Time" is followed by "One More Dub." Coming so soon after the dub reprise to "The Crooked Beat," it gives the listener pause. This was truly heavy commitment to the dub-wise principle. Yet, notwithstanding the smack of overkill—and the comments on dub mixes earlier in this text—it can't be denied that this is a highly listenable track. Dread's expert hands ensure instruments take on weird and fascinating qualities. Even the most anti-dub listener, upon hearing cymbals looming larger than life while drums resound like asteroid impacts, will end up asking, "Why not?"

"The Magnificent Seven" was so special that you can't blame the band for having another go with "Lightning Strikes (Not Once But Twice)." Unfortunately, lightning didn't strike twice for The Clash with rap. The track is a pale imitation of the album opener. The lyric, naturally, bristles with the usual Strummer wit and wordplay (he tells us that

New York's only tree can be found in a park, "But don't inspect it after dark"). However, whereas "The Magnificent Seven" had a wonderful musical nimbleness, here things are bogged down with a disjointed (and intermittently deafening) rhythm and an unattractive picked guitar riff.

"Up in Heaven (Not Only Here)" is an enjoyable track, but at the same time one can see the point of anyone who might posit it as a proof of the fact that The Clash seemed to be forgetting where they had come from. A melodic hard rock anthem in the old Clash style whose subject is the grimness of high-rise living might be assumed to be something the Towerblock Rock merchants could effortlessly make special, yet for every spot-on summation of the monochrome misery of high-rise existence in its lyric ("The wives hate their husbands, their husbands don't care"), there is a cringe-making image straight out of a pulp novel. Tower block life is bad enough that there is no need to exaggerate it, as Jones (who sings) does when he suggests such buildings tilt in high winds. Nobody would know from this creation that both Jones and Strummer had lived in tower blocks.

In "Corner Soul," discussions are taking place in "The Grove"—which sounds Third World but could also conceivably be Notting Hill Gate—about direct action. A meeting has decided that total war must ensue. Calmer heads are urging caution. Meanwhile, the forces of darkness are about to make house-to-house searches. The smoldering music and ominous chorus are given an extra spookiness by Ellen Foley's ethereal, elongated backing sighs. The track is curtailed on a resonating note from Foley, with the listener left to guess the story's resolution. A stunning mood piece.

The last time The Clash were inspired to write a song about the Notting Hill carnival, the results were impressive. "Let's Go Crazy," sadly, is no "White Riot." In place of punk fire, we have the steel drums and circular patterns of calypso, a music with far less natural vitality and momentum.

"Let's Go Crazy" is the song that "Jimmy Jazz" sounded like on the surface, as revealed by its line, "Owed by a year of SUS and suspect."

Strummer depicts black youths viewing the carnival as the one day of the year when they can get revenge against the police officers who they feel harass them. Although the portent of confrontation makes the song feel similar to the previous track, the treatment is far less haunting, something not helped by such laziness as rhyming "dread" with "dread."

The spoken-word vocal on "If Music Could Talk"—a cut stated to be composed by "Clash/Dread"—is recorded over the percolating backing track of "Shepherd's Delight," the last number on the album. Strummer is intoning two different pseudo stream-of-consciousness rants, one from each channel, neither of which are completely intelligible. An inspection of the *Armagideon Times No. 3* lyric sheet that came with the album reveals them to be of little insight or interest. The lyric's deficiencies and the facts that the backing is so easy on the ear and the saxophone so pleasantly smoky make one wonder whether this should have been left as an instrumental.

For "The Sound of the Sinners," the gospel genre is appropriated in order for Strummer to give his take on organized religion. It's difficult to know precisely where he's coming from. In one verse he is saying that the message written on Moses's tablet was "valium," indicating ridicule, in another that he himself is too drug-addled and mentally weak to live up to his delusions of being Christ, suggesting more a tone of humility. So generic is the organ work and the "Judgment Day" backing chant that it barely matters.

Jones takes the vocal on a cover of Eddy Grant's fugitive anthem "Police on My Back," which kicked off side four of the original *Sandinista!* vinyl configuration, without doubt the album's strongest.

The track doesn't quite live up to a fabulous introduction created by a barrage of synchronized keening guitar. Nonetheless, it has the kind of vitality missing from so much of *Sandinista!*'s often drab soundscape. Additionally, it's impressive the way the band prove they can turn The Equals's rather repetitive and featureless original into one of their trademark rebel-rock anthems.

"Midnight Log" is a dark slice of rockabilly which finds Strummer conversing with the devil. Crooked accountants and corrupt police officers litter it, but, barring the clear fact that it disapproves of them and those like-minded, the lyric has the opaque quality of wandering into the middle of a conversation. The quick-stepping tempo and pleasantly skeletal percussion make up for that, though, in a number that's almost as eerie as it's intended to be.

After previously proffering dub-mix alternates of songs, The Clash go the whole hog by presenting a song only in its dub version. It may be the lack of an original template with which to compare it that gives "The

Equaliser" its compelling quality, but, chances are, it would sound magnificent anyway.

Mikey Dread provides the production on this resplendent dark, staccato reggae, which condemns the iniquities inherent in capitalism. ("See the world? You have built it with shoulders of iron.") The tone is one of dejected anger, but the thought-provoking lyric—which, like several Clash reggae songs, appropriates phrases from Jamaican patois—prevents it from being depressing. Dread's tricks are ingenious: elements of instrumentation—including flecks of violin from Tymon Dogg, burps of guitar, and maniacal laughter—float in and out to almost shiver-inducing effect.

Following "The Call Up" in *Sandinista!*'s track listing comes "Washington Bullets." The title of *Sandinista!* is tied in to this track, the subject of which is the 1979 ascension to power of the Sandinista National Liberation Front in Nicaragua, Central America. (The letters in the album's catalog number constitutes said organization's initials in Spanish.) Explained Jones in *Rip It Up*, "There was a media blanket covering the whole bloody thing, and people didn't even know there was a revolution there. We really wanted to have a title that was useful for once. It was something that would draw people's attention to something that was going on at the time."

The Sandinistas were manna from heaven for someone, like Strummer, steeped in the romance and tragedy of the Spanish Civil War. So much were the Sandinistas the darlings for his generation of leftists that in the UK a semi-derogatory term was devised for them: Guardianistas, a portmanteau word the first part of which was a reference to the *Guardian* newspaper, at that point the only daily left-wing broadsheet in the country.

The Sandinista regime ran Nicaragua throughout the Eighties. As with Fidel Castro in Cuba, they came to power by toppling a murderous dictator who had been backed by the United States to protect its own territorial and financial interests in the region. Whereas Castro became in his own way as bad as the overthrown Fulgencio Batista, the Sandinistas sought to bring about the kind of social equity shaped by Castro without resorting to the totalitarianism of the man they had ousted, Anastasio Somoza. At first, they seemed set to succeed. While infant mortality and illiteracy tumbled, they held free and fair national elections, which they won overwhelmingly.

Things went less well from there. The United States formally supported the Contras, an armed opposition who refused to recognize the legitimacy of their rule. Congress ultimately stopped this support but President Ronald Reagan ordered a trade embargo of the country partly on the grounds that Nicaragua's dealings with and funding from the Soviet Union made it a Communist bulwark. The Nicaraguan economy suffered accordingly.

Although the Sandinistas sometimes behaved less than ideally, they were certainly white-bread as far as Cold War villains went. They were authoritarian but not piously disapproving of materialism in the way of Eastern bloc regimes, while the state of emergency under which they ordered the country to operate for half of the Eighties was arguably justifiable because of the fact of their being at war with opponents whose methods were often little different to those of the death squads operating in El Salvador, also armed and funded by the United States. When they lost a general election in 1990, the Sandinistas meekly yielded power, even though opposition leader Violeta Chamorro had a relationship to the Contras little different from Sinn Fein's relationship to the IRA in contemporaneous Northern Ireland, and even though her victory by 14 percent of the vote could be argued to have been blackmailed from the electorate: America had the previous year stated it would continue its embargo if the Sandinistas won.

The story, then, ended in another tragedy for the left, even if in peacetime and the post–Cold War era the SNLF—under the apparently perennial leadership of Daniel Ortega—has won further elections. All that, though, was in the future. In 1980, the Sandinistas appeared to offer a new paradigm for Third World nationalist revolution, one with which Strummer was so enamored that he, for arguably the only time in The Clash's life span, wrote a song explicitly about a formally political issue. ("Spanish Bombs" might count, but even "The Call Up" was couched in universal anti-draft terms: there were no references to Proclamation 4771.)

Parts of the lyric are risible. Strummer uses "there" to end three separate lines in the first verse. It may be a new low for laziness in lyricists that, in another verse, Strummer relies on the listener consulting *The Armagideon Times, No. 3* to understand that he is rhyming "America" with "Amerika" (Collins Dictionary: "spelling used to suggest that U.S. society is variously fascist, repressive, racist, etc."). However, the songwords otherwise impressively and thoughtfully detail the historical pattern of American intervention in the Third World, including the 1973 CIA-organized overthrow of the elected Chilean leader Salvador Allende. Strummer had some knowledge of the latter: the exodus caused by Allende's psychopathic successor Augusto Pinochet sent many Chilean musicians London-ward, some of whom he performed with. The lyric also boasts a semi-disclaimer in the form of a final verse which acknowledges that imperialism is not solely a crime of the West. Such honesty was rare among Strummer's kind: one of the defining attributes of Guardianistas was a blind spot about Soviet human rights abuses.

The track's biggest weakness is its music. It has a watery quality that doesn't do justice to the euphoria the group attempt to communicate. The joyous howl presaging the instrumental break—meant to signify the Sandinistas' victory—makes the subsequent limp steel drum solo embarrassing. This was a track where the old Clash guitar-anthem method really was the only option.

The New Orleans jazz-flavored "Broadway," which closed side four, is almost the American equivalent of "Something about England." A tramp—sorry, hobo—in that famous New York district recounts to the protagonist the story of his hard life. The desperateness of his situation is brought home to him whenever he ponders on the ambition he once harbored to possess one of the types of cars which purr obliviously past his huddled form each day. Although some of the lines are heart-twistingly sad ("Oh the loneliness used to knock me out"), the music rather lets them down, being several shades less inspired and frequently repetitive.

"Broadway" is followed by a snatch of "Guns of Brixton" sung endearingly by Mickey Gallagher's young daughter Maria. Not listed on the album sleeve, it's titled "Blowing in the Guns of Brixton" in *The Armagideon Times No.3*.

The final disc of the vinyl *Sandinista!* opened with something that wasn't even a Clash track, "Lose This Skin" being composed and sung by Tymon Dogg, an old busking mate of Strummer's. A slightly hysterical folk song of existentialist angst, it actually isn't bad. However, it would not even be present had The Clash not needed to fill up some space, not least because it had already been released as a single under Dogg's name.

From here on in, the pickings are slim. That the band reserved most of the extraneous and the substandard material for the final third is convenient for the listener but betrays the fact that they were fully aware that a triple album was, aesthetically, a disc too far.

The title phrase of "Charlie Don't Surf" originates with the 1979 Francis Ford Coppola movie *Apocalypse Now*, with which The Clash were at this point somewhat obsessed. A sideswipe at American imperialism, the song is a slight and nondescript noodle. Strangely, in concert the band developed it into something altogether more grand and impressive. An interesting piece of trivia is the fact that it contains the line, "Everybody wants to rule the world." Tears for Fears would secure a worldwide hit with a song of that title three years later.

"Mensforth Hill" is "Something about England" played backward with a few overdubs, prompting the question of whether just because something is effectively free it is above being accused of being a gesture of contempt toward one's fans.

"Junkie Slip" is yet another condemnation of the squalor and self-obsession of the life of the smack addict, almost as if Strummer was trying to communicate a message to a certain someone. (This time, the chronology would support such a theory.) Perhaps Topper didn't take the hint because he was so unimpressed by the track's tunelessness, the vocal's unintelligibility, and the instrumentation's aura of having been tossed off in a tea break. Only an indecipherable but somehow evocative primeval vocal refrain and (ironically) Headon's adroit drumming make it something more than worthless.

The inevitability of the Third World poor taking violent action is the subject of the above-average lyric of "Kingston Advice" ("Please—don't beg for your life"), which serves to make it "Corner Soul Revisited." Only it possesses none of that track's hypnotic qualities, its message blunted by a monotonous tune and lackluster instrumentation.

The above comments can be reversed for "The Street Parade": the lyric is incomprehensible (even if boasting a couple of memorable phrases, e.g., "When I was waiting for your phone call, the one that never came") but, in places, the sax-decorated, calypso-esque music approaches poignancy. Ultimately, however, it's negligible.

"Version City," the opener of side six, comes as close to substantiality as anything does on the final disc of *Sandinista!* Strummer uses the train as a metaphor for music being a means to escape ordinary career paths: the protagonist starts his rail journey from Version City, passing through A Cappella Pass and Gibson Town, picking up similar lost souls along the way to his realization of a dream. Musically, the song is subdued but not depressed. Jones contributes deft mouth harp throughout a cut that is quietly moving.

With space still to fill, another band friend gets a Clash album track of his own. At least Mikey Dread's involvement in the Clash-Dread co-write "Living in Fame" means it can boast a good production, but this reggae song is built upon a rather silly premise: namely, that all bands should live up to their names like The Clash supposedly do—for example, The Specials should be more special. Despite the risibility, some of the nimble reggae backing is enjoyable.

"Silicone on Sapphire" is a remix of the backing track of "Washington Bullets"—hardly the most powerful music to begin with—with overdubbed Strummer spoken-word that is mostly unintelligible but seems to consist of him reading out computer screen cursor messages.

"Version Pardner" is possibly better than "Junco Partner," of which it's a dub mix, but that, of course, is not saying much.

In "Career Opportunities," the classic hard-hitting track from The Clash's debut album is given an effete keyboard arrangement. The lyric is tweaked to include a reference to school rules to make it relevant to the age group of Mickey Gallagher's kids, who take on vocal duties. Pathetic.

"Shepherds Delight," the last track on *Sandinista!*, predates the album sessions proper, this Clash/Dread co-write actually a leftover from the February 1980 sessions for the "Bankrobber" single. A tranquil but essentially featureless reggae instrumental, its retrieval from the vaults provides an appropriate ending for *Sandinsita!*: the sound of a barrel being scraped.

Just as it is a Beatles fan's parlor game to nominate the tracks that would have made the "White Album" perfect, so it is common among Clash lovers to select the optimum configuration of *Sandinista!* For what it's worth, this critic's choice is:

1. "The Magnificent Seven"
2. "Ivan Meets G. I. Joe"
3. "Rebel Waltz"
4. "The Crooked Beat"

5. "Somebody Got Murdered"
6. "One More Time"
7. "Corner Soul"
8. "Police on My Back"
9. "Midnight Log"
10. "The Equaliser"
11. "Version City"
12. "The Call Up"

Looking at the track listing of this single-album fantasy *Sandinista!*, one is struck that it would have made for not only an artistically solid affair, but one with a noble and elegant tone that would have served as a fascinating contrast to the giddiness of *London Calling*.

History can't be changed, though. Not least in the illogical choice of singles released from *Sandinista!* "Fuckin' long, innit?" Strummer gasps at one point in "The Magnificent Seven." It is indeed at 5½ minutes an unusually extensive recording, but, significantly, it's not actually much longer than "The Call Up." Had "The Magnificent Seven" been chosen as its lead-off single, the fortunes of *Sandinista!* might have been far better and the single itself might have climbed higher than no. 34. Instead, it was, on April 10, 1981, the third single from the album, by which time the psychology of public reception was all different. At the time of its release, the dub-style remixing of "The Magnificent Seven" employed on the B-side of that single—"The Magnificent Dance"—was still cutting-edge but this didn't cut much ice with UK Clash fans ever-vigilant about their heroes' VFM stance: that this was no less than the third single culled from *Sandinista!* was bad enough, but that it didn't even have a "real" song on the flip was an insult.

The "Magnificent Seven" single had had to wait in line behind, insanely, "Hitsville UK." The coupling of the latter on January 16, 1981, with "Radio One"—another piggyback ride to a white audience for Mikey Dread—made for the weakest Clash single to date and indeed the poorest UK chart placing, a pitiful no. 56.

Sandinista! reached no. 19 in the UK album chart. Perhaps never fully explored or recognized is how remarkable was its achievement Stateside, where it was released in January 1981. At $15, its retail price in a market where LPs tended to be priced between eight and nine dollars was not as big a bargain as it was in the UK. Moreover, it had to contend with a campus culture where students would pin notices to bulletin boards offering to tape a selection of the album's choice cuts for a few bucks. Despite this and a hardly amenable media—U.S. radio was very conservative at the time—it climbed to no. 24, three places higher than *London Calling* had upon its January 1980 release.

By coincidence, both The Clash and The Jam sat out 1981 album-wise. The two groups were by now the clear leaders of what remained of the punk movement.

Although The Jam had undergone a musical and philosophical conversion via The Sex Pistols, they didn't copy the Pistols except in spirit. In being idealistic rather than nihilistic, The Jam instead took after The Clash. The same applies to Stiff Little Fingers, Sham 69, The Ruts/Ruts DC, The Members, Penetration, Chelsea, 999, and all the other groups of the era addressing in song the state of the United Kingdom in their natural accents.

The May 12, 1977, issue of *Sniffin' Glue* contained a Paul Weller statement never to be lived down: "All this 'change the world' thing is becoming a bit too trendy . . . We'll be voting Conservative at the next election." Weller variously claimed in later years that he was goaded by a mischievous PR or that he was taking the piss, but it wasn't his only quote of the period suffused with unambiguously Tory values. He told another punk fanzine, *48 Thrills*, "The Labour government will want everything state-owned soon." It only compounded in their detractors' eyes various other things that made The Jam a joke, regardless of the excitement and finesse of their music. Their retention of their smart mod suits made them seem the formally dressed kid at the school disco. It also made painfully transparent the pre-punk, conventional musical background which all punk bands possessed but pretended they didn't. That they were from a London suburb was also a black mark against them. ("I know I'm from Woking, and you say I'm a fraud," Weller felt compelled to write in "Sounds from the Street," before anxiously asserting that his heart was in the city.) That The Jam followed up their excellent May 1977 debut album *In the City* after just six months with the mediocre *The Modern World* had all the hallmarks of a group disgracefully trying to ride the last remnants of a New Wave they suspected was about to go flat.

Yet by 1981, for any Briton weaned on punk, it was The Clash who were the joke. The Jam, meanwhile, were the most beloved band in the land.

The Clash and The Jam were not an either-or proposition to many "kids." Although, as "(White Man) in Hammersmith Palais" indicated, there was a not-entirely-friendly rivalry between the two bands, to the public they seemed bookends. They were the two main (i.e., best) standard bearers for punk. From this end of history, the two groups can even be posited as history's last-ever great rock 'n' roll bands. However, with The Clash in the early 1980s increasingly an object of ridicule, there arose at the time an issue of ascendency.

American fans remember this period as a triumphant one in The Clash's career, culminating in them becoming a mainstream media buzz as their fans rioted in Times Square in fury at the threatened fire-hazard-related cancellation of their concerts at Bond's Casino in mid-1981, and The Clash took on the mien of the cavalry crossed with Robin Hood by agreeing to perform gigs at the venue (seventeen consecutive dates) until all ticket obligations had been met. So large did The Clash feel that this incident loomed in their mythos that, at the time, they were talking of calling a (never released) cinematic Clash venture *Clash on Broadway*. As long as ten years later, they gave their audio box set that title. Several years beyond *that*, asked in an interview the highlight of The Clash's career, Jones cited the time they had closed down Times Square.

Yet the Bond's affair had no resonance in Britain: not only was it a little-reported incident in a faraway land, it was one that perfectly exemplified the way The Clash seemed to be neglecting their home fans. (What the fackin' 'ell were they doing in Times bleedin' Square? Where was that, anyway?) This neglect, the increasing risibility of their clothing, and the declining power of their music was something for which they were paying not just in worsening chart positions but in a crescendo of contempt. Although no strangers to UK music press ridicule, at that juncture barely a week went by without a snide anecdote in music papers about their managerial, recording, drug, image, or sales misfortunes. Strummer complained to Paul Rimbali of the *NME* in 1981 of his publication, "They have a cupboard with a ruler in it which is called the Clash standard of honesty and truth . . . and they take it out and measure us with it . . ." In 1982, the singer told Charles Shaar Murray of the same paper, "There really seems to be something against us here . . . since we started going round the world."

Such was The Clash's unstoppable downward spiral that by the time of a planned British tour to promote their fifth album, *Combat Rock* (1982), interest in them had so declined in their home country that Strummer had to stage a disappearance to drum up ticket sales. Significantly, that year had started in triumph for the band who were overtaking them: January saw The Jam issue the double–A sided single "Town Called Malice"/"Precious," which not only sailed to the number one spot but saw the three-piece granted the symbolic accolade of being the first act to be allowed to "perform" two tracks back-to-back on *Top of the Pops* since The Beatles had proffered "Day Tripper"/"We Can Work It Out."

The new critical and commercial darlings in the UK seemed to be everything The Clash once claimed to be. The Jam were fulfilling all the promises of punk not just by securing number one records with social commentary sung in their own accents but also by keeping their protest to recognizably British terrain. "Town Called Malice" was a case in point, a brilliantly observed lower-waged tableau set to a Motown backing. Rather than being seen as parochial, they were felt to be a down-to-earth antidote to The Clash and their global gallivanting. Additionally, The Jam's dress style—they'd abandoned the suits for a smart-casual look—was a refreshing contrast to The Clash's mixture of cool-dude Americana and urban guerrilla posturing. Moreover, while The Jam were not averse to writing about their relationship to either the critics ("This Is the Modern World") or their fans ("Start!"), that they were not the sort of group to mythologize themselves via anthems was another factor in their favor for those a little tired of The Clash's (increasingly questionable) belief that they were the epicenter of popular music.

The Jam's success was not solely predicated on protest and Englishness, however. By those rules, Sham 69 would have been top dogs before their 1979 split. Following *All Mod Cons*, The Jam assumed an aura of greatness. *Setting Sons* (1979) was an examination of a class-bound and dilapidated Britain, and its sad timbre didn't prevent it being anthemic, courtesy of fine melodies and sweeping production. It spun off the single "The Eton Rifles," a smoldering depiction of class warfare that improbably became a top three single. Even more improbably, their scorching hard rock denunciation of militarism, "Going Underground," sailed to the top early the next year. If there was a suspicion that this was engineered by their record label Polydor—who delayed the release of the record by a week to ensure a point-of-sale spike—the fact that none of the remainder of their officially sanctioned singles over the following 2¾ years scored any lower than no. 4 showed that their success was far from being built on sand. *Sound Affects* (1981) was less thematically ambitious than *Setting Sons* but once again rock-solid in quality. Moreover, The Jam were not afraid to write love songs, and the quality of material like "English Rose," "Liza Radley," "Monday," and "But I'm Different Now" suggested that The Clash had made a mistake in denying their art this particular dimension.

Aside from "Should I Stay or Should I Go," The Clash would only return to the territory of the love song on a little-known adjunct to their canon titled *The Spirit of St. Louis*. This 1980 Ellen Foley album, recorded directly after the *Sandinista!* sessions, constitutes—apart from yet another Mott The Hoople connection: Ian Hunter had co-produced her previous LP—a very interesting digression in The Clash's career. Produced by Jones and featuring the playing of all four Clash members, it sees Strummer and Jones—who wrote six of the selections, with Tymon Dogg composing most of the others—exploiting an opportunity to experiment with their songwriting. The Clash correspondingly took the chance to branch out in the type of music they were prepared to tackle. The experiment the album comprises is not completely successful, but that's mainly due to Jones's typically amateurish production.

The album is ornate and dominated by ballads, one of which is even called "Torchlight." The overwhelming timbre is that of European theatrical pop merchants like Jacques Brel. The extent of Joe and Mick breaking out of their self-imposed Clash parameters is demonstrated by the mind-boggling title of "The Death of the Psychoanalyst of Salvador Dali." One of the songs—"The Shuttered Palace"—is a unique Clash-related creation. Transposing pronouns would not enable a man to sing what is a distaff song through and through, one which finds the narrator chiding her lover for a public machismo with which he dispenses in the boudoir. As such, it stands as one of the most impressive of all Strummer/Jones collaborations.

5

A PARADOXICAL SUCCESS

The first Clash single of 1981 not to be lifted from an album hardly helped stem the tide of their commercial and perception misfortunes. "This Is Radio Clash," released on November 20, has an angular, stuttering funk groove that is authentic, not cultural tourism, and the lyric crackles with witty lines like "This is Radio Clash—cashing in the Bill of Rights!" Yet the production is so in-your-face—the continuous, heavily echoed hand claps being particularly wearying—that it undermines the proceedings. The song's self-obsession was also the kind of thing currently turning people off the band.

The B-side, "Radio Clash," sounds like a remix of "This Is Radio Clash" but is actually the second half of a very long song. Considering that the ending of the A-side was something of a relief, there can't have been many who turned it over much. A 12-inch version of "This Is Radio Clash" featured two remix versions of the title track: "Outside Broadcast" and "Radio 5." The vainglory inherent in such a proliferation of versions of a not-very-good song was the type of thing giving The Clash an air of the ridiculous.

Can we get that world to listen? Not judging by the chart performance. The record climbed only as high as no. 47.

The first sessions for The Clash's fifth album, ultimately titled *Combat Rock*, took place in early September 1981 in the Ear Studios rehearsal room, located near Jones's old stamping ground of the Westway. These sessions doubled as rehearsals for their next live dates. After the completion of said dates, the recording—much to Strummer's disgruntlement—relocated to Electric Lady because Jones was anxious not to be parted for too long from Ellen Foley.

Recording work was completed in early 1982. Jones, who by now usually acted as de facto producer during the making of the record, initially wanted to release a double album containing fifteen tracks (none of which, incidentally, was "Overpowered by Funk"). That most double albums of the period contained around twenty selections indicates Jones's growing penchant for extended tracks more resembling groove than song in which he could use the effects pedals with which he was increasingly fascinated. The rest of the band were dismayed by this, as was Bernard Rhodes, who had at the band's invitation returned to the management helm in February 1981.

Another problem was the mix. Remixes were attempted but were done on the move in foreign studios as the band fulfilled live commitments. Finally, the decision was made by Jones's colleagues that he wasn't up to the job, and world-famous producer Glyn Johns, who had worked with luminaries like The Beatles, The Rolling Stones, and The Who, was brought in to provide both the final mix and edits. In Wessex Studios, Strummer and Johns (but not Jones) set to work creating an album that Strummer was openly acknowledging in interviews would be designed to sell. The number of tracks was scaled back to turn a double album into a one-disc set. Of those tracks that remained, running times were brutally cut, with songs losing not just codas but entire verses. Vocal re-recording was done on the tracks deemed commercial enough to be singles, while drums and guitars were brought forward in the mix to make the album acceptable to American radio. The music was also stripped of the sort of production bloops and squeals beloved of Jones.

There's little doubt that all of these things were necessary both artistically (compare the sonic warmth of *Combat Rock* to the miserably freezing *Sandinista!*) and commercially (any more VFM gestures would have bankrupted The Clash, just as, in 1982, it would their now-former management team Blackhill). Yet in their quest to regain lost ground The Clash went beyond practical into the realms of mercenary. The loss of integrity of which The Clash had been accused, often unfairly, throughout their career now actually—by their own terms—did happen.

They agreed to play second fiddle on a string of dates to The Who, a member of the supposedly discredited rock dinosaur generation, and furthermore in the sort of stadiums they had always claimed created a regrettable barrier between artist and fan. When the *NME*'s Paul Du Noyer went to visit The Clash as they played support to The Who at Shea Stadium, New York, he found them sheltering in their dressing room "two young security guards" who had "argued with their employer over whether they could keep their red plastic jackets." He also found Strummer candidly stating of The Who, "I have to say that the newer stuff they're doing doesn't get to me like the old stuff." While such things maintained their men-of-the people aura (no other group would so bite the hand that fed them), it was significant that none of the Who dates were in The Clash's homeland: they knew they would be ridiculed and that the move might even be commercially counterproductive in Britain.

Combat Rock spawned multiple singles ("This Is Radio Clash" transpired to the final stand-alone Clash single) and came with gimmicky free gifts such as stickers and stencils. "Rock the Casbah" (June 11, 1982, no. 30) featured a substandard B-side in the form of "Long Time Jerk," a song that sounds almost like a sequel to *Sandinista!*'s "Rebel Waltz" but doesn't have that track's haunting qualities, not least because of a quintessentially bleep-bloopy production by Jones, who still held sway on what might be termed non-important tracks. However, their September 17, 1982, release didn't even have the courtesy to exploit the fans by throwing on a previously unavailable B-side. The cut-down version of the parent album's "Straight to Hell" that featured on the other side to "Should I Stay or Should I Go" (no. 17) would seem an anti-enticement if anything and the sort of philistinism that would have caused an embolism in the Clash camp if imposed by the record company. Yet the record was thought worthy of being made a double–A-side.

In an apparent volte-face over their opposition to crass music industry commercialism, there was even at one point a plan to market Clash Clothes based on their latest militaristic look. Kosmo Vinyl offered the feeble justification that if anyone should make money from their image it should be The Clash. Although that doesn't seem to have reached fruition, latter-day Clash member Vince White has recalled being told that the Clash camp made a considerable amount of money from merchandising.

And could the fact of Strummer getting his teeth capped have been part of this strategy to play by conventional rock industry rules? Possibly not: he promoted the album with a startling, almost disturbing, Mohawk haircut. Either way, his singing voice was now noticeably clearer and more palatable to the mainstream.

Ironically, few in Britain could bring themselves to be outraged by all this apparent avarice and hypocrisy, simply because The Clash had long been written off as a joke. Many of those still interested in the band felt some sympathy, for these machinations smacked of a battered response to a self-imposed penury going right back to their entrée. "The Clash is everything to me. I have nothing else," Mick Jones told journalist Paul Morley in the *NME* of October 13, 1979. "I'm under the impression that I have given up everything else for it. I'm under the impression that I have lost everything: home, personal life, everything. So my dilemma in a way is that I resent the Clash." Although recent traumatic occurrences like a split with a girlfriend and a burglary played a part in his pain, he was also broke—at a point when The Clash were widely considered to be the incumbent Greatest Rock 'n' Roll Band in the World. The new hard-headed, businesslike attitude of the 1982/1983 Clash seemed less a betrayal of values than an exhausted insistence on their right to finally enjoy the fruits of their labor. If the music press didn't like the fact that some of the things they were doing would, in years gone by, have been considered by The Clash themselves to be a sellout, The Clash probably couldn't have cared less. Perhaps the fact of them having been unable to do anything right for the UK press over the last few years even motivated them to take a spiteful pleasure in this dramatic subverting of expectations.

The letters in the catalog number of *Combat Rock* are an implicitly anti-American reference to an El Salvadorian rebel grouping. Yet the album is very American. (When, several months before its release, it was announced that its working title was *Rat Patrol from Fort Bragg*, the groans of contempt at the military-esque Yankophilia could be heard all over the band's homeland.) The lyrics refer to New York as much as they do the UK, while the Vietnam War is mentioned or alluded to in no fewer than four of the album's twelve tracks. However, lyrics aside, there was no aping of American musical forms. The music of *Combat Rock* is indefinable: a new form that combines elements of rock, funk, folk, and ambient.

With the exception of "Rock the Casbah" and a couple of others, there is an overall lack of immediacy to this music, and the anthemic rockin' sound that was not long ago their trademark is almost complete-ly absent. Melodies are skeletal, even non-existent, something that is the result of the tracks' origins as lengthy mood pieces. Some of the tracks are so opaque lyrically and unresolved musically that they feel like the equivalent of abstract paintings. However, the "So what?" reaction dissipates the more one listens and warms to the insinuating rhythms and moving compassion. Symbolically, it is "Straight to Hell," one of the growers, that gradually reveals itself not just as the best track but as a bona fide Clash classic.

Nevertheless, one can fully understand *Smash Hits* reviewer Pete Silverton who on May 13, 1982, found it as "puzzlingly bitty" as *Sandinista!* and commented, "If you like the sound of someone scratching their head, you should like *Combat Rock*." Even the cover of the album seems confused. Although the new commercial realism had dictated it bear the first color Clash album photograph, Pennie Smith's picture of the band astride Thailand railway tracks is peculiar: Strummer has half his face covered by a hand; the others seem distracted—but not by the same thing.

Combat Rock contrived to become the most successful Clash work to date. The album reached no. 2 in their homeland, but that was almost immaterial in light of the fact that *Combat Rock* broke The Clash in the biggest music market in the world, climbing to no. 7 in the U.S. charts. Although The Clash's enthusiastic and business-minded touring of America helped considerably, the album's success still seems strange for a country where such left-field music, at that time, was usually commercially untenable.

"Know Your Rights" was released as the precursor single on April 23, 1982. This stripped-back, vise-tight track has the pace and tone of a Cossack dance, and packs a powerful punch through its stabbed, synchronized guitar attack. Strummer is listing three rights to which people are supposedly entitled: to not be killed, to food money, and to free speech. Except he claims they are an illusion, withheld by governments at their discretion. The lyric gives the impression of a first draft in its bittiness and naïveté, but the track's intense, lock-jaw rhythm is enough to carry the day.

The exclusive B-side of "Know Your Rights" was "First Night Back in London." A story of facing such oppressive treatment from the British police after foreign travels that it makes the protagonist want to immediately leave his homeland again, it's a brooding track that would have been a better choice for inclusion than some of the material on *Combat Rock*, even though Jones's mix is, as ever, heavy-handed. As a comeback, the single was commercially unconvincing, peaking at no. 43.

"Know Your Rights" provided the opening for *Combat Rock*. It's followed by "Car Jamming." As with several of this album's cuts, there is ostensibly no real reason why "Car Jamming" should ever command a second listen. The feeling develops of a bridge detached from the song to which it really belongs, for both musical reasons (there are modulations but no discernible chorus-verse structure) and lyrical ones (it's a stream-of-consciousness musing on the sights the protagonist observes while stuck in traffic, although as those sights include Vietnam vets reduced to homelessness, Strummer is conveniently given the opportunity to trade in his particular form of streetwise poetry). Yet something about it—the balmy air? Joe's smile-inducing singing?—draws us in and makes us happy to hear it again.

Jones both wrote and sang "Should I Stay or Should I Go," although Mitch Ryder & the Detroit Wheels's "Little Latin Lupe Lu" and/or "Sophistication" by The Sharks seem to have provided some of his inspiration. An anthem of hesitation about walking out of a love affair, it has parts rendered in Spanish for no other reason, it seems, than to show off Strummer's Spainophiliac tendencies again. It's slightly worrying that this attempt to return to their anthemic rock roots proves slightly beyond The Clash—its stiffness is already a world removed from the easy flowing rock 'n' roll of the *London Calling* album—but it's still pretty good.

Good enough, in fact, that when The Clash sanctioned its use for a Levi's TV commercial in the UK in 1991, it was re-released and became the band's only ever number one in their homeland. Unless, that is, we count "Dub Be Good to Me" by Beats International featuring Lindy Layton, a 1990 single masterminded by Norman Cook/Fat Boy Slim that brazenly sampled the bassline of "The Guns of Brixton." (The matter was settled out of court.)

The American B-side of the "Should I Stay . . ." single was "Cool Confusion," a piece of reggae which seems to start in the middle. Like most Clash B-sides of the *Combat Rock* period, its slightness is not helped by the electronic farts with which Jones riddles it.

"Cool Confusion" was not released in the band's home country at the time. The same is true of "The Cool Out," a remix of "The Call Up" which appeared on the 1981 American 12-inch "Magnificent Seven" single. (The latter's lead track was actually a remix of "The Magnificent Seven" titled "The Magnificent Dance" and its version of "The Magnificent Seven" was severely truncated.)

During the *Combat Rock* sessions, Headon was playing an increasingly smaller role in Clash recording due to his ever-worsening heroin addiction. "Rock the Casbah" was the glorious exception to the rule. The piano, bass, and, of course, drums were laid down by Topper while waiting for the others to arrive at the studio. The short piece of jaunty music was looped to make it a standard length, and Strummer came up with a caustic lyric about the fact that being a rock lover was punishable literally by the whip in fundamentalist Iran. This lyric, because it chimed perfectly with the anti-Iran sentiment then still prevalent in America only a few years after the national trauma involved in Americans being held hostage in their embassy in Tehran for 444 days, became The Clash's biggest-ever U.S. hit, climbing to number eight. Chauvinism aside, the single deserved its success, being catchy, nimble, and funny.

The June 1982 UK single version of "Rock the Casbah" showed what a remix should really be about. Mick Jones—perhaps to ensure popularity with dance-floor DJs as well as radio jocks—gave it a far more prominent rhythm track. This beefed-up version makes even the splendid *Combat Rock* original pale in comparison.

"Red Angel Dragnet" is a musically bizarre track, with an EQ-ing which produces "real" sonics, i.e., it sounds like an assortment of musical instruments playing at the same time instead of the sound painting that proper meshing engenders. There is no proper vocal melody: despite pretending not to be, it is spoken-word. The recitation in the middle by Kosmo Vinyl of Robert De Niro's "All the animals come out at night" speech from *Taxi Driver* is just a silly piece of Americana and another example of the band's enthrallment with movies that glamorize violence and psychosis. However, although the weakest on the album, the track has its musical virtues, particularly the pleasing counterpointing of chugging guitar riff and swelling organ.

Its gravest offense is contained in its lyric, inspired by the case of Guardian Angel Frankie Melvin, who in December 1981 became the first Angel to be killed while on patrol, apparently shot dead by a police officer. A Strummer composition, it sees Simonon taking lead vocal it would seem in the manner of Lennon/McCartney doling out a track for Ringo to sing on Beatles albums as a way to keep his fans happy. The alternative theory is that Strummer—just as he distanced himself from his sensitive songs by getting Jones to sing them—was anticipating some sort of backlash to his assessment of the Angels as "a fine thing."

In the Eighties, the debate on crime had been raging in America for several decades. It would fairly soon cease to be such a burning issue as the downturn in offenses that society had become resigned to never happening transpired to take place. This was the consequence of zero-tolerance law enforcement polices, higher incarceration levels, an abortion-ordained drop in the birthrate among racial groupings most likely to drift into crime or a combination thereof. Before that unexpected salvation, the nation was perennially apprehensive and pessimistic about the issue. Into this atmosphere of fear stepped the Guardian Angels, a volunteer organization who stated their objective as protecting the public in the absence of police resources to do so properly. The Angels were unarmed, but their dress code was paramilitary. Not only was the Angels's uniform not too dissimilar to The Clash's military fatigue outfits at this stage of their career, but their berets spoke to the fantasies of every person who'd ever had a Che Guevara poster on his wall, one of which was almost certainly Joe Strummer.

The Guardian Angels, though, were no leftists. Although not formally politically aligned, and although containing in their ranks many volunteers with good motives, they displayed an archetypal hard-right-wing indifference to due process. A common motif of their leadership in interviews was that the Angels never hurt anyone. Journalists who saw them beat up the likes of suspected drug dealers could, and did, state this to be a lie. Moreover, their most famous spokesman, Curtis Sliwa, was a self-aggrandizing fantasist, lodging false police reports to drum up publicity, and only admitting to them when the statute of limitations had passed. Former colleagues suggest that he was responsible for several more stunts, including a claim of an attempted rape of his wife Lisa, also then an Angel. That he is now a conservative talk show host—a profession synonymous with reactionaryism and bullying—is somehow both astounding and expected.

The ultimate vigilante action occurred in December 1984 when New Yorker Bernhard Goetz shot four black men on a Manhattan subway train after he alleged they attempted to mug him. Famously, he was acquitted of the entirety of a battery of charges brought against him except that of carrying an unlicensed firearm. Although Angels did not carry guns, both the actions by Goetz and the verdict of a jury drawn from the crime-weary populace of NYC among whom their brand of street justice had by now become popular have the whiff of a linear thread leading back to the Angels.

The Angels's popularity was located among the sort of working-class people who dismiss due process and prima facie evidence as the priorities of the "book-smart." Even though that was partly the result of the Angels operating in an era before camera phones, YouTube, and other potential means of exposing the brutal reality behind their knights-in-shining-armor image, it does bring up the issue of just how right-wing the proletariat often are. It also demonstrates that populism often causes people of leftist bent like The Clash to find themselves batting in an ideological ballpark normally distasteful to them.

Combat Rock's opus is side one's 5½-minute closer "Straight to Hell," a beautiful and moving meditation on the world's dispossessed. Punning on the Monopoly instruction "straight to jail," Strummer's vision flits all across the globe to identify the doomed-by-fate, from inhabitants of English industrial towns cast into unemployment to Vietnamese children sired by vanished GIs to the smack-addled poor of American ghettos. The lyric has the wordplay and colloquialism of beat poetry ("King Solomon he never lived round here"). Strummer's lonely vocal is bone-chilling, particularly the series of gasps he uses to lead into the final verse. Musically, the track snakes sinuously, carried by a kind of subdued bossa nova beat. Drums, in fact, are the only recognizable components: that the keening background noises are unidentifiable as instruments only adds to the song's sublime air of mystery.

The album version (more or less) of "Straight to Hell" featured on the 12-inch version of the UK "Should I Stay or Should I Go" single. The original recording featuring a verse excised from the *Combat Rock* version was one of the few good points about the *Clash on Broadway* box set.

Restored to *Combat Rock* at the Wessex remixing sessions, "Overpowered by Funk" sees Strummer playing on the fact that, before it became a term for a musical style, "funk" meant "objectionable." As the band maintain a (frankly, not that authentic) funk rhythm behind him, Strummer lists in a sort of jive-talk the irritants of everyday life, from urban isolation to overpopulation. "Don't life just funk you out?" is the defiantly depressed keynote line.

This gives way to a guest rap. The Clash by this point were comically susceptible to anyone with a semblance of an outlaw aura. This description applied to Futura 2000, one of the urban graffiti artists at the time becoming media stars. Futura 2000 designed the cover of the "This Is Radio Clash" single and handwrote the lyrics on the inner sleeve of *Combat Rock*. He turns out to be less eloquent with words than with a spray can, claiming to be as deadly as a vulture.

Note: The Clash backed Futura 2000 on 1982 single "The Escapades of Futura 2000," whose A-side was a collaboration between the artist and Mick Jones and whose B-side (same title, instrumental version of the A-side) was credited to Jones.

"Atom Tan" is a downbeat tale of nuclear catastrophe. The track has absolutely none of the vitality, or tunefulness, of the similarly themed "London Calling," something which one suspects Strummer and Jones taking alternate vocal lines is designed to disguise. The groaned, stretched-out refrain "Oh, he caught an even atom tan" hardly constitutes a classic chorus. However, once again the group's instrumental chops somehow prevent a negligible track from being completely pointless.

"Sean Flynn" is possibly the strangest thing in The Clash's corpus. Although it started life as an exploration of the disappearance of photojournalist Sean Flynn (son of movie star Errol) in Vietnam during America's war with that country, its disconnected, elliptical lines ("Each man knows what he's looking for") ensure that nobody would actually know this unless they'd read Clash members' explanations in interviews. It scarcely matters. It's an exotic, sultry mood piece sounding like it came straight off the sound track to a movie set in the Southeast Asian jungles. Gary Barnacle provides mournful saxophone before the track departs as mysteriously as it proceeded.

Although he doesn't get composing credits, from all accounts beat bard Allen Ginsberg collaborated with Strummer on "Ghetto Defendant," a composition about nineteenth-century French poet Jean Arthur Rimbaud. His spoken poem alternating with Strummer's singing is unexpectedly successful: Ginsberg's burr has a gravitas that the reedy raps of Futura 2000 and Kosmo Vinyl simply do not. The track has a genuine tune too and a good elongated, vibrating riff. Plaintive mouth harp underpins choruses which see Strummer asserting that heroin addiction, rather than the forces of darkness, are preventing the poet from instigating the revolution he desires.

The collaboration with Ginsberg came about after the poet had visited the band during their Bond's residency. The Clash provided backing to his poem "Capitol Air" on one of these dates. This recording was eventually released on the 1993 Ginsberg box set, *Holy Soul Jelly Roll: Poems and Songs 1949–1993*.

In "Inoculated City," a double-tracked Mick Jones identifies the reason for the perennial phenomenon of senseless conflict as being a chain of military command in which the individual components do not have the authority to question or overturn orders. The melody is appropriately a brisk, marching one.

The first pressing of the album featured an overdubbed cheerily voiced commercial for a toilet cleaner. One of the first examples of what would become known as sampling, it is, frankly, apropos of nothing except Jones's penchant for a hallmark of the unsanctioned rap remixes then proliferating on American radio. As it gave the track its title, said title was stripped of its meaning for a period when the commercial was erased as a consequence of legal action by the manufacturer of the implicitly ridiculed product. The commercial has in recent years been reinstated.

"Inoculated City" is a reasonably agreeable listen, but the most interesting thing about it is how it suggests that the natural shelf life of The Clash was coming to an end. The overwhelming feeling it provokes is that we have sort of heard this before: "The Call Up" was similarly pacifist and had the same marching sonics. The same theme of anti-militarism informs all or part of "The Card Cheat," "Ivan Meets G. I. Joe," and "Charlie Don't Surf." There are other examples of subject repetition in The Clash's catalog, notably the desperate plight of the unskilled worker, tower block living, the potential for riot, the dreariness of the inner city, and the dangers posed by nuclear power and weapons. While the group had incrementally broadened their subject range over the course of their career, the fact of this repetition shows that there were only so many iniquities against which to rail. The

Clash's preference for the general rather than the specific restricted their room for maneuver: narrowing the focus to individual injustices might have made for less of a sense of recurrence, and even for more powerful songs, but would have taken them into the area of Tom Robinson Band–style topicality for which they'd always shown a reluctance.

It all demonstrated a peril unique to a political band. Such a sense of decreasing returns somehow doesn't apply to musical artists who specialize in more conventional songwriting: love is a subject that seems to bear repeating in a way that tableaux of inner-city deprivation or denunciations of warmongering do not. That The Clash were, at this point, not long for this world has always retrospectively been put down to internal politics and chemistries. One wonders whether a subliminal sense of theme exhaustion also played a part.

This is a perishability distinct from that created by The Clash's increasing prosperity. After the already lucrative *Combat Rock* tour was over, The Clash were asked to perform at the Us Festival in San Bernardino, where their eighty-minute set earned them the sum of half a million dollars. By this point it seems fair to say that they had a certain interest in never again being caught in the middle of a riot, white or otherwise. How many more Clash anthems could be written from that side of the security fence?

When Mick Jones's post-Clash band—ultimately known as Big Audio Dynamite—first began playing live dates, a component of their set was a song called "She-Beast." An *NME* reviewer, taking exception to what he interpreted as misogyny, asked why it was that, in the litany of global injustices addressed by The Clash's catalog of songs, there had never been any complaint about the oppression of women.

"Death Is a Star," the closing track of *Combat Rock*, is almost that feminist Clash song for which the *NME* scribe yearned, but it doesn't quite make it. It was The Clash's response to the growing popularity of slasher movies, in which female characters were disproportionately slaughtered, especially—in an example of incongruous and twisted morality—sexually promiscuous ones. Unfortunately, only band interviews yielded this fact, the vague lyric talking merely of someone watching "the bad go down again" while smoking in a dark cinema. As in "Red Angel Dragnet," there is also some dissociative semi-spoken-word poetry which only serves to crank up the opaque quotient.

Headon uses brushes and Tymon Dogg plays tasteful piano on a track that might have been an album highlight if only its components could be properly heard: the mix is so quiet that when the song is over it has the same wisplike qualities as a dream that slips from memory even as one tries to recall it. A weird closer to a weird album.

6

A SAD FINALE

By the time The Clash had finished touring *Combat Rock* in November 1982 (with a brief addendum of a handful of gigs in mid-1983), they were, it might be assumed, sitting on top of the world.

A half decade of struggle and setbacks—many of them admittedly their own fault—were now behind them. While they could be said to have compromised some of their ideals in reaching a place of financial and career comfort, there was no suggestion that they had betrayed their musical values: *Combat Rock* rose up the most conservative album chart in the world despite its English accents, political subject matter, and almost avant garde instrumentation. (That it often quickly found its way into American secondhand shops when purchasers discovered it contained few further radio-friendly anthems like "Rock the Casbah" doesn't diminish the point too much.)

Moreover, they had somehow contrived to rehabilitate themselves in Britain. In April 1982, Strummer disappeared on the eve of a British tour and the release of the *Combat Rock* album it was intended to promote. He turned up safe and well four weeks later. ". . . it was something I wanted to prove to myself: that I was alive," Strummer explained to Charles Shaar Murray in the *NME* on May 29, 1982. "It's very much like being a robot, being in a group." The frontman didn't publicly reveal the truth behind that burnout explanation until a 1988 appearance on UK music television program *Wired*: Bernard Rhodes had told him to do it as a stunt to drum up publicity. When he did make that revelation, the penny dropped for all those who remembered that back in 1982, week after week, ads for The Clash's UK tour dates were appearing in the music press long past the point where it would have been assumed all the tickets would have been sold. (One suspects it was only at this point that the band first fully realized that they were considered by many former British fans to be distant and absurd.) In the absence of knowledge of the cynicism that motivated it, something about the vulnerability inherent in the disappearing act turned The Clash from a joke that couldn't sell tickets into something resembling the men-of-the-people they had been at the beginning. The cancelled tour was rearranged and was a triumph. Their brace of gigs at the 4,300-capacity Brixton Fair Deal not only sold out but was such a seething, joyous affair that the band quickly added another date there. Snide music press comments about the group began to decline. Even the *NME* was converted. Richard Cook's review of the opening night at Brixton gushed about "purpose in every turn" and a "florescent razor's edge."

However, fissures had started appearing in an apparently rosy picture even before *Combat Rock* was released. Shortly after Strummer returned from his disappearing act, Headon was sacked. Strummer had become exasperated beyond endurance by the drummer's increasing unreliability and the way he was making a mockery of his anti-heroin lyrics. At the time, the official reason given for Headon's departure was "a difference of opinion over the political direction the band would be taking." Music journalists in the know about the drummer's habit were generally happy to toe the line/lie. With a U.S. tour imminent, there was little time to rehearse material with a replacement drummer. It was therefore the easiest option for The Clash to ask Terry Chimes to take Headon's place onstage and help promote an album that, ironically, Topper's "Rock the Casbah" broke Stateside.

It took The Clash 3½ years to follow up *Combat Rock*. It will be remembered that in roughly that span of time, they had released their first four albums. By the time that that follow-up album saw the light of day, several further revolutions had occurred in the lives of The Clash.

Chimes played his last gig with the band in November 1982. The real reason was not revealed at the time, but he explained in Danny Garcia's 2012 documentary, *The Rise and Fall of The Clash*, that rumblings he was hearing about Jones following Headon through the exit door made him uneasy: ". . . if it was gonna be a completely new band without Mick, it would be a whole new project and I didn't really feel like getting involved in a brand new band." Chimes was replaced by Pete Howard.

Although a surprise to those not aware of his drug problems, Headon's dismissal was as nothing compared to the earth-shaking quality of the announcement on September 1, 1983, that Strummer and Simonon had fired Mick Jones. The reason given was that "Mick Jones has drifted apart from the original idea of The Clash. In future it will allow Joe and Paul to get on with the job that The Clash set out to do from the beginning." Strummer and Simonon elucidated in subsequent interviews that Jones had become prone to increasingly prima donna–ish behavior and was barely interested in conventional rock music anymore. Although Jones has since admitted that he was indeed difficult, it was still a drastic move. As one critic pointed out, it seemed as inconceivable as The Rolling Stones jettisoning Keith Richards. (Although drugs were not mentioned as a factor, some noted the guitarist's increasingly cadaverous appearance, often a telltale sign of heavy cocaine use. Interestingly, for a brief while after Jones's dismissal, Strummer took an anti-drugs line in the press, disavowing the marijuana of which he had been a heavy consumer.)

Most observers agree that Strummer made the dismissal decision after prompting by Rhodes. Jones had, of course, almost been sacked from The Clash at Rhodes's instigation in 1978. That time, Rhodes's machinations to discard him ultimately resulted instead in his own dismissal. By the autumn of 1983, with Jones's diva airs if anything worse than they had been five years previously, Strummer had come around to Rhodes's way of thinking. One wonders, though, whether Jones's behavior had something to do with a couple of festering sores. One was the fact of having been assaulted by Strummer backstage in January 1980 after an altercation caused by his refusal to play "White Riot." The other was the humiliation of being forced to accept Rhodes back the year after that: not only had Strummer threatened to quit The Clash unless their former manager returned but, in the crowning humiliation, deputized Jones to make the overture.

The 1978 attempted dismissal of Mick Jones had been linked to the intriguing prospect of Steve Jones replacing him. Although the Sex Pistol had little of his namesake's compositional and arrangement genius, he was an exciting guitarist and, in his heedless, Artful Dodger–like behavior, the very essence of punk. If only Strummer and Rhodes had sought out Steve Jones this time around, too. That one of Mick Jones's replacements was Nick Sheppard of second-tier punk group The Cortinas seems to contain its own health warning. Another seems to lie in the fact that an additional guitarist in the form of Vince White was recruited to help fill the position one man had previously occupied.

There were other worrying signs. One of the first photos released of the new-look Clash saw them posed in front of a temp agency: their combat fatigues and grim expressions looked ridiculous against a backdrop of handwritten signs advertising telephonist and receptionist vacancies. Strummer was increasingly bombastic in interviews, announcing that his new five-man Clash would turn back the clock and recapture the punk fire whose abandonment by the group over the last few years he pronounced a mistake. His punk purism seemed old-fashioned for reasons other than it being a step backward: The Clash's image and rhetoric was increasingly macho and militaristic. ("In my mind I liken us to a new platoon," Strummer told Bill Holdship of *Creem*. "We're going to go and crawl out in front of the enemy lines, get fired upon and then look at each other to see how we're bearing up.") Such talk seemed antediluvian compared to the aura surrounding new idols like Boy George. Strummer publicly ridiculed him, but the Culture Club singer, by dint of being the biggest pop star in the world despite being openly gay and resembling a transvestite, was effecting societal changes that The Clash—for all their bellicose pronouncements and campaigning— had never wrought and never would.

After extensive touring, the new Clash finally had product in the shops in September 1985. The lead-off single for their new album, surprisingly, augured well for it: it was the best Clash song since *Sandinista!* Moreover, it was, at last, another Clash song explicitly about their home country.

"This Is England" is a track in the tradition of "All the Young Punks" and "Straight to Hell": a stately paced, heart-wrenching examination of despair, in this case that of the casualties of Margaret Thatcher's "economic miracle." Its tone is one almost of subjugation, begging the listener to heed the plight of the cities in the north of Britain, where hope is a forgotten emotion and violence and hatred everyday currency. Programmed drums and wedges of synthesizer strike a surprising note but chime with the dignified tone. In any case, a fat, snub-nosed guitar riff drives the message home in more traditional Clash style. Children's voices at the beginning tug at the heartstrings. Strummer completes the job by emoting, "I'm never gonna cry no more. . . ."

It has to be admitted that many in Britain would not find the anti-Thatcher polemic of "This is England" heartbreaking at all, but preposterous. By no means were all of those people "yuppies," the young, upwardly mobile breed about which the country had recently begun to hear. While it is true that never has a prime minister divided opinion in Britain like Mrs. Thatcher, it is in no way true that those divisions were along class lines. Many proletarians saw her as a savior and did not use quote marks when they spoke of an economic miracle.

Although The Clash's career began under a nominally leftist Labour government, the threat of a Margaret Thatcher–led, hard-right Conservative administration informed their music from day one, i.e., if things were bad now, how much worse were they were going to get? The reality of "Fatcher's Britain" when she was elected to power in May 1979 did, for The Clash, fulfill their worst nightmares. Thatcher cut public spending to the bone in the middle of a recession, sending unemployment skyrocketing. Her monetarist policy, in fact, was partly dependent on unemployment: in a country where inflation had hit 25 percent as recently as 1975, wage demands needed to be suppressed, and, for the Tories, one of the most effective ways of doing this was to make people fearful for their jobs. Moreover, the overmanning of industry that was making British firms uncompetitive needed to be rectified. By 1984, Strummer's anger about the high levels of unemployment engendered by Thatcher's policies was bottomless. He was to be found strutting the stage of the Brixton Academy née Fair Deal—microphone shaft slung across a shoulder, as was his new guitar-less wont—affirming that by the time of the next election ("ten fuckin' centuries away") there would be "nothin' up north."

Yet a discomforting thought occasionally popped to the surface of the minds of left-wingers who cheered such rhetoric: that Thatcher had succeeded in conquering the dragons that stalked the land during their childhoods and adolescences. By 1982, inflation (colloquially, the "cost of living," which the Clash had referenced in the title of one of their releases) was consistently down to single figures for the first time in almost a decade. It would largely remain that way. Meanwhile, courtesy of monetarism and of the outlawing of strikes without ballots and secon-

dary picketing, the number of working days lost through industrial action was 169,000 per month when "This is England" was released, down
from 900,000 a month when Thatcher became prime minister. The
downward trend would continue. This may not have been a consolation
to the unemployed—let alone people whose relatives had committed
suicide in despair at their jobless state—but that was not exactly the
same thing as a failed policy.

There were many other glimmers of discomfort for the left during
Thatcher's 11½ -year reign. Thatcher was in no way personally likeable
in the way of her American counterpart Ronald Reagan, but the reason
she secured three successive election victories for her party was that
there was little disputing that she was improving the financial lot and
the quality of life of most: the days when the lights regularly went out,
mass walkouts over petty infringements of union rules crippled productivity, and uncollected rubbish was piled high in the streets were gone
and never coming back. Nor was she the snob that her hoity-toity voice
suggested. The Conservatives under Thatcher were not the clichéd
class of privilege and smugness that led Strummer to coin the phrase
"Tory Crimes." Under her, they became less a party of inheritance and
more a party of meritocracy, opening up areas of employment previously denied people not in possession of the right school tie, most notably
in the stock exchange. It was striking how working-class accents began
proliferating in the media as an apparent consequence of the example
of her caste blindness. Through a mixture of cutting welfare and en-
couraging self-employment, she conferred a pro-enterprise bent to the
British character common in America but hitherto considered "pushy"
in the UK. While it has to be said that this went hand in hand with a
coarsening of the culture—it was notable in the Eighties how many
Britons seemed to feel they'd been given license to be personally self-
aggrandizing, even obnoxious—it meant that by the end of her tenure
the notion of the "wrong accent" was becoming a thing of history.

Thatcher sold off nationalized industries that, previously secure in
the knowledge that they could get away with any inefficiency or bad
workmanship by virtue of the safety net of government support, gave
rise to leaner, fitter, and more customer-responsive companies. The
end of the monopoly status of such organizations made if far more
difficult for utility workers to effectively hold the country to ransom
with industrial action, thus decreasing wage inflation. When she slashed

enterprise-deterring high taxation levels from 83 to 60, then 40, percent, it did not, as warned, lead to a loss to the Exchequer in receipts. She started allowing council tenants to buy their homes. Many felt that, because she did not embark on a new program of house building, this had a catastrophic effect on the availability of affordable accommodation. Indeed, during the Eighties, the homeless began proliferating on London's streets to levels not seen since Dickensian times. Yet council housing began losing its stigma. One of the reasons the World's End Estate, on which Strummer once lived and wrote songs, is now a far more pleasant place to live is that the right-to-buy scheme, of which many residents took advantage, instilled a proprietorial pride that renting a flat one was destined to never legally own could not.

If some leftists now grudgingly concede that, on balance, Thatcher was good for the British economy, and if some go even further by saying that the changes she wrought could not possibly have been made by a government run by the Labour Party because such polices would have been resisted by the very unions that funded it, they draw the line at accepting that she was admirable beyond the economic sphere. Such people continue to assert that Thatcher's administration was indefensible from a civil libertarian perspective. While it is true that she was often cruelly socially authoritarian—many still splutter with rage when they speak of police brutality during the 1984/1985 miners' strike— even there the picture is not clear-cut. It was Thatcher's Conservative government that, by introducing the 1984 Police and Criminal Evidence Act, required police officers to record interviews with suspects and witnesses. Before this, methods of gathering evidence had sometimes resembled those in Third World countries, leading to suspicions of many confessions being concocted in police station canteens. During its periods in power, the supposedly less authoritarian Labour Party had never been responsible for such a seismic shift in police practice, any more than their hatred of class divisions had impelled them to shatter class barriers in employment the way the Conservatives did with the "Big Bang" financial deregulation in the City of London in 1986.

Not all of these revolutions had been completed or were even under way in 1985, but by this point many of the people of whom Strummer felt he was a champion had abandoned the ideological ship on which he sailed. By 2002, however, the verdict could be said to be in. That year, this writer interviewed Strummer about the first Clash album (sadly one of his last interviews before his shockingly premature death two days before Christmas). The interview contained this exchange:

> *That bit at the end [of "Remote Control"] where you're singing "Repression", I mean that's kind of embarrassing isn't it?*
>
> Well it is. But then the times were hot. Yeah. The times excuse it. The tempo of the time.
>
> *Talking of the tempo of the time, the backdrop of the album, when you look back, does it kind of surprise you that this social backdrop wasn't actually Thatcher's Britain but it was actually a Labour government in power at the time?*
>
> I know. This was the real . . . I remember the three-day week. The blackouts. Was it the Grunwick strikes and pickets? It was pretty socio-politically active times.
>
> *Does it kind of surprise you looking back that that all happened under Labour?*
>
> The surprise is when you see a film like *Rude Boy*. The beginning of that, it looks like it's a hundred years ago.

Reading that now, Strummer seems to be avoiding the questions. By this point, he had long since moved out of the inner city, which he had once felt crucial to his songwriting, into the countryside. He had also elected to send his children to private school, something he kept very quiet. Moreover, he struck up a friendship with right-wing journalist, and later Conservative mayor of London, Boris Johnson. Perhaps by now he had concluded that the reason that times whose tempo was "socio-politically active" felt like "a hundred years ago" was actually because of beneficial factors in Thatcher's policies. Certainly, film director friend Julien Temple told Pat Gilbert of *Mojo* in June 2006 that Strummer "talked in the end about respecting Margaret Thatcher." Although he may not have ever actually voted Conservative, perhaps Strummer had also concluded—at least in part—that he and his colleagues had been wrong about Thatcherism. If so, he was clearly determined to "keep schtum" about that, too.

Whatever the debatability of the anti-Thatcher message of "This Is England," its dignity and quality was the reason its parent album came as such a bitter letdown. *Cut the Crap*—released on November 8, 1985—embraces both the posturing clichés and the cacophonous music "This is England" eschews.

The circumstance of the album's genesis seem bizarre, starting with the fact that Bernard Rhodes was the producer. The band would appear to have never all been in Weryton Studio, Munich, where it was recorded, at the same time. Rhodes erased material Strummer laid down in the latter's absence. Norman Watt-Roy played bass on more tracks than Simonon. Watt-Roy's partner in the rhythm section was not human: in the deepest irony after all Strummer's scorning—public and private—of Jones's beat-box leanings, *Cut the Crap* featured un-rock 'n' roll artificial drums. (Strummer expressed doubt that Pete Howard is on the album at all.) Another irony is that the two new guitarists don't even add up to one Mick Jones, although, again, that may be because they were dispensed with, synthesizers often audibly taking their place.

Strummer took The Clash on a bizarre busking tour of the UK in May 1985, after which he quit the band. He later claimed that Rhodes tampered so much with the *Cut the Crap* tracks—vari-speeding, adding electronic brass, drenching almost everything in terrace chants—that they were unrecognizable to him. Mathematically, this tampering might even justify the "Strummer/Rhodes" writing credit that Strummer was amazed to see given all songs on the finished product. However, Strummer can't claim to be completely blameless for the low quality and peculiar soundscapes of the album. Vince White later recalled his horror when Strummer enthusiastically played him "The Dictator," apparently oblivious of how incongruous and out-of-tune were its synthesizer overdubs. It was a product a broken Strummer refused to promote on its release, being more interested in distancing himself from Rhodes and apologizing to Mick Jones for sacking him. When he begged Jones to come back to the fold, Mick declined, having spent several months setting up Big Audio Dynamite (whose debut album appeared within a week of *Cut the Crap*), thus bringing the story of the band to a pitiful end.

If Strummer was shocked by *Cut the Crap*, it was as nothing compared to the reaction of Clash fans. In the wake of Jones's sacking, The Clash had decided to have another Year Zero, only this time the enemies of music with their bloated albums and self-indulgent experimentation were not ELP and Pink Floyd, but The Clash of the last few years. As Strummer explained to Richard Cook of the *NME* on February 25, 1984, "I go back to our first record and I like the writing style on that record. It's lean. Trim! Makes a point, then another song starts."

Strummer told Cook that *Sandinista!* was "brazen stupidity"; *Combat Rock* half half-good [sic], half-awful. Strummer's stated intention to take the band back to its roots was welcomed by many fans right up to the point that they found out that this meant a cartoon idea of punk. Some people had thought Strummer at twenty-four looked a bit too old for The Clash. At thirty-three, and now a father, he had put himself in the undignified position of spouting sentiments even more youth-oriented than in 1977. That those youth-oriented lyrics did not ring true, however, was for reasons over and above his relatively advanced years. The risible clichéd Americanism of the album title is representative. Strummer's rants on *Cut the Crap* are those of a U.S. youth. His protagonists traverse the slums in cars and have a penchant for "finger-poppin.'" American or British, the depictions of poverty are stylized and unconvincing.

The crowning glory of the faux punk aura is the sea of "yobbish" chanting in which almost every song's chorus is drowned. Symbolically, this had been the trademark sound of Sham 69, a band considered a caricature of The Clash. The trashiness was exemplified by the album cover, which simulated a poster glued to a piece of corrugated iron fencing bearing a picture of a sunglassed, Mohawked punk.

Buried beneath *Cut the Crap*'s sometimes ham-fisted production, often embarrassing lyrics, and frequently weedy music, there are worthy moments. Indeed, it's notable how superior Strummer's melodies are to the tunes on *Combat Rock*. None of this, though, can prevent it being overall a cringe-making self-parody which besmirches a great band's legacy. Needless to say, the unpromoted and critically unloved *Cut the Crap* achieved miserable chart positions: no. 16 in the UK, no. 88 in the U.S., the latter a staggering, and possibly record-breaking, turnaround from the top-ten performance of their previous album.

Where *Cut the Crap* is not dismissed as a joke, it is simply ignored: official Clash product like the *Clash on Broadway* and *Sound System* box sets and the *Westway to the World* documentary give the impression that there were no Clash releases after Jones's sacking.

"The Dictator" makes for a shocking album opener. The horror induced in listeners by this track's puny synthesized horn charts, oppressive chanting and glaring, quintessentially Eighties mix was profound. *This* was supposed to be a return to the snarling power of *The Clash*?

The lyric—one of only a few reproduced on the inner sleeve—proves to be an intelligent and quasi-chilling condemnation of a U.S. foreign policy that saw death squads as a legitimate means to protect a superpower's financial interests abroad, but the music in which this articulate message is dressed up is so fatuous as to almost completely deny the song emotional resonance.

On "Dirty Punk," as in many places, we are subjected to a mix wherein the lead vocal is almost buried, and, as if to compensate, what sounds like a hired drunken mob renders the chorus with minimum subtlety. However, the Ramones/"Janie Jones" blurred guitar riff is far more like the reaffirmation of the Spirit of 1977 that this album was supposed to be about. The guitar solo is pleasantly grungy, while the anthemic lyric is quite affecting.

Yet the lyric's reference to acquiring a "great big car" is a jarring note, putting one in mind of affluent America, where punk was merely a fashion rather than an expression of class despair. These touches of self-parody are what serve to make the five-man Clash a blurred Xerox of the band that recorded *The Clash*. In 1977, The Clash were creating punk as they went along. In 1985, they were conforming to what they imagined were its rules—and not even getting those right. With tracks like this, what the new-look Clash uncomfortably reminded one of was the new wave of punks that had started springing up in Britain at the turn of the Eighties.

Punk had always been explicitly anti-nostalgia: kicking over the traces of a moribund music scene and daring to call revered rebels old farts was its raison d'etre. Inconceivably, a few years after it had exploded, it bequeathed its own revivalists. That by 1980 the original punk bands were evolving into something less ideologically confrontational and less musically primitive was a source of some grievance to new bands like Blitz, Chron Gen, Discharge, The Exploited, and Vice Squad.

These groups might be termed third-generation punks, with The Sex Pistols the first generation (and lodestar) and every band inspired by them (even early converts like The Clash) second generation. They could also be termed the Punk's Not Dead generation after a phrase frequently heard at the time. The defiant resistance to progress inherent in that phrase was a symptom of a problem. In the hands of these new groups, punk ceased to be a spirit for change and began ossifying into a set of clichés. The image became a rigid uniform of studded leather jackets, tartan trousers, bondage straps, and spiked hair. The music was wrenched back to the brutal minimalism of 1976/1977, with all subsequent advances in style, musicianship, and production dismissed as going soft and selling out.

There were some new aspects. The snottiness that had been a manifestation of the original punks' disenchantment with both the music scene and the economy now hardened into something more sinister. It came as little surprise to some how the new punk melded so indistinguishably into Oi! music, practiced and consumed by racist skinheads. The other aspect the new generation added was Mohawk and Mohican hairstyles: not part of the original punk look, they are now a routine researcher's mistake when seeking to visually represent 1976/1977 punk in magazine articles and documentaries.

"We Are the Clash" is a new sort of self-aggrandizing Clash anthem. Aimed not at detractors in the music press or anywhere else outside the Clash family, it is a message to Mick Jones, who, following his dismissal, had let it be known that he considered himself the true custodian of the band's name. At one point (although possibly after this song's composition) he even began informing promoters that the band he was setting up with fellow exile Headon would bear the name The Clash. This was something that must have made Strummer rather uneasy. That he was touring with the new Clash without record company financial backing may have suggested to him that CBS/Epic felt that they might decide to confer legitimacy on Jones's putative Clash. After all, they could only issue records by one band with that title. In the end, Jones didn't pursue his threat of laying legal claim to the name.

Another Ramones-y riff and a chorus straight from the soccer terraces decorates a lyric in which Strummer manages to rhyme "Clash" with "trash" and "lash." Despite its reductio ad absurdum of Clash self-absorption, it's not bad, even if its rabble-rousing intent is undermined simply by the fact that the chorus chanting across the album makes every track sound like a tilt at an anthem.

A track known in concert as "Are You Ready for War?" was subjected by Rhodes to a buffoonish re-titling. Ironically, considering the self-consciousness of the two preceding cuts, "Are You Red . . .Y" recaptures the old anthemic Clash sound without even trying. There's too much bubbling synth and sequencer work for a traditionalist's comfort,

but this is a punchy, powerful, and (naturally) marching anti-war number, with great call-and-response sequences between Strummer and the
backing vocalists, whose parade-ground yelling is for once the appropriate ingredient.

The message of "Cool Under Heat" is the affirmation of life in the
face of adversity, territory explored so triumphantly, so recently by The
Clash in "I'm Not Down." It's tempting to perceive the contrast between the verses and the choruses of this track as representing the
conflict between Strummer and Rhodes. A good melody and a subtle
bongo-assisted groove dominate until we get to the choruses, where the
booming terrace chanting kicks gratingly in yet again.

"Movers and Shakers" opens with a piece of unconscious self-parody
that is quite probably the worst line ever to appear on a Clash record:
"The boy stood in the burning slum." From there, Strummer enunciates basically the same message as in the previous track. The last verse
plausibly celebrates the musician's life as a way out of poverty, but it's
difficult to take seriously Strummer also portraying the poor as heroic
figures for carving out a living as traffic light squeegee merchants.

"This Is England" opened side two. "They own the pack while we
play the three card trick" is the crux of following track. What this metaphor means is not quite clear but "Three Card Trick" seems overall to
be a rejection of the type of authoritarian law and order policies that
become popular in times of recession. The melody (especially in the
chorus) proves once and for all that Strummer was, at times, capable of
writing tunes on the level of the departed Jones.

"Play to Win" is a bewildering track. The verses are free-form, with
Strummer and his bandmates engaging in conversation that drifts in
and out of earshot but never into comprehensibility. These brow-fur-
rowing passages give way to soaring (and actually pleasantly melodic)
choruses in which the band, en masse, declare that they long for the
prairie of the wild frontier. Had this appeared on any other Clash album, we would have accepted it as an example of their propensity to
explore other musical styles and cultures, but the rural reference strikes
quite the oddest note among *Cut the Crap*'s evocations of urban decay.

Against a jostling rhythm track and synth runs peppered with brass
blasts, Strummer sings in "Fingerpoppin' " of dancing the night away
while seeking to identify the best girl in sight. The notion of a thirty-
three-year-old father strutting his funky stuff for the ladies is not as

gruesome as it may sound, but one really wonders where Strummer's head was at during this stage of his life if his notions of the proletariat were located in such stylized *West Side Story* territory.

"North and South" is parody to "This Is England" 's authenticity. Strummer sings, against a slow, would-be poignant backdrop, of an impending riot whose instigators have the objective not of destruction for its own sake, but a better life. In this, they are aided by the power of youth. Ahem. What saves this from sheer contemptibility is the same thing that provides the saving grace on much of the rest of the album: Strummer's sincerity and compassion. When the melody lilts and Joe talks of a woman and a man trying to feed their child "without a coin in their hand," we, against all our better instincts, feel our heartstrings given a wrench.

There may be a good song in "Life is Wild," but it's well hidden behind those ever-present rent-a-moron massed vocals and a crowded, exhausting mix in which—bizarrely—samples of previous tracks seem to be floating. It provides an approximately confused finale to a chaotic album.

The only genuine recorded legacy of the five-piece Clash is the songs "Do It Now" (the B-side of "This Is England") and "Sex Mad Roar" (the additional track on the 12-inch version of "This Is England").

Courtesy of overwhelming massed vocals from the get-go and its anthemic celebration of the underdog, "Do It Now" doesn't sound different from much of *Cut the Crap*.

"Sex Mad Roar" is a prime example of the way that the studio versions of the Jones-less Clash songs sometimes had arrangements, lyrics, or titles often almost unrecognizable to people who had seen the band live. "Sex Mad Roar" is one of the few feminist Clash songs but, like "Death Is a Star," possesses that status not because of its content but via public pronouncement, in this case statements made by Strummer from the stage (e.g., "This is dedicated to all the victims of the sex mad war, either woman or woman or woman!"—San Francisco, January 21, 1984). The song that had been known in concert as "Sex Mad War" appears not just to have had its title changed but to have been diluted. The lyric preserved for posterity by its commercial release has none of the anti-porn content claimed for it in live reviews. It's also somewhat hard to decipher, but what can be gleaned from the track sounds, if anything, like a lament about horniness, a fairly standard, ideologically neutral rock motif. The brisk and clean music is actually quite decent, if still burdened by those massed vocals.

7

REHABILITATION

Mick Jones performed and recorded with Big Audio Dynamite (designed, of course, to reduce to the acronym BAD) over the course of twelve years. This means he was in BAD a third longer than he was The Clash, even if BAD's personnel changed so thoroughly and repeatedly during that time that it brought into question whether it was a group or a solo project. The music BAD made was most certainly cutting-edge in its mixture of rock and hip-hop, and they even secured a couple of enjoyable hit singles in "E = MC2" and "Medicine Show." However, while *This Is Big Audio Dynamite* (1985) and *No. 10, Upping St.* (1986) were good albums, nobody will suggest they are classics, and after that opening brace the law of diminishing returns set in, not least because Jones's weedy, substandard production and his use of artificial drums never did justice to BAD's hard-socking intentions. One can, however, admire on one level his refusal to perform Clash songs throughout the entire life span of the group. BAD collapsed in 1997 when their record label refused to release their ninth album, at which point Jones effectively retired from making music for a decade. He subsequently performed and recorded with ex–Generation X bassist Tony James as Carbon/Silicon, after which he revived BAD.

Because Joe Strummer's solo career was hindered by a legal dispute with Sony, who had taken over CBS/Epic, he had only released three albums by the time of his 2002 death. They were enthusiastic, but noticeably lacked Jones's melodic skills. He did, though, engage in ample acting and sound-track work, even if he did seem to lose his enthusiasm for both. Both Jones and (eventually) Strummer ceased being *Top of the Pops* refuseniks in their post-Clash careers. (The ex-members of The Clash also allowed the program to air the promotional film for the 1991 re-release of "Should I Stay or Should I Go.")

Headon's post-Clash career was hindered by his heroin addiction. He stayed with Mick Jones's post-Clash band only long enough to see it go through a name change (from Real Westway to Top Risk Action Company/TRAC). He made a 1986 soul-inflected solo album called *Waking Up* that is quite well regarded—and impressive for the fact that almost all of it is self-composed—but that was the extent of the good news. Having already squandered his arguable status as greatest drummer of his generation, he proceeded to blow his *Combat Rock* fortune. Taking up a job as a mini cabdriver, he was known to, unsolicited, apprise fares of the fact that he had once been a rock star. He was reduced to homeless hostels before kicking his habit. Now on the straight and narrow, he is a wiser and mellower personality than he ever gave the impression of the potential for while in The Clash.

Paul Simonon was at one point prepared to participate in a post-Strummer Clash that Rhodes was intending to assemble in the manner of the worst example of pre-punk acts who—as personnel splintered—treated group names less as a means of enabling creativity than an opportunity to perpetuate a franchise. Mercifully, that last-dregs Clash never reached fruition. After attempting a post-Clash career with band Havana 3AM, Simonon concentrated on the painting gift that few had known about during the days of The Clash. He is now a successful artist, restricting his musical activities to dabbling with the likes of Gorillaz and The Good, the Bad and the Queen.

The Clash never formally regrouped. The closest it came to happening was *No. 10, Upping St*. BAD's second album saw the revival of the Strummer/Jones publishing credit. As well as co-writing some of the tracks, the pair co-produced the album. There was a serious, formal plan for a Clash reunion at a point Strummer estimated as "perhaps when the first Big Audio Dynamite left Mick," which would make it approximately 1990. It was stymied by Strummer's insistence that Rhodes resume his role of group manager. No doubt thinking an X-rated variant of "When will he ever learn?" Jones declined this suggestion. Strummer and Jones remained good friends, however.

Although a gathering of the classic Strummer-Jones-Simonon-Headon lineup would have been profoundly more worthwhile than the post-Strummer Clash, it's perhaps merciful that it too didn't happen. The group might have matured into something along the lines of U2—who co-opted their anthemic rebel rock for something more ideologically generalized to vast, decades-spanning success—but U2 had never nailed their colors to the youth-oriented mast of punk in the way The Clash had. There's nothing wrong with going bald, as Jones has, or emaciated as Headon, courtesy of his once drug-addled lifestyle, has. Nonetheless, The Clash exploited being young, thrusting, and beautiful for everything it was worth, and juxtapositions with their previous selves would have possessed a shock factor over and above such yore-comparisons suffered by veterans like Mick Jagger and Elton John. In addition, the idea that Strummer might no longer have believed what he wrote in Clash lyrics is further strengthened by his revelation in post-Clash interviews that he had been given pause by people who asked him what were the answers to the questions posed in Clash songs.

As well as being a sad coda to The Clash's career, *Cut the Crap* served to squander the goodwill extended to the band following Strummer's 1982 disappearance. They returned to a joke status in their homeland and remained like that for several years. Unexpectedly, though, their reputation was subject to a posthumous soaring.

Talk of betrayal of values and self-parody began to be forgotten once removed from the relentless scrutiny prompted by the fact of their existence. They were helped in this respect by changes in the music industry and society generally. A new atmosphere evolved in which rock's past was treasured instead of being dismissed as old hat whenever a new critical darling emerged. Symptoms of this change were box sets, *Mojo* and *Spin* magazines, and the massive success of the *ABBA Gold* CD. People now concerned themselves less with image than recorded legacy.

In many ways The Clash's rehabilitation was underserved. Not artistically—their legacy of great recordings is hardly in dispute for people with their hearing faculties intact—but in the sense of the Value-for-Money/Artistic Integrity ethos they once shouted from the rooftops. When it was stated by Strummer in *Sounds* magazine in 1979, "There will be no six-quid Clash LP, ever!," it was not only a gesture of defiance to CBS but to inflation and reality. Only someone as foolhardy as the twenty-six-year-old Joe Strummer who made that pledge would be up-set about the inevitable shattering of it. However, it is rather eyebrow-raising that The Clash have become just another Heritage Act, to use a music industry phrase not in existence in their lifetime. Once inclined to lament fellow musicians who turned rebellion into money, they (in collusion with CBS/Sony) did precisely that after their split. Of course, The Clash never took a vow of poverty, nor is there any reason they should have. However, it is objectionable that they paid less attention to tending properly to their catalog than to their royalties, something illus-trated by the various collections of Clash music that hit the shelves after their demise.

Excepting *Black Market Clash*, the first Clash compilation was *The Story of The Clash Volume 1*, originally released in 1988 as a double vinyl album and double CD. (The strange addendum has been given several explanations ranging from a genuine plan to have a live set as volume two to a sarcastic response to Sony vetoing the title *Revolution Rock* to the subtitle being Joe Strummer's semi-desperate attempt to assert that the story of the band was not yet over and that he might still be able to persuade Jones to re-form the group.) Compiled by Jones, it was a disappointingly standard "Best of" when it could and should have rounded up all the singles, B-sides, EP tracks, and rarities not yet avail-able on album, regardless of the inevitable omission of the type of hits and famous songs that make such releases more attractive to the casual buyer. The CD version retailed for £22.99, which seems expensive even from today's perspective. Former Clash-lover Robert Christgau was one of those disgusted. In *Village Voice*, he wrote, ". . . this two-disc repack-age could have been programed by a random-play button. It tells only one 'story'—they fought the corporation and the corporation won."

Even when in 1991 The Clash got around to compiling a box set—a format tailor-made for the mopping-up exercise—they spurned a per-fect opportunity to prove that, even posthumously, they still cared about the value-for-money issue that was once as crucial to them as the quality of their music. *Clash on Broadway* was a three-CD affair that stuck to the standard format of a mixture of previously released material plus a few never-heard-before live and studio recordings. This meant, of course, that their die-hard fans—who would already have the previ-ously released material—had to pay an exorbitant price merely to ob-tain the less than a dozen fresh selections (which were mostly pretty unspectacular themselves—including a protest song about Roger Moore's acting abilities). It wasn't even as if the band were merely dancing to the record company's tune: in a petty reprise of an argument a decade-and-a-half old, "Remote Control" was the only song from *The Clash* not included. Also petty is the fact that the set completely ignored the post-Mick Jones lineup: "This Is England" would have constituted a preferable final track—both artistically and historically—to "The Street Parade." The booklet's discography was appallingly bad: the list of American singles didn't even include their biggest U.S. hit, "Rock the Casbah," while the UK discography managed to invent a new variant of "This Is Radio Clash" in the shape of "Radio 6."

Additionally, *Clash on Broadway* revived old grievances about The Clash neglecting their home country. As well as the Americana of the title, the liner note contributions were by Americans with little cultural understanding of Britain. In the final insult, *Clash on Broadway* was given to the States first. In the fully 2½ years before a UK release, fans who wanted it were shelling out steep import prices. Both they and the British fans who waited for the UK release (RRP: £33.49) were, if they had already bought *The Story of The Clash Volume 1*, being double fleeced: the entire contents of that latter compilation, in one form or another, could be found on *Clash on Broadway*.

It's interesting that when six years later Polydor put together a Jam box set, it was pretty much perfect. *Direction Reaction Creation* featured the group's entire studio output across five discs.

Even when Clash compilations set out with the purpose of rounding up the rare and the obscure (e.g., *Super Black Market Clash, 1977 Revisited—a Collection of Rare Tracks and B-Sides, Twelve Inch Mixes*), there were always infuriating selection polices. This resulted in a fairly substantial list of tracks that could only be obtained by hunting down vinyl, a list not made completely redundant by 2013's *Sound System*.

The impression gained from all of this was that The Clash thought none of their previous stances mattered anymore simply because they originated so long ago. Yet if being conscientious about value for money and quality of product mattered from 1977 to 1985, why should it not matter now? As Marcus Gray said in his 1995 Clash biography *Last Gang in Town*, "There is no statute of limitations on integrity."

There was at least one Clash member willing to break ranks by speaking up about this. Headon said to Billboard.com in October 2008, "I don't think there's any need for another Clash product on the market . . . Joe [Strummer] would be turning in his grave if he'd seen what the band have become today. You know what The Clash originally stood for and we don't stand for that anymore. The Clash were 30 years ago. None of us are really that bothered anymore and so people are moving in and making money out of it."

His comments came on the occasion of the release of the concert album *Live at Shea Stadium*, the DVD *The Clash Live—Revolution Rock*, and a lavish book, *The Clash by The Clash*, of which he said, "I was against the book coming out because it's a transcript of [2000 documentary] *Westway to the World* with photos."

By the time of the release of *Sound System*, he'd changed his tune a little. This twelve-disc project rounded up and re-mastered most of The Clash's recorded studio output, with the only omissions debatable pleasures like extended mixes and, of course, Strummer's post-Jones Clash records. The euphoria of working with his old colleagues again, plus the fact that *Sound System* was a worthier project, led to the drummer telling *Vive Le Rock!* magazine, "It's pure Clash quality as it was back in the day. If we wanted to make money we'd have re-formed or we'd get a replacement for Joe like Queen did with Paul Rodgers. This is just producing something that is the ultimate Clash collection. You look at the price of some box sets . . . When you see it, you'll realize what great value for money it is."

Perhaps so, but it came housed in a replica of a ghetto blaster stuffed with the sort of merchandise (owner's manual, fanzines, dog tags, badges, stickers, poster, cigarette-effect poster holder) that The Clash once scorned. It was also wreathed in the sort of reverence for the past to which punk was once the antithesis. The product retailed for a princely £100 or more.

There is a school of thought that states that the game has changed in ways unimaginable in the Seventies and Eighties and that, in the Internet file-sharing age, the only way to combat the contempt of the public for intellectual property rights may be to offer them a beautiful artifact—like *Sound System*—that no geek can download. Even leaving that aside, though, the political certainties in which the notion of a "sellout" was forged have been undermined.

Following the creation of the welfare state and the establishment of the post-war consensus, it was sometimes remarked by British right-wingers that what constituted modern conservatism would have been condemned in the past by conservatives as something approaching communism. A similar repositioning of values occurred after the Seventies. Margaret Thatcher once remarked that her most enduring legacy was New Labour, the remolded version of Britain's most left-wing party that Tony Blair was given permission to create by a membership traumatized by repeated electoral rejection of their polices: continuous Conservative rule in Britain following Thatcher's first victory ultimately lasted eighteen years. In America, there was a similar turning away of the left from the notion that the state was the only or even main way to protect the underprivileged. The collapse of Soviet Communism in the late Eighties only further strengthened the idea that collectivism had failed, even if it didn't quite herald the end of history that one academic famously mistakenly asserted. Social Democracy would continue to be a force in Western Europe and its equivalent, Liberalism, would continue to exist in the States but in both cases in much watered-down versions. Although people did very quickly become embarrassed by the excesses of the free market–leaning Eighties ("That's *so* Eighties" could be heard as a condemnation of flashiness or avarice not far into the Nineties), it did not mean that people wanted to return to a time when it was reflexively assumed to be the duty of the government to improve their lives—with all the negative impact on enterprise and taxation levels that entailed. New generations were brought up who never heard entrepreneurialism and aspiration dismissed as the traits of someone who was giving in to "the system" or who was selfish.

In such a less confrontational atmosphere, the pledges and slogans of bands like The Clash were massively reduced in impact, even validity. The days were over when people got angry about the release of a single their favorite rock group had not authorized, or the release of a record by a rock group that included free stickers designed to persuade a fan to buy songs he already possessed, or the consenting by a band to play support to a group who were perceived to possess different values. The reaction to such matters was not to consider it a betrayal but a fact of life in a capitalist society that might be occasionally tawdry, sometimes unjust, but would appear to be better than any alternative. If one did object to the product or service offered, the rational response was not to brood over or complain about it but to exercise the choice to not purchase it.

Meanwhile, lavish examples of merchandise like box sets are not necessarily considered elitist for being out of reach of the low-waged. Consumer goods have fallen in price in real terms —partly because of economies improved by the conservative era's shake-out of bad practice, partly because of supply-and-demand patterns for which no political faction can take credit.

During The Clash's lifetime and for many years afterward, the only book on the band, with the exception of chord books and a couple of slim cuttings jobs by Barry Miles, was Pennie Smith's brilliant collection of photographs *The Clash Before and After* (1980). Following Marcus Gray's *Last Gang in Town*—a 1995 tome that debunked many of the myths the band had perpetuated without straying into Albert Goldman maliciousness—there was a flood of Clash biographies and critical analyses, a flood accelerated by Strummer's death in 2002. The very fact that a group that existed as a recording entity for merely eight years (five, if you discount the *Cut the Crap* lineup) is the subject of approaching a dozen substantial books is another yardstick of how the world decided after The Clash's demise that it missed what it no longer had.

It's certainly interesting to see that The Clash's esteem has quietly but unmistakably come to eclipse that of The Jam. The ignominious reputation of The Clash when they expired was a stark contrast to the mood among music lovers in Britain when The Jam split. Paul Weller decided to bring the curtain down on the Woking three-piece at the end of 1982, feeling it had gone as far as it artistically could. A series of farewell concerts and a good-bye EP were greeted rapturously by public and critics alike. Their act of falling on their sword—in contrast to the way bands like the Stones and The Who insisted on keeping the show on the road long past the point where they were considered to have anything worthwhile musically to say—was seen as a confirmation of the cast-iron integrity for which The Jam had been celebrated.

Nobody would have imagined from that state of affairs the way the reputations of both groups would fare subsequently. Although The Jam could hardly be said to be discredited, their holy aura began to fade shockingly quickly after their disbandment. As Paul Weller plowed a new furrow with The Style Council—a sort of "continental" Jam: Estuary accent and social commentary retained against a backdrop of café culture sophistication—his previous group fell off the critical radar. The paucity of discussion of The Jam hardly suggested the status of one of history's major recording artists which it seemed inarguable that they possessed when extant. It was as though, now that both they and the times they had so acutely explored had become a thing of memory, it was incumbent on people to address The Jam's artistic legacy in less gushing terms. Very rarely is a Jam album now to be found in the upper echelons of critics' polls, even ones organized by UK publications.

Conversely, the suspicion and ambiguity contemporaneously surrounding the reception to almost anything The Clash released from *Give 'em Enough Rope* onward has been transformed into a consensus that theirs is a formidable body of work. The first and third Clash albums—*The Clash* and *London Calling*—are universally regarded as iconic works that can stand beside the classics of The Beatles, The Rolling Stones, Bob Dylan, and the other immortals of the medium. Many agree that The Clash are third behind only The Beatles and The Rolling Stones as the greatest group of all time.

The Clash's rhetoric was frequently silly, self-dramatizing, and unachievable. Rock artists, however, are not ultimately judged on such things, but rather their body of work. The Clash's recorded legacy is as grand, powerful, and exciting as one would expect of a band whose slogan came to be "The Only Band That Matters."

SELECTED READING

BOOKS

Bracknell, Steve; Humphries, Patrick. *Top of the Pops 50th Anniversary* (McNidder & Grace, 2013)

Buckler, Rick; Foxton, Bruce; Ogg, Alex. *The Jam Our Story* (Castle Communications Plc, 1993)

Burchill, Julie; Parsons, Tony. *"The Boy Looked at Johnny": The Obituary of Rock and Roll* (Pluto Press, 1978)

Chimes, Terry. *The Strange Case of Dr Terry and Mr Chimes* (Wilkinson Publishing Pty, 2014)

Clash, The. *The Clash Songbook* (Wise Publications, 1979)

———. *The Clash Second Songbook* (Riva Music, 1979)

The Clash Retrospective: A Visual History (Retro Publishing, 1996)

Coon, Caroline. *1988: The New Wave Punk Rock Explosion* (Omnibus Press, 1983)

Fletcher, Tony. *The Clash: The Complete Guide to Their Music* (Omnibus Press, 2005)

Gambaccini, Paul; Rice, Tim; Rice, Jonathan. *British Hit Albums* (Guinness Publishing, 1990)

———. *British Hit Singles* (Guinness Publishing, 1993)

Garcia, Danny. *The Rise and Fall of The Clash* (Thin Man Press, 2013)

Gilbert, Pat. *Passion Is a Fashion: The Real Story of The Clash* (Aurum, 2004)

Gimarc, George. *Punk Diary, 1970–79: An Eyewitness Record of the Punk Decade* (Vintage, 1994)

Gray, Marcus. *Last Gang in Town: The Story and Myth of The Clash* (Fourth Estate, 1995)

———. *Route 19 Revisited: The Clash and London Calling* (Jonathan Cape, 2009)

———. *The Clash: Return of the Last Gang in Town* (Helter Skelter Publishing, 2001)

Green, Johnny; Barker, Garry. *A Riot of Our Own: Night and Day with The Clash* (Orion, 1997)

Grundy, Stuart; Tobler, John. *The Record Producers* (BBC, 1982)

Hennessy, Val. *In the Gutter* (Charles River Books, 1982)

Knowles, Chris. *Clash City Showdown: The Music, The Meaning, and the Legacy of The Clash* (Pagefree Publishing, 2003)

Long, Pat. *The History of NME* (Portico, 2012)

Miles. *The Clash* (Omnibus Press, 1980)

Miles; Tobler, John. *The Clash: A Visual Documentary* (Omnibus Press, 1983)

Needs, Kris. *Joe Strummer and the Legend of The Clash* (Plexus Publishing, 2005)

Popoff, Martin. *Goldmine Standard Catalog of American Records 1948–1991* (Krause Publications, 2010)

Quantick, David. *The Music Makers: The Clash* (Unanimous, 2000)

Reed, John. *The Complete Guide to the Music of Paul Weller & The Jam* (Omnibus Press, 1999)

———. *Paul Weller: My Ever Changing Moods* (Omnibus Press, 2009)

Salewicz, Chris. *Redemption Song: The Definitive Biography of Joe Strummer* (Harper Collins, 2006)

Savage, Jon. *England's Dreaming: The Sex Pistols and Punk Rock* (Faber and Faber, 1991)

Smith, Pennie. *The Clash: Before & After* (Eel Pie Publishing, 1980)

Strummer, Joe; Jones, Mick; Simonon, Paul; Headon, Nick "Topper." *The Clash* (Atlantic Books, 2008)

Topping, Keith. *The Complete Clash* (Reynolds & Hearn, 2003)

Turner, Alwyn W. *Crisis? What Crisis?: Britain in the 1970s* (Aurum Press, 2009)

Whitburn, Joel. *The Billboard Book of Top 40 Albums* (Watson-Guptill Publications, 1995)

———. *The Billboard Book of Top 40 Hits* (Billboard, 2004)

White, Vince. *Out of Control: The Last Days of The Clash* (Moving Target, 2008)

Willmott, Graham. *The Jam: Sounds from the Street* (Reynolds & Hearn, 2003)

WEBSITES

en.wikipedia.org
http://clash.wikia.com
http://issuu.com
http://www.45cat.com
http://www.aceweekly.com
http://www.allmusic.com
http://www.bankofengland.co.uk
http://www.billboard.com
http://www.discogs.com
http://www.sexpistolsofficial.com
www.bbc.co.uk

SELECTED LISTENING

The Clash Discography

Note: UK releases except where indicated. Only important compilation albums included. Not included: reissues, guest appearances, various artists releases.

White Riot/1977
   CBS 5058 Released 18 Mar 1977

THE CLASH
   CBS 82000 Released 8 Apr 1977
   Side one
   Janie Jones
   Remote Control
   I'm So Bored with the U.S.A.
   White Riot
   Hate & War
   What's My Name
   Deny
   London's Burning
   Side two
   Career Opportunities
   Cheat
   Protex Blue

Police & Thieves
48 Hours
Garageland

Capital Radio [EP]
CL 1 Released April 1977 [mail-order only]
Side one
Listen
Interview—Tony Parsons—The Clash
Side two
Interview—Tony Parsons—The Clash
Capital Radio

Remote Control/London's Burning (recorded live at Dunstable)
CBS 5293 Released 13 May 1977

Complete Control/The City of the Dead
CBS 5664 Released 23 Sep 1977

Clash City Rockers/Jail Guitar Doors
CBS 5834 Released 17 Feb 1978

(White Man) in Hammersmith Palais/The Prisoner
CBS 6383 Released 16 Jun 1978

GIVE 'EM ENOUGH ROPE
CBS 82431 Released 10 Nov 1978
Side one
Safe European Home
English Civil War
Tommy Gun
Julie's Been Working for the Drug Squad
Last Gang in Town
Side two
Guns on the Roof
Drug-Stabbing Time
Stay Free
Cheapskates

All the Young Punks (New Boots and Contracts)

Tommy Gun/1-2 Crush on You
CBS 6788 Released 24 Nov 1978

English Civil War/Pressure Drop
CBS 7082 Released 23 Feb 1979

The Cost of Living [EP]
CBS 7324 Released 11 May 1979
Side one
I Fought the Law
Groovy Times
Side two
Gates of the West
Capital Radio

London Calling/Armagideon Time
CBS 8087 Released 7 Dec 1979

LONDON CALLING
CBS CLASH 3 Released 14 Dec 1979
Side one
London Calling
Brand New Cadillac
Jimmy Jazz
Hateful
Rudie Can't Fail
Side two
Spanish Bombs
The Right Profile
Lost in the Supermarket
Clampdown
The Guns of Brixton
Side three
Wrong 'Em Boyo
Death or Glory
Koka Kola

The Card Cheat
Side four
Lover's Rock
Four Horsemen
I'm Not Down
Revolution Rock
Train in Vain [originally not listed on sleeve]

London Calling/Armagideon Time/Justice Tonight/Kick It Over
[12-inch single]
CBS 12-8087 Released ?? Jan 1980

Bankrobber/Rockers Galore . . . UK Tour
CBS 8323 Released 26 July 1980

The Call Up/Stop the World
CBS 9339 Released 21 Nov 1980

SANDINISTA!
CBS FSLN 1 Released 12 Dec 1980
Side one
The Magnificent Seven
Hitsville UK
Junco Partner
Ivan Meets G. I. Joe
The Leader
Something about England
Side two
Rebel Waltz
Look Here
The Crooked Beat
Somebody Got Murdered
One More Time
One More Dub
Side three
Lightning Strikes (Not Once But Twice)
Up in Heaven (Not Only Here)
Corner Soul

Let's Go Crazy
If Music Could Talk
The Sound of the Sinners
Side four
Police on My Back
Midnight Log
The Equaliser
The Call Up
Washington Bullets
Broadway
Side five
Lose This Skin
Charlie Don't Surf
Mensforth Hill
Junkie Slip
Kingston Advice
The Street Parade
Side six
Version City
Living in Fame
Silicone on Sapphire
Version Pardner
Career Opportunities
Shepherds Delight

Hitsville UK/Radio One
CBS 9480 Released 16 Jan 1981

The Magnificent Seven/The Magnificent Dance
CBS A1133 Released 10 Apr 1981

The Magnificent Seven/The Magnificent Dance [12-inch single]
CBS A121133 Released 24 Apr 1981

This Is Radio Clash/Radio Clash
CBS A1797 Released 20 Nov 1981

This Is Radio Clash/Radio Clash/Outside Broadcast/Radio 5 [12-inch single]
> CBS A131797 Released 4 Dec 1981

Know Your Rights/First Night Back in London
> CBS A2309 Released 23 Apr 1982

COMBAT ROCK
> CBS FMLN 2 Released 14 May 1982
> **Side one**
> Know Your Rights
> Car Jamming
> Should I Stay or Should I Go
> Rock the Casbah
> Red Angel Dragnet
> Straight to Hell
> **Side two**
> Overpowered by Funk
> Atom Tan
> Sean Flynn
> Ghetto Defendant
> Inoculated City
> Death Is a Star

Rock the Casbah/Long Time Jerk
> CBS A2479 Released 11 Jun 1982

Rock the Casbah/Mustapha Dance [12-inch single]
> CBS A132479 Released 18 Jun 1982

Should I Stay or Should I Go/Straight to Hell
> CBS A2646 Released 17 Sep 1982

Should I Stay or Should I Go/Straight to Hell [12-inch single]
> CBS A132646 Released 17 Sep 1982

This Is England/Do It Now
> CBS A6122 Released ?? Sep 1985

This Is England/Do It Now/Sex Mad Roar [12-inch single]
  CBS TA 12 6122 Released ?? Sep 1985

CUT THE CRAP
  CBS 26601 Released 8 Nov 1985
  Side one
  Dictator
  Dirty Punk
  We Are The Clash
  Are You Red . . . Y
  Cool Under Heat
  Movers and Shakers
  Side two
  This Is England
  Three Card Trick
  Play to Win
  Fingerpoppin'
  North and South
  Life Is Wild

SUPER BLACK MARKET CLASH
  Columbia—474546 2 Released ?? Nov 1993
  1977
  Listen
  Jail Guitar Doors
  The City of the Dead
  The Prisoner
  Pressure Drop
  1-2 Crush on You
  Groovy Times
  Gates of the West
  Capital Radio Two
  Time Is Tight
  Justice Tonight/Kick It Over
  Robber Dub
  The Cool Out
  Stop the World

The Magnificent Dance
This Is Radio Clash
First Night Back in London
Long Time Jerk
Cool Confusion
Mustapha Dance

CLASH ON BROADWAY

Epic/Legacy E3K 46991 Released ?? June 1994 [U.S. release: 19 Nov 1991]

Disc one
Janie Jones (demo)
Career Opportunities (demo)
White Riot
1977
I'm So Bored with the U.S.A.
Hate & War
What's My Name
Deny
London's Burning
Protex Blue
Police & Thieves
48 Hours
Cheat
Garageland
Capital Radio One
Complete Control
Clash City Rockers
City of the Dead
Jail Guitar Doors
The Prisoner
White Man in Hammersmith Palais [sic]
Pressure Drop
1-2 Crush on You
English Civil War (live)
I Fought the War (live)
Disc two

Safe European Home
Tommy Gun
Julie's in the Drug Squad [sic]
Stay Free
One Emotion (previously unreleased)
Groovy Times
Gates of the West
Armagideon Time
London Calling
Brand New Cadillac
Rudie Can't Fail
The Guns of Brixton
Spanish Bombs
Lost in the Supermarket
The Right Profile
The Card Cheat
Death or Glory
Clampdown
Train in Vain
Bankrobber
Disc three
Police on My Back
The Magnificent Seven
The Leader
The Call Up
Somebody Got Murdered
Washington Bullets
Broadway
Lightning Strikes (Not Once But Twice) [live]
Every Little Bit Hurts (previously unreleased)
Stop the World
Midnight to Stevens (previously unreleased)
This Is Radio Clash
Cool Confusion
Red Angel Dragnet (edited version)
Ghetto Defendant (edited version)
Rock the Casbah
Should I Stay or Should I Go

Straight to Hell (unedited version)
The Street Parade [unlisted track]

FROM HERE TO ETERNITY [live album]
Columbia 496183 2 Released Oct 4 1999

Complete Control
London's Burning
What's My Name
Clash City Rockers
Career Opportunities
(White Man) in Hammersmith Palais
Capital Radio
City of the Dead
I Fought the Law
London Calling
Armagideon Time
Train in Vain
The Guns of Brixton
The Magnificent Seven
Know Your Rights
Should I Stay or Should I Go
Straight to Hell

LONDON CALLING—25TH ANNIVERSARY EDITION
Columbia 517928 3 Released 20 Sep 2004

Disc one
As per original *London Calling* track listing

Disc two
The Vanilla Tapes (rehearsal versions of songs)
Hateful
Rudie Can't Fail
Paul's Tune
I'm Not Down
4 Horsemen
Koka Kola, Advertising & Cocaine

Death or Glory
Lovers Rock
Lonesome Me
The Police Walked in 4 Jazz
Lost in the Supermarket
Up-Toon
Walking the Slidewalk
Where You Gonna Go (Soweto)
The Man in Me
Remote Control
Working and Waiting
Heart & Mind
Brand New Cadillac
London Calling
Revolution Rock

Disc three
DVD

LIVE AT SHEA STADIUM [live album]
Sony BMG Music Entertainment 88697348802 Released 6 Oct 2008

Kosmo Vinyl Introduction (concert introduction)
London Calling
Police on My Back
The Guns of Brixton
Tommy Gun
The Magnificent Seven
Armagideon Time
The Magnificent Seven (Return)
Rock the Casbah
Train in Vain
Career Opportunities
Spanish Bombs
Clampdown
English Civil War
Should I Stay or Should I Go
I Fought the Law

SOUND SYSTEM
Columbia 88725460002 Released 9 Sep 2013

Disc one
As *The Clash* (UK version)
Disc two
As *Give 'em Enough Rope*
Disc three
As *London Calling* (album) sides one and two
Disc four
As *London Calling* (album) sides three and four
Disc five
As *Sandinista!* sides one and two
Disc six
As *Sandinista!* sides three and four
Disc seven
As *Sandinista!* sides five and six
Disc eight
As *Combat Rock*
Disc nine
White Riot (single version)
1977 (B-side)
Listen (Capital Radio EP)/Interviews (Capital Radio EP)
Capital Radio (Capital Radio EP)
London's Burning (live B-side Remote Control)
Complete Control (single version)
City of the Dead (B-side)
Clash City Rockers (original single version)
Jail Guitar Doors (B-side)
(White Man) in Hammersmith Palais (A-side)
The Prisoner (B-side)
1-2 Crush on You (B-side)
Time Is Tight (Black Market Clash)
Pressure Drop (B-side English Civil War)
I Fought the Law (Cost of Living EP)
Groovy Times (Cost of Living EP)
Gates of the West (Cost of Living EP)

Capital Radio (Cost of Living EP)
Armagideon Time
Bankrobber (A-side)
Rockers Galore on a UK Tour (B-side)
Disc ten
Magnificent Dance (12-inch)
Midnight to Stevens (outtake)
Radio One (B-side Hitsville UK)
Stop the World (B-side The Call Up)
The Cool Out (U.S. 12-inch, B-side of The Call Up)
This Is Radio Clash (A-side)
This Is Radio Clash (B-side 7-inch, different lyrics)
First Night Back in London (B-side Know Your Rights)
Rock the Casbah (Bob Clearmountain 12-inch mix)
Long Time Jerk (B-side Rock the Casbah)
The Beautiful People Are Ugly Too (outtake)
Idle in Kangaroo Court (outtake listed as Kill Time)
Ghetto Defendant (extended version, unedited)
Cool Confusion (B-side Should I Stay or Should I Go, 7-inch)
Sean Flynn (extended Marcus Music version)
Straight to Hell (extended unedited version from Clash on Broadway)
Disc eleven
I'm So Bored with the U.S.A. (Extracts from The Clash's first-ever recording session at Beaconsfield Film School 1976. Recorded by Julien Temple.)
London's Burning (Extracts from The Clash's first-ever recording session at Beaconsfield Film School 1976. Recorded by Julien Temple.)
White Riot (Extracts from The Clash's first-ever recording session at Beaconsfield Film School 1976. Recorded by Julien Temple.)
1977 (Extracts from The Clash's first-ever recording session at Beaconsfield Film School 1976. Recorded by Julien Temple.)
Janie Jones (Polydor Demos. The Clash's second recording session January 1977. Produced by Guy Stevens.)
Career Opportunities (Polydor Demos. The Clash's second recording session January 1977. Produced by Guy Stevens.)
London's Burning (Polydor Demos. The Clash's second recording session January 1977. Produced by Guy Stevens.)

1977 (Polydor Demos. The Clash's second recording session January 1977. Produced by Guy Stevens.)

White Riot (Polydor Demos. The Clash's second recording session January 1977. Produced by Guy Stevens.)

City of the Dead (live at The Lyceum, London, 28 Dec 1979)
Jail Guitar Doors (live at The Lyceum, London, 28 Dec 1979)
English Civil War (live at The Lyceum, London, 28 Dec 1979)
Stay Free (live at The Lyceum, London, 28 Dec 1979)
Cheapskates (live at The Lyceum, London, 28 Dec 1979)
I Fought the Law (live at The Lyceum, London, 28 Dec 1979)
Disc twelve
DVD

U.S. RELEASES

SINGLES

I Fought the Law/(White Man) in Hammersmith Palais
Epic 9-50738 Released 26 Jul 1979

Train in Vain (Stand by Me)/London Calling
Epic 9-50851 Released 12 Feb 1980

Hitsville UK/Police on My Back
Epic 19-51013 Released 17 Feb 1981

The Magnificent Dance/The Magnificent Seven/The Call Up/The Cool Out [12-inch single]
Epic 48-02036 Released 27 Mar 1981

This Is Radio Clash/Radio Clash/Outside Broadcast/Radio 5 [12-inch single]
Epic 49-02662 Released 25 Nov 1981

Should I Stay or Should I Go/Innoculated City
Epic 14-03006 Released 10 Jun 1982

Should I Stay or Should I Go/Cool Confusion
  Epic 34-03547 Released 24 Jun 1982

Should I Stay or Should I Go/First Night Back in London
  14-03034 & 14-03061 Released 20 Jul 1982

Rock the Casbah/Long Time Jerk
  Epic 14-03245 Released 2 Oct 1982

Rock the Casbah/Mustapha Dance [12-inch single]
  Epic 4903144 Released 2 Oct 1982

SELECTED U.S. ALBUMS

GIVE 'EM ENOUGH ROPE
  Epic JE35543 Released 10 Nov 1978 (as UK version)

THE CLASH
  Epic JE36060 Released 23 Jul 1979

  Side one
  Clash City Rockers
  I'm So Bored with the U.S.A.
  Remote Control
  Complete Control
  White Riot
  (White Man) in Hammersmith Palais
  London's Burning
  I Fought the Law
  Side two
  Janie Jones
  Career Opportunities
  What's My Name
  Hate & War
  Police & Thieves
  Jail Guitar Doors
  Garageland

LONDON CALLING
Epic E2 36328 Released ?? Jan 1980 (as UK version)

BLACK MARKET CLASH
Epic 4E3 6846 Released ?? Oct 1980

Side one
Capital Radio One
The Prisoner
Pressure Drop
Cheat
The City of the Dead
Time Is Tight
Side two
Bankrobber/Robber Dub
Armagideon Time
Justice Tonight/Kick It Over

SANDINISTA!
Epic E3X37037 Released ?? Jan 1981 (as UK version)

COMBAT ROCK
Epic FE37689 Released ?? May 1982 (as UK version)

CUT THE CRAP
Released ?? November 1985 (as UK version)

INDEX

ABOUT THE AUTHOR

Londoner **Sean Egan** has contributed to, among others, *Billboard, Book Collector, Classic Rock, Record Collector, Tennis World, Total Film, Uncut,* and RollingStone.com. He has written or edited two dozen books, including works on The Beatles, The Rolling Stones, Bob Dylan, Manchester United Football Club, *Coronation Street,* James Kirkwood, William Goldman, and Tarzan. His critically acclaimed novel *Sick of Being Me* was published in 2003, while his 2008 collection of short stories *Don't Mess with the Best* carried cover endorsements from Booker Prize–winners Stanley Middleton and David Storey. His 2002 book *Jimi Hendrix and the Making of "Are You Experienced"* was nominated for an Award for Excellence in Historical Recorded Sound Research by the Association for Recorded Sound Collections.